THE STUDY
OF POLITICS

Nelson's Political Science Library

Editor: K. W. Watkins, Ph.D.,
University of Sheffield

MAURICE DUVERGER
Party Politics and Pressure Groups

MAURICE DUVERGER
The Study of Politics

L. J. MACFARLANE
Modern Political Theory

MICHAEL RUSH and PHILLIP ALTHOFF
An Introduction to Political Sociology

JOHN W. SPANIER
American Foreign Policy Since World War II

JOHN W. SPANIER
Games Nations Play: Analyzing International Politics

THE STUDY OF POLITICS

MAURICE DUVERGER

Translated by Robert Wagoner

MARITIME COLLEGE OF THE STATE UNIVERSITY OF NEW YORK

NELSON

32

Foreword

If the study of politics is to be rewarding both intellectually and practically it must, by definition, concern itself with the great issues which arise in the real world and with the fundamental arguments which occur about their nature and the possible solutions to them.

Abstract political philosophy which is not informed by the experience of practice will become sterile. A study of constitutions and the machinery of government can become dry-as-dust and hence boring unless the underlying principles are analysed and grasped. But theories of political change divorced from an understanding of constitutions and institutions will degenerate into mere phrase-mongering. Attempts to apply the techniques of the natural sciences to politics will lead to model building for its own sake and thence to arid and barren intellectualism unless it is understood that it is impossible to quantify the intangible. Indeed, any one-sided approach to politics and consequent failure to grasp the essential wholeness of the subject is bound to end in disaster.

The study of politics is a study of changing human relationships in dynamic societies. Thus it involves, since the present and hence the future are shaped in part by the past, an appreciation of history. Conflict of interest over the use of relatively scarce economic resources is central to the subject. A failure to understand the role of technological change and innovation entails the neglect of a vital facet of the process. Above all, since it is ideas that lead to action, it is the de-

Contents

velopment of conflicting theories about men in society that is central
to the subject.

It is the great virtue of Duverger's book that he has sought to
achieve a presentation of the essential wholeness of the subject, and
has succeeded. He has structured his book so as to illumine the basic
theoretical conflicts between Marxism and liberal democracy. In so
doing he sheds light on what has been for a century now the most
important intellectual and practical issue in the field of politics. The
book is thus supremely relevant for the contemporary reader.

The Study of Politics first appeared as the major part of *Sociologie Politique,* which was published in France in 1966. The appearance of an English edition will make available both to the student and the interested layman an outstanding introduction to the
subject—an introduction which will undoubtedly be used as a basic
book for many years to come.

K. W. WATKINS.

University of Sheffield.

37158
320·01
Dur

Thomas Nelson and Sons Ltd
Lincoln Way Windmill Road Sunbury-on-Thames Middlesex TW16 7HP
P.O. Box 73146 Nairobi Kenya
Thomas Nelsor (Australia) Ltd
19-39 Jeffcott Street West Melbourne Victoria 3003
Thomas Nelson and Sons (Canada) Ltd
81 Curlew Drive Don Mills Ontario
Thomas Nelson (Nigeria) Ltd
8 Ilupeju Bypass PMB 1303 Ikeja Lagos

THIS WORK WAS ORIGINALLY PUBLISHED UNDER THE TITLE
Sociologie Politique 3d ed. (PARIS: PRESSES UNIVERSITAIRES DE FRANCE, 1968)
COPYRIGHT © 1966 BY PRESSES UNIVERSITAIRES DE FRANCE

Designed by Barbara Kohn Isaac

ISBN 017 711098 8 (boards)
017 712098 3 (paper)

Printed in Hong Kong

Introduction

Neither the word "sociology" nor the word "political" has a clearly defined meaning by itself, so we must start off by explaining how the words are used in this book. One of the difficulties of the social sciences is the lack of any fixed terminology. Every scholar must define his own vocabulary.

THE CONCEPT OF "SOCIOLOGY"

The term "sociology" was invented in 1839 by Auguste Comte (in his *Cours de philosophie positive*, vol. 4) to designate the science of society. Comte had earlier used the term "social physics" in the same sense, but later replaced it with "sociology," because the Belgian mathematician Quételet had applied the term "social physics" to the statistical study of moral phenomena (1836), which Comte called "a vicious attempt at appropriation" of this term. Since Comte's time, the use of the word "sociology" has changed little. There are those who would like to restrict it to a kind of general social science, a science of synthesis which would combine the conclusions of special research conducted within each particular social discipline. This concept is just not acceptable since research and synthesis cannot be separated in scientific matters: every piece of research is linked to hypotheses, to theories, to some provisional initial synthesis. Consequently, for most sociologists, "sociology" continues to designate the entire body of the social sciences, and we will use the term here in this sense. Accordingly, each particular social science can be indicated by adding a modifier to the word "sociology"—economic sociology, religious sociology, political sociology, sociology of the family, and so forth.

The Development of a Scientific Sociology

Comte placed great emphasis on the scientific notion of sociology. Even the birth of the discipline is tied to the fundamental idea that one must apply the methods of observation used by the natural sciences to the study of social phenomena. Emile Durkheim later concurred, saying that we must treat social facts "as we treat things." We will see later on that modern sociologists do not entirely subscribe to this view.

This positivist attitude marked a genuine intellectual revolution. Until the eighteenth century, social facts were studied primarily from a philosophical and ethical point of view. An effort was made to define not what society is but what *it ought to be* in terms of metaphysical and religious beliefs about the nature of man, the purpose of life, and the like. The very notion that man and society could be studied "like things," in a scientific manner, seemed sacrilegious.

In this initial phase, the method for analyzing social facts was essentially deductive, predicated on certain principles, certain objects of belief. There was no possibility of experimentally proving the basic premises. Conclusions were drawn from these principles through logical reasoning. The results were thus "normative," that is, they were used to define the rules (or "norms") that would allow "a good society" to function in accordance with the metaphysical and moral principles laid down as the basis for reasoning. Instead of being based on "reality judgments," expressing the true nature of men, things, and events, this method was based upon "value judgments" which confronted men, things, and events with a priori definitions of good and evil, right and wrong, definitions that were regarded as absolute and sacrosanct. Rules of conduct or "norms" were deduced from these value judgments.

From the earliest times, certain writers did, of course, endeavor to study social facts scientifically. Aristotle was a pioneer in this respect, and, later, Machiavelli (*The Prince,* 1532) and Jean Bodin (*The Republic,* 1577), but their works were exceptions. Moreover, they reflected to a considerable extent the general tendency toward a philosophical and ethical study of social facts. Scientific analyses were interlarded with value judgments. The general orientation of research continued to be normative.

The turning point occurred with Montesquieu, whose *Spirit of Laws* (1748) is the first treatise in political sociology. "We report here what is and not what ought to be," declared the lord of the manor of La Brède, who provided the world with a good definition of laws in the scientific sense of the word: "the necessary relationships that derive from the nature of things." But his work, too, long remained an isolated effort. Aside from economic sociology, it was not until the nineteenth century that research in social science made successful strides in the direction of objectivity. If Comte first thought of christening the new science "social physics," he did so with the clear intent of using a term that would denote the importance of adopting the same methods of observation that characterize the natural and physical sciences. This basic attitude still serves to define sociology in our time. The social sciences are sciences to the extent that they seek, like the natural sciences, to describe and explain real phenomena by means of observational techniques and to formulate "reality judgments" rather than "value judgments." But in the meantime, the general concept of science has also changed.

The Modern Conception of Scientific Knowledge

Within the last fifty years the concept of science has undergone radical changes, with reverberations in the field of sociology.

THE QUESTION OF DETERMINISM Lively debates first occurred among the philosophers of the 1930's on the subject of the limits of determinism, the very basis of scientific research. For science to be able to explain "the necessary relationships that derive from the nature of things," these relationships must indeed be necessary; in other words, a specific antecedent A must always and inevitably produce a specific result B. This is what we mean by "determinism." Now atomic studies have suggested that physical relationships are not strictly deterministic, that for a given antecedent A there may be several results B, C, D, and so on, without our knowing for certain which one will prevail. We know only the relative probability of each (Louis de Broglie [1]). On the other hand, in certain other areas we have been able to formulate a kind of "relationship of uncertainty": the more precise and determined one element in a group of elements becomes, the less true this

[1] French physicist, known for his research on quantum theory.

is of its correlative element. Heisenberg [2] demonstrated that the more accurately we determine the position of a moving object, the less possible it is to determine its velocity. This makes it impossible to define its trajectory with absolute certainty. But the philosophers generalized from specific cases of scientific analysis which they were not fully competent to understand. Their analyses never warranted the generalizations they read into them.

FROM ABSOLUTE DETERMINISM TO STATISTICAL DETERMINISM   The important thing we must remember first is the fact that science and determinism are no longer thought of today as they were at the end of the nineteenth century and the beginning of the twentieth, when the great debates raged over these fundamental issues. Determinism has acquired a much more statistical meaning. We no longer declare that condition A inevitably results in the appearance of condition B, but rather that the likelihood of B's occurrence as a consequence of A is of a certain order of probability. In most of the physical sciences, the degree of probability is of an extremely high order, and the contrary probability is almost zero. However, on the atomic level, the situation is somewhat different. Here the possibility exists for the realization of several hypotheses (B, C, D, and so on) as a consequence of factor A, with the respective probabilities of a fairly high order. Science seeks to determine with precision the relative likelihood of the occurrence of each.

This type of situation is most common in the social sciences: the same "cause" can produce several different "effects" for which we can measure the respective degrees of probability. Hence our point of view today is the reverse of the one held at the close of the nineteenth century. Formerly, the aim was to put the social sciences on the same basis as the physical sciences by postulating the existence of a social determinism analogous with a physical determinism viewed as absolute. Today we no longer conceive of physical determinism as something absolute, but as something relative, like statistical determinism, a concept furnished by the social sciences. The current tendency is to base the physical sciences on the social sciences, on the principle of statistical determinism.

This change favors the development of the social sciences by removing the old objections based on the question of human freedom, freedom of the will. The notion of free will is diametrically opposed to that of traditional determinism. Freedom means having the possibility

---

[2] Werner Heisenberg, a physicist, who announced the principle of indeterminacy.

of self-determination, which is to say, not being controlled by external forces. The positivists of the last century reached the point of denying man any freedom of the will, which they regarded as purely illusory, and did so for the purpose of creating the social sciences. Consequently, they engaged in many inconclusive philosophical debates. We have gone beyond them today, at least in matters respecting the social sciences. Statistical determinism does not contradict the notion of freedom, which existentialist philosophy has revalidated in another context. It simply expresses the results of concrete conditions within which freedom can operate. To say that 60 percent of the population of Paris leaves the French capital on August 15 does not prevent any particular individual from being free to remain in the city on that day or to leave it if he so chooses. Our statistical observation merely means that the pressure of social conditions prompts Parisians to flee the city on August 15 and that 60 percent of them probably prefer this course of least resistance as long as collective social circumstances remain the same and there is no change in the desire of individuals to oppose the general exodus. While expressing group behavior in terms of probabilities, statistical determinism takes into account the possible free choice of individuals within the group.

THE "OPERATIONAL" NATURE OF THE SCIENCES Today our primary concern is no longer with knowing whether or not scientific research describes the "reality" of things. Indeed, we do not know exactly what this expression means. Likewise, the term "phenomena," which replaced it from the Kantian critique of knowledge, scarcely seems any clearer. The true objective of the modern scientist is not to describe "reality" or "phenomena," but to focus upon rules of action. Science is no longer an ontological research, a search for "the being" of things. Science is now seen primarily as a collection of coordinated prescriptions enabling one to act upon things and individuals. The concern is not to prove that the universe is really formed of atoms having the configuration described by physicists. We simply note that such descriptions allow us to achieve practical results such as the liberation of atomic energy. For the old notion of "reality judgments," which science was supposed to express, the tendency today is to substitute the notion of "operational concepts," meaning concepts permitting one to take action. Of course, if one can act upon things with these concepts, they clearly correspond to a certain reality. But we no longer claim that they are "the" reality, which is unknowable. There are most likely "several" realities—multiple, diverse, complex—for every aspect of the universe, for every point of view observed. We seek not so much to describe them all—which is perhaps impossible—as to isolate certain elements enabling one to take action, to arrive at precise operational concepts. As Edouard LeRoy [3] has put it, contemporary science grants scientific concepts only "the strict sense conferred upon them by their definition." From a scientific point of view, reason is not the ability to perceive facts, according to the classical definition; it is "the capacity to remake a concept" (Jean Ullmo [4]).

Limits to the Scientific Character of Sociology

Whether science is considered in the traditional sense (the search for reality) or in the modern sense (the means of acting upon things), it is not possible to fully assimilate the natural sciences and the social sciences (the study of mankind). Sociology is not entirely scientific.

LIMITS TO THE USE OF SCIENTIFIC METHODS   Though it is possible to employ scientific methods in sociology, a large body of social phenomena eludes this kind of investigation. There are no doubt many facts in the natural sciences that also defy scientific investigation, but the situation in the social sciences differs in two respects.

First, the area in which scientific methods can be utilized at present is very small. They are of great importance in disciplines like economics and demography, but elsewhere their use is quite limited. To try to describe reality or discover operational truths, basing oneself solely on scientific observations, is (in the words of an American political scientist) "like imitating a drunk, who has lost his watch in a dark alley and who insists on looking for it under the street light at the entrance to the alley because it is the only bright spot he can find." Any in-depth analysis of a social group depends much more on approximations and hypotheses than on scientifically established facts. Scientific methods remain far less applicable to social studies than they do to the physical sciences.

Now in some respects this is a temporary situation. It is partly the result of the underdevelopment of the social sciences, the youngest child of all the sciences, still in its infancy, so to speak. But it is possible that this condition will last for quite some time. We have reason to wonder if human activity will ever lend itself to fundamental analysis by truly scientific methods—whether there is a mystery about man that makes his actions largely unpredictable.

[3] Edouard LeRoy, French philosopher and mathematician, author of *Les origines humaines et l'evolution de l'intelligence* (1928).
[4] Jean Ullmo, *La pensée scientifique moderne* (1958).

THE PLASTICITY OF SOCIAL PHENOMENA   Social facts differ from "things," Emile Durkheim's dictum notwithstanding. That is to say, they differ from physical facts by a very important characteristic which we may call their "amorphism" or their "plasticity." Material things can be distinguished rather easily from one another. Even if everything is composed of atoms, the latter combine into objects with rather clearly defined forms—a chair, a table, a floor, walls, an animal, a plant. The psychology of form has certainly demonstrated that the perception of separate groups of objects is based not only on their objective separation, but also on social conditioning. Education, which transmits civilization and the sociocultural heritage in general, influences the way in which we interpret the physical universe. We see things through our education as through colored glasses. Individual psychology also influences our interpretation. Certain tests, designed to analyze personality, are based on this sociopsychological influence upon our perception of physical facts. There is, for example, the Rorschach test based on the interpretation of ink spots of unusual shapes. What these shapes suggest to each individual sheds light on his personality. It is nevertheless true that the possibilities of personal interpretation by each individual are restricted by material facts that affect everyone. Whatever one's cultural background or individual psychology, a chair is perceived as distinct from the floor (or else one suffers from a serious mental illness). In like manner, we can determine classifications among animals, plants, and minerals, among material elements in general, among "things."

Social phenomena, on the contrary, are much more amorphous, much more plastic. They present themselves in the guise of a continuum whose different elements are very difficult to isolate—as if no shoreline separated the land from the sea, as if the chair or the table were indistinguishable from the floor, and the floor from the walls. There are, of course, objective separations among social phenomena, but they are much less distinct. They are also much more flexible and a great deal more fragile. Accordingly, it is very difficult to discover the natural classification of social facts. The main outlines of their structures and their articulation are changeable, easily modified, with the result that they can mold themselves and organize into forms that the observer gives to them. The observer takes as a natural and objective classification a projection of the subjective system he himself has built and given the society in which he lives. Social phenomena have a tendency, like iron filings, to acquire the configuration imposed by a magnetic field when a magnet is placed under a metal sheet on which the filings have been deposited. Only, in this case, it is the observer who acts as the magnet.

It has been possible to argue, for example, that the interesting results of the great American inquiry into the subject of the authoritarian personality [5] were already inherent in the conceptual scheme that
served as a basis for the questionnaires. The conclusions drawn from
an analysis of the answers tend to fall into the "categories" that were
predetermined by the investigator. Other "categories" would have
given different results. These examples reflect a general phenomenon
of great importance. The truth is that no science is ever a purely empirical quest for facts. Research is always guided by hypotheses, conjectures, models, theories, systems, that is, by a construct of the imagination. Hypotheses, theories, models, and systems are confronted with
facts through empirical research, and the results of the latter enable
one to determine to what extent these hypotheses, models, theories,
and systems express reality and to what extent they fail to do so and
must therefore be modified.

In the physical sciences we are dealing with true verifications, for
physical facts are hard, solid things which resist the pressures of conceptual structures. In the social sciences, on the other hand, facts tend
to cluster around conjectures and hypotheses to a much greater degree,
to fit into the molds of theories and systems, as we have just noted,
with the result that we always obtain, in part at least, the hoped-for response.

We must qualify, however, two points regarding the scope of the
foregoing remarks. In the first place, we must not exaggerate the
amorphism and plasticity of social phenomena. Though they are more
pliable and imprecise than physical phenomena, they do possess a certain objective reality. The difference between the two categories is one
of degree rather than kind. Second, new concepts of science are reducing the obstacles placed in the way of scientific research in sociology,
obstacles posed by the plasticity and amorphism of social phenomena.
In a certain sense, it matters little if it is difficult to determine whether
or not a particular theory, model, or hypothesis corresponds to "reality,"
since we are no longer trying to know this "reality" but only to act with
practical results. The important thing is that the hypothesis, theory, or
model must be "operational"—it must work. Experimentation gives us
a clear answer to this question. Indeed, we can classify theories and hypotheses quite well according to their practical applicability, which is
the purpose of scientific research.

THE IMPORTANCE OF SOCIAL VALUES   We have already used the term
"value" in speaking about value judgments as opposed to reality judg-

---

[5] T. Adorno and others, *The Authoritarian Personality* (New York, 1950).

ments. Generally speaking, values are beliefs relative to good and evil, right and wrong, to what ought to be and what ought not to be. Values play a very important role in social life. Most human relationships are based not only on positive, objective facts, but also on value judgments.

At first glance, this would seem to preclude any scientific study of social phenomena, at least in the traditional sense of science as defined in terms of reality judgments, to the exclusion of value judgments. Yet this difficulty can be overcome if we study the value judgments developed within a society as elements of the social reality. We may note, for instance, that at a given moment in a given country, the majority of the population believe in the values of a monarchy and judge their rulers in terms of this criterion; that at another moment or in another country, the majority believe in democratic values and judge the rulers according to another criterion. In either case, no position is taken on the validity of the criterion. We do not ask which values are "true." The values in which a society believes are treated as facts. With the same objective approach we can explain, at least in part, the birth, development, and transformation of social values. Analyses of this kind are also "operational." They enable us to measure the influence of values on human conduct, to determine the degree of their effectiveness, and hence to be able to act accordingly.

Even an objective analysis of values presents some degree of distortion. To observe that 80 percent of the citizens of a country are attached to democratic values and 20 percent to authoritarian values does not precisely reflect the society's system of values, for the relationships between two co-existing types of values are not mathematical. The overall value system of a society is not simply an arithmetical addition of the different value systems within it. On the other hand, we must not forget that value systems determine the ultimate conditions in terms of which basic choices are made which control the society as a whole. An objective study never goes beneath the surface of the value systems, never penetrates their deeper meaning. He who has never experienced faith cannot fully understand the religious phenomenon.

In the social sciences, the observer is always to some extent a part of the reality he is observing. Even the most fair-minded, dispassionate sociologist is never entirely neutral with respect to any society. This fact becomes obvious when he is scrutinizing the society in which he himself lives. He necessarily shares one of its value systems and can never totally divorce himself from it. When he is studying a society remote in time and space, he is less involved in its value systems. But even so, he continues to make comparisons in some measure, consciously or unconsciously, between the unfamiliar society and his own.

He projects upon the former something of the value systems of the latter. This is especially noticeable in the formulation of hypotheses, outlines for research, and intellectual guidelines. But as we have just pointed out, these have a special importance because of the plasticity of social phenomena.

In the modern concept of science, based on operational results, the importance of social values poses far fewer obstacles to scientific research. It matters little that the methods of analyzing these values do not achieve a high degree of objectivity when we try to explore them in depth. The important thing is that these methods allow us to understand the values of a given society and to measure their importance so that we may put them to practical use. Opinion polls, motivation studies, psychoanalytical methods, and associated testing give good results in this area. Commercial advertising and political propaganda have been able to utilize them with singular success. Likewise, the new concept of scientific research has favored the development of the social sciences.

THE PERSONAL DISTORTION FACTOR OF THE SOCIOLOGIST We noted above that the study of social phenomena differs from the study of physical phenomena since, in the former, the observer is simultaneously an element in the phenomena under study. We must come back to this question of which we mentioned only one aspect: the sociologist's attachment to one of the value systems of the society he lives in. Another aspect is the natural tendency of the sociologist to project upon the outside world the results of his own personal thoughts and reflections.

Now, on the one hand, any human problem concerns in some way the man who observes it and is, consciously or not, attached to a system of values. Up to a point, he may regard as facts the value judgments of others, but such an attitude is much harder to maintain with respect to his own value judgments. Hence, a sociologist always risks taking a position revealing preferences with respect to the facts he is examining. His own value judgments naturally cause him to see social phenomena in a distorted manner—to overestimate the importance of whatever conforms to his own beliefs and to underestimate the importance of whatever is contrary to them. Prolonged practice with scientific methods helps, of course, to overcome this tendency. Moreover, dedication to scientific methods and a belief in science constitute an essential value system for the scientist, helping to free him from the warping influence of other value systems. Yet, in spite of everything, he can never completely rid himself of his personal preferences.

On the other hand, in the study of human facts, the sociologist has at his disposal another means apart from scientific observation—the analysis of his own mind, the awareness of his own thoughts and introspection. He must be wary of knowledge acquired in this manner because it lacks scientific precision. But he cannot entirely overlook it. With regard to the future, he must adopt the attitude of the Eternal One in Anatole France's *Penguin Island:* "I am ignorant of what I know. I cover my eyes thickly with the veils I have pierced." We can surmise how difficult it is to do this, especially since the relatively few really scientific observations in sociology leave in the dark a vast number of basic problems on which introspective analysis can often shed some light—or the illusion of light.

THE CONCEPT OF "POLITICS"

It is more difficult to assign a precise definition to the term "political" than to the term "sociology." The latter is a relatively new word that preserves a technical meaning and is still seldom used in everyday speech. The word "political," on the other hand, is very old and is found in everyone's vocabulary. Through time and usage it has become very vague and general.

Of course, along with its everyday usage, it is used in a more specific sense by sociologists. The expressions "political sociology" and "political science," which are almost synonomous,[6] have now acquired a legitimacy in France to designate a particular branch of sociology, one of

---

[6] In certain countries the distinction is purely administrative or pedagogical. In the United States, where sociology and political science are usually two separate "departments," they speak of "political sociology" when a professor from the Sociology Department is dealing with the phenomenon of power, and of "political science" when the same subject is taught by a professor from the Political Science Department.

In Europe, the term "political science" (which is not yet widely used) often serves to indicate the field of research of a scholar whose training is grounded in history or law. The term "sociologist" more often refers to professional philosophers or, less frequently, to people trained in the purely sociological disciplines.

The term "political science" may reflect a certain tendency toward isolating the study of political phenomena by limiting its contacts with other branches of the social sciences. The term "political sociology," on the other hand, may indicate a desire to restore political phenomena to its proper place within the broad spectrum of social phenomena, to remove barriers between disciplines, and to emphasize the essential unity of all the social sciences. In this sense, the term "political sociology" is preferable. It also suggests a firmer intention to use empirical and experimental methods of research instead of philosophical reasoning.

the social sciences. The terms are still more common in the Anglo-Saxon countries, especially in the United States. But there is no agreement among specialists on the precise limits to the field of political sociology. There are several conflicting concepts of the word "political" which we must examine in some detail.

Political Sociology, the Science of Power

There are, first of all, two conflicting notions of political sociology. One considers political sociology the science of the state, the other, the science of power. The second concept, the more "operational" of the two, is more widespread than the first, and we will adopt it here.

THE CONCEPT OF POLITICAL SOCIOLOGY AS THE SCIENCE OF THE STATE   This concept uses the word "political" in its usual connotation, that is, dealing with the state. The word "state" is taken to mean a particular category of human groups or societies. In practice there are two meanings: the nation-state and the government-state. The state, in the sense of nation-state, designates the national society, that is, the community that appeared at the end of the Middle Ages and has today become the most strongly organized and the most completely integrated. The government-state designates the rulers and leaders of this national society. To define political sociology as the science of the state is to place it in a classification of the social sciences which is based on the nature of the societies studied. Political sociology would thus be in a category distinct from family sociology, urban sociology, and the sociology of ethnic or minority groups.

THE CONCEPT OF POLITICAL SOCIOLOGY AS THE SCIENCE OF POWER   The above-described concept, which corresponds to common sense, has, in the last analysis, found few adherents among contemporary scholars. Only a few important writers—the German sociologist Jellinek, who wrote before World War I, and French historian Marcel ` Prélot— have connected political sociology with the science of the state. Theirs . is the old concept of political sociology.

The more modern conception holds that political sociology is the science of power, of government, of authority, of command, in all human societies, not only in the national society. This conception derives from what Léon Duguit [7] called the distinction between the governors (gouvernants) and the governed (gouvernés). He believed that

[7] French jurist, author of Des fonctions de l'état moderne (1894) and Traité de droit constitutionnel (1911).

in every human group, from the smallest to the largest, from the most ephemeral to the most stable, there are those who command and those who obey, those who give orders and those who comply with them, those who make decisions and those who abide by them. This differentiation constitutes a fundamental political fact that calls for comparative study in every society and on every social level.

This view places political sociology in another classification of the social sciences, one that is based, not on the nature of the societies studied, but on certain kinds of phenomena which reappear in every society. Political sociology would thus be distinct from economic sociology, religious sociology, the sociology of art, and so on. Many contemporary writers accept in principle this definition of political sociology, with perhaps a few modifications—notably Max Weber, Raymond Aron, Georges Vedel, Georges Burdeau, and the author of this book.

THE IMPLICATIONS OF THE DEBATE   The scientific debate over the definition of political sociology is interesting for its hidden implications.

Behind what would seem to be a mere question of definition lies an ill-concealed lack of agreement on the nature of the state and the national society with respect to other human groupings. To make political sociology the science of the state by isolating the study of the national society from that of other societies is to imply that the state and the national society are different in nature from other human groups. This tendency is linked to a theory that was born with the state itself at the close of the Middle Ages, the theory of "sovereignty" which pervaded juridical thinking down to the time of World War I. It envisaged the state as a kind of perfect society, independent of any other, yet dominating all others. The state was thus regarded as "sovereign." The rulers of the state therefore possessed a particular quality which the heads of other groups could not share with them and which was also called "sovereignty." The two notions of "sovereignty of the state" and of "sovereignty within the state" correspond respectively to the concepts of "nation-state" and "government-state" described above.

Those, on the other hand, who equate political sociology with the science of power tend to believe that power within the state does not essentially differ from power in other human societies. They differentiate only in terms of the efficiency of its internal organization or the degree of obedience it obtains. By implication, they reject the idea of sovereignty. Or more precisely, they regard it as a system of values, historically important, which still has some significance but has no scientific meaning and does not correspond to any objective reality.

From a scientific point of view, equating political sociology with the science of power is the preferable interpretation. We cannot say that it is closer to reality, because the definitions of the various branches of science serve merely to establish lines of demarcation within which specialists carry on their particular research. Such classifications are necessarily artificial. The real advantage of the power interpretation is that it is more useful, and, further, is the only one whose basic premises can be verified. A comparative study of power in various human groupings would reveal how power exercised within the state differs from that exercised within other groups—*if* such differences exist. But, if we limit the study to power within the framework of "the state alone" (as Prélot suggests), we cannot compare it with the power wielded by other groups and so learn whether a difference in nature, predicated a priori, corresponds to the actual facts.

The Concept of Power

It is not enough to say that political sociology is the science of power. We must analyze the concept of "power," which is very broad and vague. The distinction made by Duguit between those who govern and those who are governed is not as clear as it first seems. In every small group only the person at the bottom of the ladder is governed without being a governor, and only the head of state is a governor without being governed. Can we speak of "power" then, whenever there is inequality in a human relationship, whenever one individual can impose his will on another individual? If every human relationship of an authoritarian nature were to fall within the province of political sociology, then political sociology would be as broad as sociology. We must therefore find a more precise and more limited definition, one that will distinguish political power from other kinds of authority. Several bases could be used for our definition.

ELEMENTARY GROUPS AND COMPLEX GROUPS   The most common practice is to compare authority in small or "elementary groups" with that of "complex groups," which are made up of small groups interlocked and overlapping one another. These large groups would be the concern of political sociology, whereas the elementary groups would fall within the domain of social psychology. This concept corresponds more or less to the actual division of labor between political scientists and sociologists working in the other branches of the social sciences. The former study primarily power in complex social groupings, while the latter examine its role in elementary groups.

However, this distinction is very precarious. It is difficult to draw the line between elementary groups and complex groups. In the first place, within any group, no matter how small, a process of differentiation produces cliques, coalitions, and subgroups. Groups that are truly undifferentiated are rare; even small groups are complex. The notion of a limited group also eludes definition from another point of view. For example, let us take an industrial firm. If we are dealing with a small enterprise, it is an elementary group. If we are dealing with a large enterprise, it is a complex group. Size is as important a factor as complexity in distinguishing between social groups—indeed, one is partially a function of the other. But the boundaries are impossible to define in this area. Is it possible that questions of authority in the Council of Ministers—a group that is definitely limited and elementary—lie outside the province of political sociology? We shall see later that the size of a group is of great political importance and that one must distinguish the "macropolitics" occuring within large communities from the "micropolitics" of small groups. Yet both types fall within the scope of political sociology.

THE UNIVERSAL SOCIETY AND PRIVATE SOCIETIES   A second distinction rests, not on the size and complexity of social groups, but on the nature of their organizational ties. Thus "private" societies are often compared with "universal" societies. Private societies are groups with certain specialized interests and a limited sense of solidarity—trade unions, athletic organizations, literary, artistic, and religious associations, and commercial and industrial enterprises—and each corresponds to a certain category of human activity. Generally speaking, everyone belongs to a number of private organizations or societies, depending on the variety of his tastes, needs, and desires. The members feel only a partial commitment to each group, namely, to its special activity. Hence the name "private" societies; hence the limited sense of solidarity that develops. But every individual also belongs, in a more physical sense, and is aware of belonging in a psychological sense, to a universal society, one that encompasses and supersedes all these private societies. The universal society is a general category of some sort to which one belongs as a human being and not merely as one interested in a specific activity. The feeling of solidarity is not only greater than in private societies, but it is also deeper and more intimate.

For some writers the object of political sociology is to analyze power in "universal" societies, not in private societies. In private societies, authority is regarded as having only a technical nature; it does not raise problems about the dependency of certain individuals with respect to others, problems that constitute the very basis of power, properly speaking. This distinction corresponds, in a certain sense, to the popular notion of the word "political." It is true, for instance, that we are referring to authority in a universal society when we speak of political leaders and rulers. It is true that "politics" is concerned with collective issues, with general objectives that transcend the demands of any particular group, and that the purpose of politics is to reconcile the demands of these various groups. In fact, one of the distinctions between political parties and pressure groups is that the former have generalized objectives while the latter have only special interests.

But having said all this, the distinction between the universal society and private societies cannot serve as a basis for the definition of political sociology. First, the distinction is decidedly vague. For some persons, the nation is the universal society, for others it is the family, for still others it is a group which would seem to be "private." The trials of the OAS in 1962 revealed that, for some of the military, the Foreign Legion represented a universal society, one in which its members found complete personal fulfillment. Similarly, for monks, their religious community is the universal society. Second, there are two notions of the universal society. One is defined by the feeling of belonging, the sense of fellowship, that affects the totality of human activity. The other, a more formal and juridical concept, holds that the universal society is the one that embraces all others. For many sociologists, the universal society of our time is the nation-state. In other eras, it has been the city, the tribe, and so forth. In effect, we end up then with the theory that equates political sociology with the science of the state.

In the last analysis, it matters little which concept is adopted. Both have the same shortcoming. To say that authority in a private society is qualitatively different from authority in a universal society is a hypothesis that needs to be verified. And this can be done only to the extent that no a priori obstacles are placed in the way of comparative studies between the two types of societies. We are no better off defining political sociology as "the science of power in the universal society" than as "the science of power in the state." Besides, the two expressions are generally synonymous in the minds of those using them.

Instead of distinguishing different types of societies in order to define political power, it seems preferable to distinguish the different kinds of authority relationships within all societies, be they small or large, simple or complex, private or universal. By "authority relationship" we mean any unequal relationship in which one or several individuals dominate the others and bend them, more or less, to their will.

Most human relationships are like this and, in practice, very few are truly egalitarian. Juridical thought formerly fostered the opposite view by its emphasis on the notion of contract. But the equality of contracting parties is, in general, illusory. Behind the appearance of equal rights, one person more or less imposes his will on another. Behind idealistic theories, laws camouflage a very different reality. Yet we must not go too far in the opposite direction. There do exist human relationships that are truly egalitarian. Many human relationships exist outside the sphere of force and coercion, such as those based on sympathy, admiration, affection, and love. Be that as it may, the problem is to distinguish, among authority relationships, those that involve "power" in the precise sense of the word, and those that do not. The point is to avoid overextending the field of political science and to prevent it from encompassing all of sociology.

The solution can be found by distinguishing among relationships in the broad sense of the term—on the one hand, "institutional" relationships, and, on the other, purely personal relationships. Power, from our point of view, is comprised of the entire range of social institutions connected with authority, which is to say, with the domination of some men over others. It excludes simple, unequal relationships that have no institutional character and that do not derive from an institution. Political science is thus defined as the science of institutions in relation to authority. There remains the task of clarifying what we mean by "institutions" as opposed to "relationships." We will return to this problem later on, for the study of the concept of institution is an important part of "political" sociology. We will limit ourselves here to an initial summary of the problem in order to define more clearly our notion of the term "political."

The distinction between "institutions" and "relationships" rests on two complementary criteria: one is physical, the other consists of our collective attitudes and beliefs. On the physical side, we speak of relationships in the strictest sense of the term—human relations that are not tied to any preexisting models and do not usually endure in any permanent form, relations of a sporadic, ephemeral, and unstable nature. By "institutions," on the other hand, we mean various models of relationships which serve as patterns for concrete relations. Such relations are, therefore, stable, lasting, and cohesive. If we pursued the analysis further, we would have to examine the institutional models themselves and the relations they engender. Institutional models closely correspond to the notion of "structures" in the modern sociological sense. In practice, the distinction virtually disappears. "Structures" are systems of relationships with no existence apart from the relationships themselves, and the originality of these relationships is determined by their connection with the structural model. In this sense, we may say that parliaments, cabinet ministers, heads of state, and elections are all institutions.

The distinction between simple "relationships," in the strict sense of the word, and "institutions" is based at the same time on a second criterion—man's beliefs. Power is felt as power by those who obey it and those who wield it. To them, it is not just a physical phenomenon, a domination. It is also a psychological phenomenon. Here, we are confronted with the notion of "legitimacy," which we will often return to because it is a key concept. Power, properly speaking, is always regarded as something "legitimate," to a greater or lesser degree, meaning that we find it more or less natural to obey it. On the contrary, plain domination appears only to be the result of our inability to resist its pressure; we obey because we cannot physically do otherwise. But power is obeyed because we think that we ought to do so, because we believe that it is legitimate to obey. As long as there is cohesiveness, physical stability, and adherence to a structural model, it is this sense of legitimacy that distinguishes power from simply authority relationships. Clearly, the two phenomena are linked to each other. Stability, continuity, and ties to a structural model engender a sense of legitimacy.

A GENERAL VIEW
OF POLITICAL SOCIOLOGY

Since men first began thinking about politics, they have oscillated between two diametrically opposed interpretations. For some, politics is essentially a struggle, a battle. Power enables those groups and individuals who hold it to maintain their domination over society and to exploit it; other groups and individuals oppose their domination and exploitation by striving to resist and destroy them. The second interpretation regards politics as an attempt to establish order and justice. Power protects the general welfare and the common good from the pressures and demands of special interest groups. For the former, politics serves to maintain the privileges of a minority over the majority. For the latter, it is a means of integrating everyone into the community and of creating the "City of the Just" that Aristotle spoke of.

The adherence to one view or the other is in part determined by one's social status. Oppressed individuals and classes, the poor, the unfortunate, and the dissatisfied agree that power guarantees order, but only a caricature of order, which conceals the domination of the privileged few. For these people, politics is a struggle. Individuals and groups that are secure, affluent, and contented find that society is harmonious and that power maintains a valid social order. For them, politics is integration. In Western nations, the second group have more or less succeeded in convincing the first group that political battles are dirty, unsavory, and dishonest and that those who engage in them are merely pursuing selfish interests with dubious methods. By thus discouraging and demoralizing their opponents, they assure themselves a great advantage. Every "depolitization" favors the established order, the status quo, and conservatism.

Of course, each of these attitudes represents only part of the truth. Even the most optimistic conservatives cannot deny that if the purpose of politics is to achieve integration, it rarely does so in a very satisfactory manner. Like characters in the plays of Corneille, conservatives present politics as it ought to be, while their opponents, more like Racinian characters, show politics as it really is. But they too can hardly deny that their picture is too black. The most oppressive and unjust of rulers perform some functions in the interest of all, at least in the technical domain, if only by regulating traffic, providing postal services, and ensuring the removal of garbage.

Finally, it is the very essence of politics, its real meaning, that it is always ambivalent. The two-faced god Janus is the true image of power and expresses the most profound political truth. The state—and in a more general way, the institutionalized power of a society—is at all times and in all places the instrument of domination by certain groups over other groups, utilized by the former to their own advantage and to the disadvantage of the latter. At the same time, it is also a means of guaranteeing a certain social order, a kind of integration of all within the community in the interest of the common good. The proportion of one element or the other fluctuates greatly according to time and circumstances and from one country to another. But the two elements continually coexist.

The notion that politics is both a conflict between individuals and groups for the acquisition of power, which the victors use to their advantage at the expense of the vanquished, and an attempt to establish a social order beneficial to all constitutes the basis of our theory of political sociology. It will serve as a guideline through all the developments that follow. Not everyone accepts this theory. One of the most serious flaws in contemporary political sociology is the absence of any general theory accepted by the community of scholars, of any theory that could serve as a basis for their individual researches. Each scholar is obliged to fill the gap by erecting his own synthesis. It would be better if this were done candidly, admitting that one is setting forth personal ideas, rather than giving opinions an outward appearance of objectivity and generality that does not correspond to reality.

Nevertheless, the theory behind this book aims at being general—if not by the number of political scientists who rally to its defense, at least by the range of subjects it examines. Its originality lies in going beyond the particular framework of each of the two great, contending political cosmogonies of our time: Western theory and Marxist theory. Each one is regarded as a partial and relative synthesis which needs to be integrated into a universal synthesis. Just as the better economists are beginning to build a "generalized economics" that goes beyond the different economic systems currently applied, so we are attempting here to lay the foundations for a "generalized politics." We are not so presumptuous as to believe we have already succeeded, but we hope we are on the right track.

The general outline of political sociology, given here, will naturally center around the theme of the two faces of power, that it is both oppressor and integrator. In Part I we will describe the political structures in which the dialectic of antagonisms and integration unfolds, that is to say, the context of political phenomena. In Part II, we will examine the dialectic itself in its primary manifestation, the existence of antagonisms. Since integration represents an attempt to suppress or reduce these antagonisms, it is appropriate to begin by studying their underlying causes. Lastly, in Part III, we will describe how antagonisms are resolved and integrated, as well as the apparent limits to this procedure.

PART I

Political Structures

UNDER THEIR dual aspect of antagonisms and integration, political phenomena occur within many kinds of human communities—nations, provinces, cities, international societies, associations, trade unions, clans, bands, cliques, and other assorted groups. From our point of view political sociology is the study of power in every human grouping, not just in the nation-state. Each of these groups therefore serves as a structure, a framework for the enactment of conflicts and integration. Political structures are, first of all, the different social groupings. We can study them only in a summary manner, for their detailed analysis belongs to the field of general sociology. But such a cursory examination is indispensable since it enables us to relate political phenomena to all the other aspects of collective living.

There are two possible ways of conducting this study. We could take as a basis the various categories of human communities, with each category representing a certain type of political structure. Or we could base the study on the different elements found in all, or almost all, human communities—geographic, demographic, technological, institutional, cultural, and so on. The difference is simply one of classification. In the first case, we classify the political structures "vertically," with each community defined by a combination of different elements. In the second, we classify them "horizontally," with each element appearing in the various types of communities. The second classification seems preferable for our analysis of political sociology since it allows

21

us to define more clearly the relations between political phenomena and the various elements of the human communities within which these phenomena occur. We will therefore adopt the second approach.

Thus defined, political structures can be divided into two broad classifications: physical structures and social structures. But the separation between the two is not rigid. The term "physical" is applied here to those factors closest to nature (geography and demography); the term "social" refers to the more artificial, essentially human factors (technology, institutions, cultures, beliefs). There is no sharp line separating them. Men do not perceive physical structures in their original, material forms, but through acquired ideas, beliefs, and social traditions. Indeed, today they are as much a product of social change as of physical evolution. Man's manipulation of the earth, the soil, the things he cultivates, and his means of communication makes geography no less social than physical. And human intervention in the demographic area—through medicine, hygiene, and birth control—is even more significant.

Inversely, many social elements are based on physical substrata. Sometimes the foundation is obvious: the sexual and parental instinct underlies the institution of the family; the forces of nature are the sources of animistic religions. Broadly speaking, almost every social institution corresponds to some physical factor. For example, the purpose of economic institutions is to satisfy material needs; competition between men in this area explains many theologies; finally, the way in which these material needs are satisfied determines numerous cultural elements.

1

Physical Structures

As a rule, human communities are more or less attached to a geographical area. Even nomadic tribes move about on certain routes within specific zones. Likewise, the populations of these communities have various characteristics—such as number, density, and distribution. *Territory* and *population* are traditionally recognized as basic elements of nations in the theory of the state, but actually they are components of every human group. To define the nation-state in the traditional way, as "a population fixed to a given territory," is to ascribe to one kind of community a characteristic that applies to almost all communities.

The phenomena of power are closely tied to and greatly influenced by the physical structures within which they occur, whether we are speaking of antagonisms whose purpose is the acquisition of power, or of integration that those in power are trying to achieve. Conflicts over territorial borders, over raw materials, over transportation and communication routes illustrate the political importance of geographical structures. Theories which explain wars and revolutions in terms of population pressures indicate the importance of demographic structures.

Nevertheless, it appears that the influence of physical conditions upon political life diminishes in proportion to the technological development of a society. Ancient states were more dependent upon geographical and demographic factors than modern states, and today, industrialized nations are less dependent than underdeveloped nations. Man is progressively tending to dominate nature instead of being dominated by it.

GEOGRAPHICAL STRUCTURES

"The politics of states is in their geography." This Napoleonic maxim expresses an idea that goes back as far as the fifth century B.C. in Hippocrates's *Treatise on Airs, Waters, and Places*. Herodotus applied it in his *Histories*. In his *Politics*, Book VII, Aristotle formulated a theory concerning the relationship between climate and political liberty, which was to be restated throughout the later centuries, notably by Jean Bodin, and by Montesquieu in his *Spirit of Laws*, Books XIV and XV. At the end of the nineteenth and the beginning of the twentieth centuries, these traditional themes received systematic treatment by geographers. A German named Frederick Ratzel published a *Political Geography* in 1897; later, his disciples called this new discipline "geopolitics." In reaction to the overly deterministic concepts of the German school, there developed the French school of "human geography," founded by Vidal de la Blache and Jean Brunhes.

Conservatives, fascists, liberals, Marxists—none of them deny that politics is dependent upon geography, but they disagree about the degree of dependency. Conservative ideologies tend to exaggerate its influence, while the newer ideologies tend to minimize it. For Maurice Barrès (1862–1923),[1] politics is based "on the earth and the dead," that is to say, on geography and history, with the latter largely dependent on the former. The German school of geopolitics was closely associated first with the pan-Germanists, and later with the National Socialists. The notion that man is locked in a determinism of earth and environment, that he cannot escape from nature, is at the very heart of the philosophy of the right. On the left is the opposing view that man is free, that he can escape from natural conditions and is, in fact, moving in that direction. Generally speaking, the influence of geography cannot be divorced from man's technological inventions, which enable him to overcome the difficulties of his natural surroundings. Thus, geographical factors are sociological as well as geographical, and social as well as physical, and the social element increases at the expense of the physical in proportion to technological progress. In primitive so-

[1] A French writer and politician; his novels preached the restoration of France's national energy.

cieties political phenomena depend greatly upon geographical conditions; in modern states the dependency is less.

Climate and Natural Resources

Climate and natural resources are closely linked together, especially with respect to plants and vegetation, which depend on both climate and soil for their existence. Practically speaking, these factors are inseparable. Ancient writers made the mistake of treating them separately. We will examine them here successively to determine the role each plays in their interrelationship.

CLIMATE   From Aristotle to Montesquieu, early theories on the relationship between geography and politics centered on climate. These theories still have a certain hold on the public, which, although not really familiar with the theories, visualizes the influence of geography on political phenomena in a similar fashion. Modern geographers and sociologists hold rather different views.

Montesquieu gave the best-known and most precise formulation of the theory in his *Spirit of Laws,* Book XVII (1748): "Great heat enervates human energy and courage," whereas "in cold climates there is a certain strength of body and mind which makes men capable of performing acts that are long, painful, great, and daring." The conclusion follows that "we must not be surprised if the cowardice of peoples in hot climates has almost always made them slaves and that the courage of peoples in cold climates has kept them free." "Civil servitude"—in other words, slavery—is linked with climate in the same way: in hot countries "men are driven to perform painful duties only by fear of punishment; slavery is less shocking to human reason." Montesquieu's theories are simply restatements of Aristotle's views. Having observed that a cold climate is conducive to liberty and a hot climate to slavery, Aristotle examined the question of temperate climates, which obviously perplexed him. He judged that men are free in temperate climates but that they also know how to command others, and he failed to explain why this is so. Jean Bodin (1530–93) restated the same ideas, but this native of Anjou was more anxious to defend the peoples of the south than Montesquieu, a native of the Gironde. Bodin believed that the southerners' intellectual qualities offset their lack of physical energy, with both factors dependent upon climate.

Popular notions of the political influence of climate have changed very little from these traditional theories. In the nineteenth century, French historian Jules Michelet emphasized the role of heat and its influence upon the revolutionary days of 1789 (which occurred, for the most part, between May and September). His thesis applies to the Revolution of 1830 (July) and the days of June, 1848, but not to the outbreak of the Revolution of 1848, which occurred in February. Need we recall that the Soviet revolutions took place in October and November (1905, 1917, respectively) in a country already cold at that time of the year? Some forty years ago it was fashionable to speak of "sun spots" to explain wars and revolutions, a notion no longer taken seriously. Nevertheless, a climatic influence on events of this nature is not improbable. If the Romans named the third month after the god of war, it was because March constituted the ideal moment to begin a military campaign in Europe. "General Winter" played a role in Napoleon's defeat in Russia in 1813 and in Hitler's defeat in 1941.

Although the direct influence of climate on political phenomena cannot be denied, it is neither as simple nor as absolute as Aristotle and Montesquieu thought. In a few instances we can perceive a rather clear, direct influence of climate upon politics. The ancient Mediterranean democracy, whose center was the agora or the forum, was clearly linked to a climate that favored outdoor living. The same can be said of African *palabres* and Berber *djemaas*. But other factors must also be taken into account, and the influence of climate is extremely indirect. Rather it is a people's way of life that is linked to climate; political forms are only one aspect.

There are climates that preclude almost all social or political development—excessively cold climates, climates at high altitudes. There are others that make such development difficult—hot and humid climates or desert climates. Nevertheless, we find Eskimo societies as well as civilizations high in the Andes and in Tibet. And there are certain tropical or equatorial regions that have experienced great development (the city of Rio de Janeiro, for example). On the other hand, some climates favor social and political development. These regions are found mainly in the temperate zones. Human societies are thus placed, from the outset, in disparate circumstances that weigh heavily upon their future development. But the effect of climate is felt less as an immediate influence of the human psyche (as ancient writers believed) than through an indirect influence on the country's natural resources. Man's political and social life is conditioned, not so much by a direct climatic influence, as by the collective influence of his "climato-botanical" environment.

NATURAL RESOURCES   By natural resources we mean all the things provided by geography that are necessary to man's physical existence—

such as food, clothing, and shelter. Animal and vegetable resources are essential in underdeveloped societies, while mineral resources become increasingly important with industrial growth. As in the case of climate, political theorizing about natural resources has long been psychological in nature. To some extent it remains so today. But the psychological theory rests on a basic contradiction. On the one hand, an abundance of natural resources would appear to be a source of power, hence a means of social and political development. But on the other hand, this wealth tends to cause human energy to slacken and willpower to weaken, leading to stagnation and decadence.

Theorists of the past generally took the second view. Montesquieu, for example, believed that fertility of the land and an abundance of wealth were conducive to slavery, whereas a dearth of natural resources nourished a people's desire to be free and independent of foreigners. In fertile lands "rural people, who make up the majority of the population, are not jealous of their liberty. They are too preoccupied and too much concerned with their private affairs. An abundant country is afraid of being pillaged, afraid of an army." In poor countries, on the other hand, "liberty . . . is the only possession worth defending." Moreover, "a land that is sterile makes men industrious, sober, hardened by labor, courageous, and fit for warfare. They must secure for themselves what the terrain refuses to yield. A fertile country imparts, with its abundance, a spirit of indolence and a certain fondness for the preservation of one's own life." We can discern in this argument traces of the moralistic views of Cato and other writers of antiquity, linking frugality to democracy.

Modern theories, which posit a close correlation between a democratic society and material abundance, are at complete variance with the earlier views. Poverty is seen as an aggravating factor in political antagonisms, making free governments more difficult. General affluence, on the other hand, is seen as tending to reduce political conflicts and to favor the cause of freedom. However, international competition interferes with internal rivalries. The prosperity of some can generate antagonisms instead of reducing them. The race for raw materials is a very influential factor in this matter; it explains a number of conflicts and intrigues between states, as well as internal upheavals.

With the development of international and industrialization, the problem of raw materials became crucial. In the nineteenth century, for example, Great Britain was "the workshop of the world," receiving from all parts of the earth raw materials that were converted into manufactured goods sold everywhere. Such a system was possible only so long as the sources of raw materials remained available. Today, the

United States consumes more than 50 percent of the world's raw materials, and access to raw materials is fundamental to it. Competition and rivalries also arise among the great industrial nations, as well as between them and the states with raw materials. Thus the existence of raw materials on a nation's territory (which is a geographical fact) becomes an important factor in its politics and, indirectly, in the politics of other nations, especially industrial nations.

This race for raw materials explains many wars, alliances, and international intrigues. Sometimes the internal politics of a state also reflects its foreign policy, which is dictated by the presence of coveted raw materials on its soil. Certain revolutions in oil-producing nations and certain authoritarian regimes charged with maintaining "order" are directly tied to pressures from nations that purchase their raw materials. But we must be careful not to exaggerate these influences. There exists today a certain myth about oil and its political influence, just as there was a myth about coal and steel in the nineteenth century.

No less important are the routes used to find and bring back raw materials in every era since the dawn of civilization. It has been shown that the political influence of Paris and its inhabitants, the *Parisii*, was dependent, even before the Roman conquest, upon their location along the tin route. The trade route for amber and silk and spices was already important under the Roman Empire. The importance of the Parthian kingdom derived from its location on the silk and spice route. We know the role played by the Indian trade route in British politics of the nineteenth and the first half of the twentieth centuries, even if it was sometimes exaggerated. Markets for the acquisition of raw materials often influenced the political structures of states or served as focal points for national rivalries. But this topic leads us away from strictly geographical factors.

GEOGRAPHY AND UNDERDEVELOPMENT   Early theories about the political influence of climate and natural resources deserve to be reexamined. When brought up to date, they probably provide the best explanation for the contemporary imbalance in the development of nations. Racists claim that this imbalance is due to an inequality of the races, but every experiment shows that Africans, Asiatics, and American Indians, when placed in the same living conditions as persons of the white race, reveal the same aptitudes and the same level of intelligence, as we shall see further on.

The relation between levels of socioeconomic development on the one hand and the great climato-botanical zones on the other is striking. The highest degree of underdevelopment occurs in the two glacial zones of North and South, the equatorial zone, and the subtropical desert zones. The highest degree of development occurs in the temperate zones (North America, Europe, Russia, and the fringe of North Africa in the northern hemisphere; Australia, New Zealand, parts of Chile and Argentina, and the fringe of South Africa in the southern hemisphere). The Asiatic steppes end in a kind of halfway development. We find there, for example, patriarchal societies which form the nucleus of conquering tribes. Local circumstances which improve the climato-botanical situation (as in the valley of the Nile, the Tigris and Euphrates rivers; the Asiatic monsoon region; the altitude of the Inca and Aztec empires) lead to a higher level of development than in the surrounding zone.

These climato-botanical influences are of secondary importance in today's industrialized societies, but they played a fundamental role for centuries. Because of their geographical handicap, countries in the glacial zones and in the equatorial and tropical regions were long held back from developing, and it is very difficult for them to catch up. If they were industrialized, the effects of their climate and natural resources would be far less significant. But it is precisely because of their long difficulties with climate and resources that they have not been able to industrialize. Technology, on the other hand, permits those nations with the capability to greatly increase their rate of production, and this results in an ever-widening gap between them and the underdeveloped nations. The curse of geography still weighs heavily, and it weighs even more so on peoples in the nontemperate zones.

Space as a Political Structure

Climate and natural resources cannot be divorced from another geographical factor that is the subject of much study today—territorial space. A specific example will illustrate its importance and relation to other social factors. In ancient Egypt, the geography apparently had a great deal of influence on politics. The Nile valley, isolated by deserts, provides a natural setting for social development. Its lands are extremely fertile, thanks to regular fluvial inundations. To use this natural phenomenon the Egyptians must have developed a system of dams and reservoirs, and then continued to maintain the canals and pumps —which required a highly advanced and centralized social organization. Here we find both the pressing need for a strongly organized state and the factors necessary for the development of such a state: natural wealth, easy communication through the Nile, no places of refuge for dissidents, protection by the deserts from foreign invaders, and so forth. In the valleys of the Tigris and Euphrates, a combination of climate, resources, and location provided the same possibilities for civilization, but the absence of regular flooding by the rivers failed to bring about the same degree of centralization.

Geographers a. e increasingly convinced that the study of living space is one of the main branches of their science. The natural space within which human activity develops can be studied from three points of view: (1) the delimitation of societies, (2) the internal arrangement of societies so delimited, and (3) the location of these societies with respect to one another, and their mutual contacts.

DELIMITING THE SPATIAL STRUCTURES OF POLITICAL SOCIETIES The spatial structure of a political society (of a state, for example) is not solely the result of geographical factors. Many other influences are involved, particularly the nation's history. But geography does have its importance, to a greater or lesser degree depending on the circumstances, and sometimes it is decisive.

Geographical space is more or less divided up, partitioned in one way or another. Certain divisions, certain partitions, are illusory, resulting more from human interpretation than from physical realities. But other divisions are based upon undeniable geographical facts. This is especially true of islands, using the word "island" in its broadest sense. In addition to oceanic islands (or islands in lakes and streams), which fit the narrow definition of insularity, we must include oases, those islands of the desert; the valleys of certain rivers (the Nile, for example); clearings, those islands in the forests; and so on. Island peoples have no neighbors; they are separated from other peoples by "voids." This fact not only gives them a greater degree of security, but it also confers on their citizenry the notion that they live in a natural setting. For insular peoples, the concept of natural boundaries is clear, precise, and undebatable, provided, of course, that a single people occupies the island's territory and occupies it entirely. Otherwise, insularity has no meaning.

But except in the case of island territories, geographical divisions are always more apparent than real. Nothing is less natural than "natural boundaries," an incontestable fact with regard to rivers, which unite more than they separate. There are civilizations in river valleys which have developed on both banks of the stream. Rivers have been chosen as frontiers because they constitute convenient landmarks. But only the course of a stream is natural, not its role as a wall or boundary which it is forced to play. The concept of rivers as natural boundaries has been forged by history, not by geography. There is, for example, a Rhenish civilization that almost became the basis of a nation, the famous Lotharingia. History decided otherwise and made the Rhine a frontier. There is also a Danubian civilization which has sometimes served as a basis for political alliances.

Mountains form more natural boundaries than rivers, although everything depends upon their height. For every mountain that serves as a wall, how many mountains have served as thoroughfares? Civilizations have often developed and gravitated around mountain ranges as if they were magnets. The Basques and Catalonians are examples of peoples unified by mountains, not separated by them, and who developed civilization on both sides. Switzerland was born in the mountains, and its unity derives from them. We must, of course, distinguish the peoples of the plains on either side of the mountains, who are separated by them, from the people within the mountains who occupy their slopes and valleys and are united by them. But this distinction is not always sharply defined.

The political influence of geographical divisions has always been considered important. "Island peoples are more inclined to cherish freedom than peoples on the continent," Montesquieu wrote. "The sea separates [islands] from great empires, and tyranny cannot lay its hand on them. Conquerors are halted at the water's edge. Island dwellers are not engulfed in conquests and they preserve their laws more easily." It has often been said that insularity enabled Great Britain to do without a standing army until the twentieth century, whereas France was forced to provide one from the time of Charles VII for its own defense. Deprived of this effective means for exerting pressure against the noblemen in his kingdom, the English monarch was unable to establish his absolute power. His attempts in this direction met with rebuffs and accelerated the development of a parliamentary regime. In France, on the other hand, the existence of a standing army enabled the king to dismiss the Estates General in 1614 and to rule without control or limitation. The broad outlines of this analysis are correct, but many other factors entered into the picture.

The existence of natural obstacles to invasions has had a similar if somewhat less significant influence. Even though they do not constitute natural boundaries, rivers, and more especially mountains, do hinder would-be conquerors. The vast plain of northern Europe was far more susceptible to invasions than the mountainous zones of central Europe. The unstable and ephemeral nature of the states that were formed there, the uncertainty about their borders, and the many changes they went through over the years clearly have political consequences.

The administrative divisions within states are often based on natural divisions resulting from geography and history. The French communes, which replaced the church parishes of the Old Regime, more or less reflect the Gallo-Roman administrative pattern. The *départements* created by the Constituent Assembly (1791) made use of older divisions established by Charlemagne, which, in turn, dated back to earlier divisions of ancient Gaul. In every country we find similar situations. To be sure, this parceling out of the land for administrative purposes was as much the work of man as of nature, but geography played its role in the operation.

In certain cases, moreover, the geographical role seems to have been decisive. Swiss federalism, for example, differs from all other federalisms by the size of its federated units. As a rule, federalism exists in the very large states (like the USSR, the United States, and Brazil), with each member state quite sizable by itself. Switzerland, on the other hand, has made federalism survive in a very small state, one in which the federated units are diminutive. This arrangement gives every appearance of being geographical in origin. The natural partitioning of the country by mountains produces clearly defined valleys or groups of valleys set apart from one another. The valleys form cantons which, collectively, constitute the Swiss Confederation. To be sure, historical factors have entered the picture, but geography appears as the overriding element.

We could cite many comparable cases. The example of Norway impressed the followers of Le Play (1806–82),[2] who attached great political importance to the fjords, regarding them as isolating factors encouraging close family ties and a spirit of individualism. While these conclusions are debatable, it is clear that the country is divided by fjords, which inevitably has political consequences. By the same token, a tendency toward political separatism in certain regions of a country is often explained by the region's geographical location— being remotely situated (Brittany, for example) or part of a mountain complex (the Basques and Catalonians).

There are two traditional forms of rural settlements—dispersed and conglomerate. Though it is not easy to define them precisely, we can quickly grasp the essential difference. The dispersed settlement is

---

[2] A French engineer and economist, regarded as the founder of the modern study of social economy in France.

made up of farms that are isolated or grouped into tiny hamlets of two or three farmhouses close to the lands being cultivated. In the conglomerate settlement, the farmers are grouped into villages of varying size, which they leave each morning and return to each evening, often making a fairly long journey to reach the fields.

Whether the settlement is spread out or concentrated depends in part upon geographical factors. A well-known theory has been formulated to account for this variation. In countries with porous soil (chalky soil, for example), the rain penetrates deeply and water is hard to find, especially if the climate is generally dry. Consequently, the homes cluster about a well wherever this rare and indispensable necessity is located. In countries with nonporous soil, rain trickles and runs freely and water is everywhere, especially if the climate tends to be humid. Wells are then easily located, and the population can thin out. This explanation is valid, if it is not pushed too far. In the Causses [southern France], where the soil is porous and the rainfall light, settlement is often dispersed. In the Woëvre [Lorraine] and the Hungarian Putza, where the soil is nonporous and the rainfall abundant, settlement is concentrated. Human factors clearly enter the picture, particularly security—which seems to have played an important role in the concentration of Sicilian population, as well as those in southern Italy and the Hungarian Putza. Regardless of its explanation, the dual nature of rural settlement has had a definite influence on political phenomena. In a study of western France in 1913, economist and historian André Siegfried observed that regions with a widely scattered population were rather conservative, while those with more concentrated population tended to be more receptive to change and innovation. He explained this fact by the isolation of the former, leading them to turn inward on themselves and their traditions, whereas, in the latter case, more frequent contacts with other individuals permitted a faster and easier dissemination of new ideas. This analysis seems valid, even though people spy on one another in villages and social pressure is in the direction of conformity and conservatism. Perhaps we should take into account the size of the villages. When they amount to real cities, as in southern Italy and Sicily, the atmosphere is different from that of tiny, rural hamlets.

Cities do not always have a geographical origin. By this we mean that their location is not always the result of natural conditions, but of human factors. The examples of Brasilia and Washington, D.C., are fairly typical, even though geographical considerations intervened in their choice (the location of Brasilia was determined by the fact that it is in the center of the country). Many different elements underlie the urban phenomenon. A city may grow up around a religious shrine, a marketplace, a port, or a center of natural resources. It can also be the result of military requirements (fortifications) or of political needs (capital cities and smaller administrative units).

Whatever the origin, the political consequences of the urban phenomenon are considerable. Democracy was born in cities, the cities of antiquity, and socialism developed in modern industrial cities. Revolutions are essentially urban phenomena; peasant revolts are rare, and even more rarely are they constructive. Cities not only have a direct political influence on people by the numerous contacts they afford and by the opportunities they offer for political action (the right to assemble and the right to demonstrate are essentially urban rights); they also exert an indirect political influence because of their leading role in the development of civilization and in material and intellectual progress. Language has reflected this fact by treating as synonyms the terms "urbanity" and "civilized character."

The use of geographical space within the cities is also a phenomenon with considerable political consequences. It has been said that the invention of the elevator aggravated the class struggle by accentuating social segregation. Prior to its invention, the aristocracy and the bourgeoisie occupied the lower levels of an apartment building, those above the ground floor and mezzanine. The first of these was the "noble" floor, the second slightly less "noble," the third still less, and so forth. Common people thus lived on the top floors and on the ground floor. This arrangement allowed for daily contacts between the social classes. However, in revaluing the upper floors, the elevator increased the tendency of the common people to form separate neighborhoods. These facts have probably been exaggerated, for segregation into neighborhoods predated the invention of the elevator (in 1848 and 1871, the political division of Paris into two parts, east and west, was already striking). Certain laws concerning low-cost housing have reinforced this tendency. On the other hand, in Great Britain and other countries, urban planners tend nowadays to create mixed neighborhoods, often for political reasons—like weakening the impact of the workers' demands. As a matter of fact, in such neighborhoods, working-class voters are often more conservative than in neighborhoods made up entirely of workers.

CONTACTS We have mentioned the political importance of contacts between societies a number of times. These contacts depend in part upon geographical factors.

It is difficult to make a sharp distinction between "natural" highways and those created by man. Formerly, the adherents of geographical determinism tended to believe that highways followed the natural patterns of the soil or the earth's topography. It has since been noted that many of these highways, regarded as "natural," were the results of history rather than of geography. They became natural, but they were not so originally. Be that as it may, the fact remains that there are natural highways (rivers, plains, seas), and the course of "artificial" highways always takes natural conditions into account.

The influence of routes and highways upon politics is undeniable. Trade routes, the routes of religious shrines, invasion routes—all led to contacts. They transport merchandise, armies, diseases, and ideas. Studies in electoral geography illustrate their role as penetration routes for new political doctrines. But highways also favor contacts between people and political power, between the governors and the governed. The police and the military use them to put down revolts; islands of resistance are located far from the main arteries in hard-to-reach areas. "Civilization is first of all a highway," said Kipling. But centralization is also "first of all a highway." This ambivalence is always present and precludes rigid determinism. If the valleys of certain rivers, surrounded by deserts (the Tigris, the Euphrates, and the Nile), were the privileged political sites in antiquity, producing the first great States, it is perhaps because two contradictory yet advantageous factors were present: isolation by deserts and contacts by means of waterways.

This same ambivalence probably explains the advantages conferred by a maritime location, for the sea is simultaneously a protection, a barrier, and a means of communication—the only highway on which important and heavy cargo could be transported over long distances in ancient times. Great empires, such as the Greek and Roman, grew up around the sea. And can we not speak today of an Atlantic empire? Less so nowadays, because modern technology has transformed the problems of communication and diminished the advantages of a maritime situation. The influence of the sea on internal political structures is not as clear. "Free man, thou shalt always love the sea," wrote the poet. But, if maritime peoples have often been free peoples, we can not generalize from this fact. Further, they do not want to talk about it; but their attitudes vary a great deal. Many peoples of the sea—such as the Corsicans, Italians, and the people of Provence in southern France—are not really sailors.

Highways are but one factor in a more general concept that we might call *location*. Let us take as an example present-day France, with its 50 million inhabitants, its cities, factories, universities, and its technological and intellectual capabilities. If we transported it into the Pacific, to the site occupied by New Zealand, its political importance in the world would be reduced by 75 percent (this figure being purely symbolic). Hence, the political importance of France is three-fourths dependent on its geographic location. Now, of course, such a supposition is absurd. If France were situated in New Zealand, it would be a very different country, but this in itself illustrates the importance of location. We could provide many similar examples. Swiss neutrality is obviously linked to Switzerland's location in Europe. The possible development of communism in Cuba is important only because of the island's proximity to the United States. Moreover, a country's location can be evaluated from various points of view: its situation in relation to other states, to the great arterial highways, and to raw materials and natural resources, and so on. It also depends upon history. The displacement of politically important centers from the Mediterranean to the Atlantic has changed the situation for the peoples bordering these seas.

DEMOGRAPHIC STRUCTURES

For a long time, it has been widely believed that demography influences politics. The public readily accepts the idea of population pressure as a cause of wars and revolutions. And the notion was popular for several hundred years before becoming the basis of Hitlerian propaganda on "vital living space" and being revived again by contemporary sociologists.

The prominent political theories have attached very little importance to demography. Liberals and Marxists barely touch on the problem. Christians, nationalists, and communists are all critical of Malthusian theories and are opposed to birth control. However, a rapid increase in population produces serious political consequences. The size of a population—which defines the size of a community—is by itself a political fact of great importance.

The Size of the Population

The distinction between large and small states was familiar to ancient writers before it was obscured during the nineteenth century by the development of legal theories on national sovereignty and equal rights. Voltaire believed that democracy was suited only to small states. Rousseau conceived of different constitutions for Poland and the city-state of Geneva because of their differences in size. Today, the question of the size of a community has come back to the forefront of political discussion, whether on the national level or on other levels such as "large cities," "large complexes, or "small groups." From a theoretical point of view, it seems that the very nature of political phenomena changes with the size of the community, and that basic differences separate "macropolitics" from "micropolitics."

The size of a community depends primarily on the size of its population, which is to say, on the number of people who are members of the community. Territorial size is of secondary importance. Australia is an average-sized state in terms of population, though its territory is very extensive. The relationship between the size of the territory and the size of the population defines the population density, which forms the basis of the concept of "demographic pressure," to be examined later.

THE DISTINCTION BETWEEN MACROPOLITICS AND MICROPOLITICS   The distinction between micro- and macropolitics is very important. The difference in the size of a community leads to a difference in the nature of the social relationships and political phenomena that develop within it.

Micropolitics is the political activity within small communities; macropolitics, the political activity within large communities. But how can we distinguish large communities from small ones? Obviously, there are many intermediate-sized communities which we hesitate to call large or small. We cannot establish a precise point at which a community ceases to be small and thenceforth becomes large. Yet, the general distinction is clear enough. In a small community, all members know one another personally. Their relationships are thus primarily interpersonal, man to man, so to speak. "Small groups" are defined in this manner by English and American sociologists. In a large community, on the other hand, personal acquaintance of all members does not and cannot exist. A Frenchman cannot know every other Frenchman, or a Belgian, every other Belgian. The mass of people who make up the community is, for each of its members, an abstraction, an image, a myth to some extent, and not something living and tangible. Human relationships are largely carried on through organizations.

In the last analysis, man serves as the basis for differentiating between the two types of communities. Small communities are founded on direct human relationships; large communities, on relationships we could describe as "mediated." The citizen of a large metropolis is never likely to have the opportunity to see his mayor, unless it is at some civic function at which the mayor makes an appearance, or during a brief audience at which protocol and social distance make human relations artificial, formal, and impersonal. The citizen of a small town, on the other hand, can see his mayor, talk to him, get to know him personally, and develop a human relationship. Normally, the citizen of a large city will have a very different kind of contact with the municipal authorities. The same is true for the citizen of a large nation; the head of state is even more mythical and remote, and relationships with those in power are even more strictly administrative.

Thus, differences in the size of a community entail differences in the nature of their social relationships. Direct human contacts and mediated relationships are fundamentally different, a difference especially noticeable on the political plane. In small communities, the political struggle takes on an essentially personal character. Of course, coalitions, cliques, and factions are formed, which roughly resemble the political groupings of a large community. But small communities have no formal political organizations, merely alliances among individuals and personal affinities. By the same token, integration is simply a question of harmonizing interpersonal relationships.

In large communities, however, the political struggle is as much collective as individual. Complex organizations are set in motion. Institutions, political "machines," and party "apparatuses" of varying importance and complexity confront one another. The struggle goes on simultaneously between these contending groups and within each group. In the latter case, the struggle sometimes takes on the personal character of smaller communities; thus, an intermingling of macropolitics and micropolitics occurs. But more often than not, individual relationships within these organizations are less direct, less personal, more anonymous and bureaucratic. The situation is comparable to the difference between an artisan's shop, privately owned and operated, and a large department store. Relationships between the artisan-manager of the small store and his fellow workers are really micropolitics; those between the owner-manager of the large store and his employees, macropolitics. In large communities, integration involves problems of community organization rather than interpersonal relationships, as well as problems of beliefs and public attitudes, which make the society as a whole meaningful to its members (the flag, nation, and so forth).

PROBLEMS OF MACROPOLITICS   Political power in large communities poses special problems that are becoming increasingly acute in modern societies, precisely because these societies are based on very large groups of people. The main problems concern bureaucratization and decentralization.

The governments of large communities tend to become bureaucratic. For one thing, those who govern are unable to make direct contact with the citizenry except by such artificial means as radio, television, and the press. Furthermore, as the community expands, the intermediate echelons also expand, increasing the distance between the ordinary citizen and those holding power. This growth in the administrative apparatus forces the relationship between government officials and the public to become standardized. This is reflected in vast amounts of paper work, forms, questionnaires, and so on, which tend to give an anonymous and mechanical aspect to the concerns and requests of the citizenry. Within the administrative hierarchy, government reports become equally standardized among the various departmental agencies. Eventually, power loses contact with the social reality it is based on and comes to know only an abstract picture, consisting mainly of generalities translated into statistics. The development of automatic copying machines has aggravated this tendency towards abstraction. Such then are the principal aspects of bureaucracy. We will come back to this subject later (pp. 55–67) since it is tied to the question of technological progress.

Bureaucracy is not confined to the upper echelons of power. Political organizations, struggling to acquire power, also tend to become large communities in which human relationships are no less bureaucratic. The bureaucratization of trade unions and of large political parties has long since been studied and analyzed. The political contest tends to become a battle of robots in which the individual citizen feels like an outsider. A reaction against this tendency doubtless accounts in part for the present-day attempt to personalize political power. The admiration and confidence that the citizen bestows on the head of state or a party leader gives him the impression of making a direct human contact, one that breaks the bureaucratic barriers. But such an impression is illusory. Moreover, the bureaucratization of power makes it more oppressive, adding to the psychological danger of power a technological danger as well.

In large communities, the real political struggles in the inner circles are waged by big political machines and big organizations, in which the average citizen participates in only an abstract and episodic way. The resulting sense of alienation is only partially dispelled by the personalization of power, since this retains an illusory character. Genuine participation by the citizen in reaching decisions is possible only if the community is divided into smaller groups, groups organized on a human scale and with the power, the authority, and the means of making decisions. This is what is meant by "decentralization."

Decentralization is not to be confused with regional power arrangements. Even in a centralized government there is a need for authority to have its local headquarters. But these regional offices do not imply any local political life, whether they are in the hands of ordinary administrative agents, who carry out decisions made in the capital city, or whether they are in the hands of persons who have been invested with decision-making power, which they exercise in the name of the central government, the only body to which they are accountable (French prefects, for example). Local political life can exist only when local authorities are independent of the central power, when their authority springs from local political competition, and when they have the power to make their own decisions. In addition to regional decentralization, there is a kind of decentralization we may call "corporative." Here the individual community is given back the power to make decisions and the right to choose the men who will exercise this power —such as associations, unions, organizations for economic growth, universities, and so on.

Decentralization has become one of the major problems in the political life of large communities. Indeed, without it, political life withers away, competition occurs only on the level of huge bureaucratic organizations, social integration becomes a formal, impersonal process, and individuals feel alienated. Technological progress moves in the opposite direction from decentralization. First of all, by reducing distances, it facilitates decision-making at the top echelon. (The telephone, for instance, is an obstacle to local autonomy; it is so easy to have a question resolved by placing a call to the capital.) Second, technology tends to encourage mass organization, universal programs and planning in very large units. But we must not exaggerate this paradox. Even from a technological point of view, excessive centralization is harmful—a fact which became apparent in Soviet efforts to centralize economic planning for the entire country. In the last few years there has been a noticeable rebirth of decentralization in many large centralized societies, such as the USSR, France, and the people's democracies.

Demographic Pressure

Demographic pressure may be defined as a certain relationship between the size of a population and the amount of territory it occupies —for instance, if a population is too large for its territory. The present and future situation of most underdeveloped countries furnishes one of the most striking examples of demographic pressure with all of its political consequences.

DEMOGRAPHIC PRESSURE AND POLITICAL ANTAGONISMS It is a notion as old as mankind that in overpopulated countries social tensions are violent and wars and revolutions are frequent. In less-crowded countries, on the other hand, antagonisms are presumably diminished, rulers less likely to be challenged, and peace more likely to prevail.

Even Aristotle and Plato believed that an excessive growth in population provoked social disturbances. In his *Essais* (Chapter XXIII), Montaigne found a close correlation between the demographic theory of wars and the theory of revolutions. He considered wars "the bloodletting of the Republic," purging the body politic and freeing it of such harmful fluids as an affluxion of blood (a notion consistent with the medical views of the time and the concept of "humors"). It was a familiar idea then, and many Renaissance writers explained the conflicts of the day in terms of population pressures. "War is necessary in order that youth may emerge and the population may decrease," wrote Ulrich von Hutten, a friend and supporter of Luther, in 1518. And German free thinker Sebastian Franck added, in 1538: "If war and death did not come to our aid, we would have to leave our land and wander like gypsies." In the eighteenth century, the notion that population pressure produces political antagonisms directly inspired the theories of Thomas Malthus. He feared that a population increase among the poor, who would be condemned to ever greater poverty because of this increase, would intensify the poor man's envy of the rich man's property and eventually lead to a destruction of the social order.

There is some impressive evidence in support of theories of demographic pressure. Between 1814 and 1914, the population of Europe doubled; then the great wars of the first half of the twentieth century occurred. At the end of the eighteenth century, France was probably overpopulated relative to her natural resources and the technology of that era. It was at that moment that the Revolution of 1789 took place, as well as the great wars of the Napoleonic era (1792–1815). In today's underdeveloped countries, overpopulation coincides with numerous revolutionary movements and with attitudes that are often bellicose. In the 1930's, Germany in Europe and Japan in Asia were noticeably overpopulated. Their expansionist policies, and the wars they unleashed, were instigated to procure the space that these countries vitally needed. Inversely, it appears likely that the underpopulation of the United States in the nineteenth century, and the possibility for dis-

satisfied people to move west, weakened social tensions and notably reduced the class struggle. We can understand the views of Gaston
Bouthoul,[3] who maintains that wars today serve a regulatory function
formerly exercised by the great plagues and epidemics: they provide a
"demographic relaxation" and act as a kind of safety valve. Montaigne
held virtually the same view.

However, theories of demographic pressure are open to criticism
when viewed in this simplistic form. The most densely populated
countries are not the most bellicose; if that were so, Holland would be
the most warlike nation in Europe, given the density of her population. Overpopulated China was a peaceful nation for centuries,
whereas the Indian tribes of North America, scattered over a vast terrain, were continually engaged in hostilities. Many other factors, besides overpopulation, unleashed the French Revolution of 1789. The
Russian revolutions of 1905 and 1917 occurred in an underpopulated
country where it was hardly possible to speak of demographic pressure. Moreover, the concept of demographic pressure remains vague. It
cannot be defined merely in terms of population density. Alfred
Sauvy [4] has noted that we must also take into account the age of a
population, which increases as the population grows, thus causing a reduction in demographic pressure. Collective ideas and popular images
are also important factors. "The yellow peril," an image that was widespread at the end of the last century and has recently become popular
again, is based less upon any realistic appraisal of Asian power than
upon some vague notion of teeming masses of slant-eyed Orientals
about to sweep over the Caucasian nations in a vast wave. There was
also "the steamroller" myth, which had a definite effect on French
morale in 1914. Similar images contributed to the demoralization of
the Germans, beginning in 1942.

The first requirement is to assess a nation's natural resources and
the means available for exploiting them. In certain respects, the
theory of population pressure is a theory of poverty; it is more economic than demographic. It was precisely in this sense that Malthus
envisaged the problem when he formulated his famous law in *Principles of Population* in 1798: "Population, when unchecked, increases
in a geometric ratio. Subsistence only increases in an arithmetical
ratio." Accordingly, the gap between the two would grow ever wider
as the population increases at a rate of 2, 4, 8, 16, 32, 64, 128, and so
on, while the means of subsistence increase at a rate of 4, 6, 8, 10, 12,

[3] *Les guerres* (1951).
[4] Author of *La population*, 6th ed. (1961), and *Théorie général de la population*
(1952–54).

14, and so on. Humanity would thus be doomed to famine, unless there was a voluntary restriction on the birthrate; and this famine would produce very serious conflicts.

In the mathematical form given by its author, the Malthusian law has never been verified, nor is it capable of verification. What is meant by the "natural" growth of a population or of foodstuffs? Yet the very idea that the former increases more rapidly than the latter has remained deeply rooted in the human mind. At the present time, the acceleration in the rate of population growth has given the theory a new lease on life, and Malthusianism is experiencing a genuine rebirth among population analysts, particularly in the United States. A large number of demographers have been struck by the almost unlimited possibilities of population expansion as opposed to the clearly limited possibilities of expanding the food supply. Some believe that intensive cultivation tends to exhaust the soil, and that the means of subsistence are also threatened with gradual depletion. The most optimistic, those who think that a rational exploitation of the earth's resources will suffice to feed more than 6 billion persons, are struck by the fact that this figure is liable to be passed by the year 2000. Even if one concedes the possibility of feeding 10 billion persons, this level will be reached in less than seventy-five years. It is quite clear that the blind optimism of expansionist theories is inadequate to solve a problem of such magnitude.

DEMOGRAPHIC PRESSURE IN UNDERDEVELOPED COUNTRIES   For the present, the theory of demographic pressure describes the situation in underdeveloped countries, where population growth proceeds at an extraordinary rate, greatly aggravating political antagonisms. A mere glance at population statistics reveals that the general growth in population moves at different rates in different countries. We can discern two general rates of growth—a relatively slow rate in industralized countries and a very rapid rate in underdeveloped countries, which places these countries in a critical situation.

Impartial observation suggests that two kinds of demographic equilibriums tend to arise naturally from an interplay of physiological and psychological factors: a population balance in primitive societies, and one in highly developed industrial societies.

The equilibrium in primitive societies is like that which occurs among many species of animals, deriving from a combination of birth rate and death rate, both of which are very high. We might call it "the sturgeon equilibrium." Of the tens of thousands of eggs the female sturgeon lays, if all were to reach maturity, and if all of the eggs of the

new generation were to do the same, then every other species of animal would be displaced by sturgeons, the earth becoming an immense
sturgeon preserve. But, of course, thousands of eggs never reach maturity, and thousands upon thousands of baby sturgeons are doomed to
an early death. Hence, a relative demographic balance is established in
the sturgeon world. The population balance that arises in a primitive
society is similar in nature. A very strong reproductive drive, combined with a total lack of birth control, produces a very high birth
rate. But hygienic deficiencies, difficulties in providing food, diseases,
and premature aging produce a death rate that is equally high.

In highly developed societies, the situation is different in both respects. The mortality rate drops sharply, because of better hygiene, a
more abundant and better balanced diet, and improved medical care.
But at the same time, the birth rate also tends to drop as a result, first
of all, of biological factors not yet fully understood but whose effects
are clearly evident. Contrary to popular opinion, undernourishment
and physical weakness are accompanied by great natural fecundity.
The latter seems to diminish, however, when more food is available
and general vitality is stronger. In addition, increased personal comfort, education, and the development of individuality encourages voluntary controls on the birth rate. In short, a certain demographic balance tends to come about by the concurrence of a lower birth rate and
a lower death rate.

The situation in underdeveloped countries seems to stem from the
fact that the primitive population balance has been disturbed, while
the equilibrium of industrialized countries has not yet been reached.
The introduction of a few basic rules of medicine and hygiene, and
particularly the introduction of easy and inexpensive measures for
combating endemic diseases (the massive and regular use of DDT, for
example), cause a sharp decline in the death rate, especially the infant
mortality rate, which is the single most important factor in population
growth. Prolonging the life of the elderly, after they have lost the capacity to reproduce, is not significant in this connection. But birth
rates tend to remain at the same level over long periods of time, first
because a people's way of life and food habits change very little, and
their natural degree of fecundity is not affected; second, because traditional social habits and general educational patterns evolve very
slowly, and they have long been opposed to the current practice of voluntary birth control. Consequently, the population of a country on the
verge of industrial development tends to increase at a very rapid pace,
faster than its normal pace.

The results of this demographic imbalance are even more serious since it occurs at a time when the need for rapid population growth makes it very difficult to keep the food supply at its usual level; for workers must be removed from the production of current consumer goods and put to work constructing factories, highways, dams, and so forth, in other words, on the things needed to build the foundations of a modern country. During this intermediate stage, the food supply tends to increase, while the population tends to increase at a rapid rate. Underdeveloped countries thus find themselves in an explosive situation, one that is even worse than the picture drawn by the most orthodox Malthusians. Violent political antagonisms develop because of the demographic pressure. Revolutions, war, and dictatorships threaten to arise unless stringent measures are taken to propagate contraceptive practices.

THE DISPROPORTIONATE INCREASE AMONG THE POORER CLASSES Does the disruption of the natural demographic balance, which characterizes underdeveloped countries, also apply to the poorest classes of industrialized societies? Certain sociologists think so and have constructed on this premise a theory known as "differential fecundity," which, in turn, has led to the doctrine of eugenics. Both theories are open to criticism.

Throughout history, observers have been struck by the fact that the birth rate is lower among the wealthy classes than among the poor, and certain people have drawn political inferences from this fact. The laws of Caesar Augustus, designed to increase the birth rate, applied only to Roman nobles. The emperor hoped to maintain the power of the aristocracy and prevent its being usurped by the more rapid population growth of the common people. For his part, Malthus preached voluntary birth control only to the poorer classes, fearing that their rapid increase would create an explosive situation that could jeopardize the property of the wealthy.

Certain contemporary observers have drawn even more pessimistic conclusions from what they call "differential fecundity," that is, the faster rate of population growth among the poor. Considering that the poor have the highest rate of illiteracy and are generally less advanced intellectually, these theorists conclude that the most intelligent humans are dwindling in numbers, submerged by a mediocre mass. Through a natural demographic process, they see mankind as tending to regress, moving toward an ever greater degree of universal stupidity.

Some have used this seemingly scientific theory to advocate policies systematically encouraging an increased birth rate among the upper classes and discouraging an increase among the lower classes. This is known as "eugenics." The imperial laws of Augustus were a form of eugenics long before the term came into being. Modern eugenicists advocate comparable measures, such as abolishing family allowances for the most backward elements of society and granting systematic inducements to increase the birth rate among the upper classes. The more doctrinaire eugenicists go much farther, some of them demanding the sterilization of individuals afflicted with hereditary diseases or mental disorders. They would even create actual "human stud-farms" designed to reproduce individuals of superior quality. We find here, by a circuitous route, racist theories. Sterilization and human breeding were practiced in Hitler's Germany.

All of these theories are highly debatable. First of all, in terms of social classes, differences in human fertility, or rather in birth rates, are not as great as they are claimed to be. There is a natural tendency for them to level off. In the most industrialized societies, the birth rate has been rising for some years among the middle class, while declining among the working class. The case of the United States is typical. In France, government allotments for families have retarded the movement, but it is becoming noticeable all the same. Besides, in an industrialized society the status of the wealthy in comparison with the poor is not comparable to the situation that exists in two different societies, one developed and the other underdeveloped. Industrial workers and farm workers are as well informed as the middle class concerning the availability and use of contraceptives. In addition, the death rate has long remained much higher among the poorer classes, especially infant mortality, which offsets the effects of a higher birth rate (infant mortality in certain populous sections of Paris is twice that of the wealthy sixteenth *arrondissement*).

Above all, nothing is more false than a belief in the intellectual superiority of the so-called upper classes. Eugenicists make the same mistake here as racial theorists. They claim to base their views on a certain number of studies conducted in various countries on the aptitudes of school-age children. These studies, based on a series of tests, have indeed shown that, on the average, the intellectual level was greater among middle-class children than among working-class and farm children of the same age group. But these tests do not prove that the innate aptitudes of the groups are different. Even disregarding physical factors (better food, diet, and so on), so important for the intellectual development of a child, the obvious differences in social environment and education suffice to explain the different performances on the tests.

Intellectual growth by "osmosis," the kind of learning a child absorbs from conversations with his parents and from the general social environment, is of major importance. Without a doubt, the children of workers and peasants are handicapped in this respect, as compared with middle-class children, and this handicap is enough to explain the different results on the tests. One fact in particular reinforces this interpretation: the disparity in the average performance on testing, in terms of the social classes, decreases as the children grow older and are all exposed to the influence of a common educational experience. Initial differences, those resulting from parental assistance in the preparation of homework and explanations given outside the classroom, and from the permanent effects of education by environmental "osmosis," account for the persistence of a relative disparity.

The Composition of the Population

The composition of the population in terms of age, sex, the sociocultural level, ethnic groups, and geographical distribution plays a role in the political life of a community. While less important than the role of population pressure, it is by no means negligible.

BY AGE AND BY SEX   The role of sex in influencing political behavior is more apparent than that of age, even though it is not especially significant. Women are generally more conservative than men, and young people are often less conservative than older people.

In highly developed countries, where life is long and the birth rate is low, elderly people are numerous in relation to the younger generations; but in underdeveloped countries this is not the case. Now it is generally conceded that older people are more attached to the existing social order, hence more conservative, whereas young people are more radical. However, youth's taste for novelty can easily turn to a fondness for specious innovations, whose shocking, provocative, and outwardly violent nature corresponds rather closely to the psychological manifestations of youth's identity crisis and its search for originality. Among the middle class, this crisis often generates a conflict between the need for change that it arouses, and a deep, instinctive attachment to a privileged social status. The desire to hold on to the latter can lead to fascism with its authoritarianism and pompous affectations (*style muscadin*). The likelihood remains, however, that young nations are more inclined to revolutions and social upheavals than old nations, which find them extremely distasteful.

Various studies have shown that young people vote less for conservative and moderate parties than for parties advocating change, both on the left and on the far right (but more on the left than on the far right, in the last analysis, except under special circumstances). The average age of the population is mirrored in its political leaders. The youthful leaders of today's underdeveloped countries, like the youthful leaders of France in 1789, reflect the average age of the population. These demographic observations partly explain why industrialized nations, with a generally older population, are becoming more conservative, while underdeveloped countries, with a much younger population, are, on the contrary, more revolutionary. Thus the age composition of the population reinforces the demographic pressure, further aggravating political antagonisms.

On the other hand, in the youthful population of an underdeveloped country, the percentage of elderly people who need to be cared for is relatively unimportant. However, in industrialized societies, the elderly are a significant factor, and it is anticipated that the proportion may well rise to 25 percent (it is already 16 percent in France and Great Britain, 12 percent in Italy, and 10 percent in Spain)—a heavy responsibility for the population that is still active. One may even speak of an outright conflict between generations. In any event, the greater the proportion of elderly people in a society, the less dynamic the society becomes, and the more it tends toward social immobility. While these notions are somewhat vague, they nevertheless correspond to a certain reality. A falling back upon established values, a concern with security above anything else, the mental outlook of "retirement"— these attitudes reflect a definite way of life, one that tends to prevail as the average age of the population rises. And, naturally, this is reflected in a country's political life.

Differences based on sexual distribution probably have a certain political influence. As we noted above, it is more obvious than the influence of age differentials. Yet, in the long run, it may prove less significant. The legend of the rape of the Sabine women has helped perpetuate the memory of "wars over women," which were probably fairly common at a certain stage of civilization. It is by no means certain, however, that a population shortage was their only cause; a taste for novelty may have entered the picture. The folklore of American pioneer settlements, and of colonists in various countries, have also popularized the image of internal conflicts provoked by the scarcity of women. Such antagonisms, born of frustration, are undoubtedly real, but we must not exaggerate their extent.

Of greater importance are the lasting effects the scarcity of women has had on the development of certain social institutions and modes of social behavior. The scarcity of white women and the attitude of European colonists towards colored women played a definite role in the formation of racist sentiments (or nonracist sentiments, as was sometimes the case). Brazilian sociologist Gilberto Freyre has made some penetrating, although somewhat exaggerated, observations on this subject. During the pioneer period of the United States, the shortage of women caused them to be held in the highest esteem. Thereafter, a kind of moral matriarchy developed, which was more or less embodied in the law of the land; it still exercises a strong influence on American society. Most American wealth is in the hands of women, giving them a definite influence over the press, radio, television, and so forth. In addition, there is the enormous role played by women's clubs in the political and social life of the United States.

A predominance of women in the population seems to reinforce conservatism, at least in modern Western societies where female voters are generally more oriented to the right than male voters. In the 1965 French presidential elections, a majority of the women seem to have voted for de Gaulle, while a majority of the men voted for François Mitterand.[5] Certain analysts believe these differences are more a matter of age than of sex. Since women generally live longer than men, and there are many more older women than older men, the greater proportion of older women pushes the entire female vote toward the conservative side. For in both sexes, voting is more conservative among the older segment of the electorate. The fact that a great many older women are widows, looking back on the past, accentuates this general conservative tendency.

This is an interesting theory. However, various investigations have shown that the female vote was also more conservative among younger women, especially in working-class neighborhoods. Some people see in this the influence of "the tug on the heart strings" and of the mentality young, working-class women derive from their reading matter, television, and movies. According to these sources, the best way for women to escape from their present circumstances and climb the social ladder is to discover a "Prince Charming" and marry into wealth—a prospect that encourages them to adhere to the value system of the bourgeoisie and takes away any revolutionary ardor. We must not exaggerate the validity of this explanation, but it does contain an element of truth.

In underdeveloped countries, the political influence of women sometimes appears to be just the opposite—against the established order and in favor of change and heightening political tensions. The social

[5] A member of a small center-left group close to the Radicals, Mitterand became a candidate in the 1965 presidential election and was endorsed by the Socialists, Radicals, Communists, and the United Socialist party.

position of women is generally worse than that of men, particularly in Moslem countries, in Asia, and in Latin America. As the most oppressed social group, it would be natural, therefore, for women to be the most revolutionary element in the population. However, the theme of emancipation for women can also camouflage the failure to make any basic changes in the social structure. This was the case in North Africa among the partisans of *"l'Algérie française,"* with their campaign against the wearing of the veil, and in South Vietnam in the public pronouncements and public speeches of the overly publicized Mme. Nhu.

THE QUALITATIVE COMPOSITION OF THE POPULATION   The idea of analyzing population according to age and sex is quite clear. The concept of the qualitative composition of the population is not so clear; many factors are involved. We will limit ourselves here to examining the political consequences of different techno-cultural levels, on the one hand, and of ethnically mixed populations, on the other.

Except for a few very backward countries, we find in every nation groups that are highly developed from an intellectual and technological viewpoint, other groups that are less developed, and some that are not at all developed. But the relative distribution of these categories —whose limits are difficult to define—differs a great deal from country to country. This variation is politically very significant.

In underdeveloped countries, the politico-administrative elite, capable of staffing the top echelons of government, is very small. Those capable of staffing the middle echelons are also scarce, likewise technical workers trained to operate machinery with the precision and regularity required in modern society. The mass of the population consists of uneducated people who can neither read nor write, and who are accustomed to traditional ways of life, in which divisions of time are vague, continuity often unknown, and work methods very primitive. A population of this kind is ill-suited to the demands of a modern state, especially to industrial production and to democratic political processes. (We will undertake a careful study of this phenomenon later.)

In thoroughly industrialized countries, on the other hand, the proportion of people that are uneducated, illiterate, and untrained in modern skills is quite small. Most of the population has adjusted to machinery, regular work hours, continuity of effort, and precision. And this adjustment makes certain countries much more powerful than others with a population of the same size. The importance of Western Europe, of North America, and, to an ever greater degree, of the USSR and Eastern Europe derives in part from their situation with respect to technically trained reserves of manpower. As we shall see, democracy functions better in populations of this kind, although we must not consider this factor out of context.

Certain states have composite populations, formed of several groups differing in language, religion, traditions, and race. The popular tendency is to call them "polyethnic societies," but this term is not very satisfactory since it calls attention to the notion of race, which usually has no bearing on the matter, at least in the biological sense of the word. For our part, we prefer the expression "multicommunity states."

Sometimes the problem is simply a temporary one, related to the rate of immigration and its diversified character; the immigrants will eventually be assimilated into the national community. The most notable example occurred in the United States in the nineteenth century, when people coming from all parts of the world were united in the American melting-pot. It was not a complete fusion, however, especially for the colored races, but also for the Italians, the Irish, the Jews, and others with closely knit ethnic groups that often play a great political role. Certain political phenomena were observed, moreover, at the various stages of assimilation. Following their naturalization, new Americans often manifest an aggressive nationalism, which reflects their eagerness to become Americanized and, at the same time, their serious doubts about its true nature. Nationalism is often still very strong among their children, who reject the language of their origin and resent their parents' accent and any trace of foreign behavior. Eventually this aggressiveness subsides.

In other cases, the "multicommunity" situation endures. Each group refuses assimilation and preserves its originality. Numerous examples show that this does not prevent the formation of highly unified and closely integrated nations in which patriotic feelings are strong. But political structures must take into account the multicommunity situation. Federalism is the most common solution in these circumstances, the case of Switzerland proving that it can succeed very well. Sometimes particular conditions force the government to resort to more subtle solutions, especially if the different communities are not fixed to particular segments of territory. Lebanon is an interesting country to study in this connection.

It is usually more difficult to find a political solution when there is a considerable difference in the size of the communities, when one of them is quite obviously in the minority. Its fear of being engulfed by the majority community makes it emphasize its individuality; as always, aggressiveness and intolerance are the result of great weakness. If the minority borders on a large state with the same civilization, the same language, and the same way of life, the problem is even more complex. There is a great risk that the minority community will turn to its large neighbor to defend itself against the state it belongs to, and sometimes even attempt to break it up. A typical example was the action of the Sudeten German minority in Czechoslovakia in 1938–39. Although the treaties of 1919 had envisaged international systems for the protection of minorities, the results were not impressive. And so, in 1945, there were wholesale transfers of populations, often dramatic in nature, to alleviate the most serious cases of political incompatibility.

GEOGRAPHICAL DISTRIBUTION The average density of a population means nothing in itself. Egypt is an immense desert. Its population is very heavily concentrated in the triangle of the delta and along the thin ribbon of the Nile valley. Disparities in the distribution of population within a state lead to political antagonisms. They often produce inequities in the apportionment of political representation, which sometimes has a great influence on the exercise of power.

The political consequences of unequal population distribution are quite variable depending on the country. Generally speaking, a long-established, traditional inequality has fewer repercussions than an aggravation of existing inequalities. The depopulation or overpopulation of a region as a result of internal migrations is more important than the traditional coexistence of highly populated and sparsely populated regions. No doubt a low-density population poses certain permanent problems, such as greater per capita expense for the maintenance of highways, transportation, and public services, and a lack of capital funds for investments. A rapid rate of depopulation adds to the feelings of frustration which cause political unrest. This is rarely translated into a revolutionary spirit, just a repressed feeling of revolt. The population is too sparse to risk any violent manifestation of this feeling.

Tensions are more explosive in overpopulated areas. In Western Europe in the nineteenth century, the great migrations to the cities produced overcrowding of the poor and unfortunate. Ill-housed, ill-fed, and forced to endure dreadful working conditions, they played a key role in revolutionary movements: the revolutions of 1789, 1848, and 1871 started in urban areas and were put down finally by the rural populations. The formation of shanty towns around urban centers in underdeveloped countries today produces analagous situations. Population density is only one factor in a complex situation that includes a low standard of living, low wages, exploitation by employers, local political conditions, and the development of ideologies.

In almost every country, unequal distribution of the population produces inequities in political representation. Underpopulated areas have a larger proportion of delegates than they should have in terms of the total population; they are overrepresented. Heavily populated areas, on the other hand, have a smaller proportion of delegates than they are entitled to; they are underrepresented. Technically, these inequities in representation could be greatly reduced. Even if we adopt the principle that there must be one representative per x-number of inhabitants, we cannot regroup certain regions that are too thinly spread out to attain this minimum figure of inhabitants. We must simply accept the fact that certain sparsely inhabited areas must have representation based on a lower number of inhabitants. This could be a matter of little importance, but the truth is that inequities in representation are generally quite large, for reasons that are politically motivated.

In most countries of Western Europe during the nineteenth century, the conservative aristocracy relied upon the peasants in its struggle against the liberal bourgeoisie. Gradually, as the aristocracy was forced to yield on the question of extending the voting right, it tended to favor the rural population at the expense of the cities in order to maintain its domination. Then, the middle class perceived in turn that the socialists and communists, who were threatening them, relied primarily on the cities for their support. Like the aristocracy, they discovered that the conservatism of the rural population could be of assistance in maintaining their power. The middle class therefore followed the example of the aristocracy by establishing inequities of representation that favored less-populated, rural areas, but the peasants did not receive any real benefits. In both cases, the peasantry played the role of a supporting class for another class.

This imbalance is often very great. In the French Senate, an absolute majority of the electoral body (51 percent) represented, according to the 1954 census, villages of less than 1,500 inhabitants, which, at that time, included only 35 percent of the total French population. The disparity has since been intensified by the rapid depopulation of the rural areas. Moreover, this situation is an old one. Reestablished in 1948 under the Fourth Republic, after a brief interruption of two years, it goes back to 1875, when rural predominance in the Senate was the price the moderate monarchists demanded for supporting a republican constitution. Overrepresentation of rural areas is, moreover, a very widespread phenomenon. The reverse case of an urban overrepresentation is extremely rare. It existed in the USSR before the Constitution of 1936, when the Soviets sought to favor the minority working class, concentrated in the cities and regarded as the strongest supporter of the revolution.

2

Social Structures

In our definition, the social structures of politics—as opposed to the physical structures (geographic and demographic)—are those that derive from human creation rather than nature. This would include material inventions (a tool, a machine), systems of collective relationships (a business corporation, a matrimonial system), and even doctrines and cultures (Marxism, Western humanism). Bear in mind that the distinction between "physical" and "social" structures is not clear-cut. Physical structures today are intermixed with many social factors, as we have already indicated, and the collective beliefs that have grown up about them are often as important as their material reality. Inversely, physical factors are involved in the structures we call social: the natural needs of mankind form the basis for economic institutions; the physical conditions of a child's development play a major role in social relationships and even in the formation of ideologies, myths, and civilizations (if we are to believe the psychoanalysts, who perhaps exaggerate but are surely partially right).

Thus defined, social structures may be divided into three classifications: technological skills, institutions, and cultures. Technological skills are the means men have devised to act upon things—tools, machinery, and so forth. Institutions are the means of maintaining a stabilized order of social relationships—the legal status of the family, laws governing goods and property, and political constitutions. Finally, cultures are the ideologies, beliefs, and collective ideas generally

54

held within a given community. Of course, technological skills, institutions, and cultures are not really separable from one another. As with all classifications, this one should not be interpreted rigidly. Nevertheless, it is a reasonably accurate description of the essential aspects of social life, viewed as the framework within which political phenomena take place.

TECHNOLOGICAL SKILLS

The Littré dictionary defines technological skills (la technique) as "the collective processes of a specific art or manufacture." By "techniques" we mean the various material inventions men have devised—tools, machinery, and so on—which give them a mastery over nature or other men. Some people, notably Jacques Ellul,[1] use the term in a broader sense, including in it the social organization, regarded as a technique for organizing men. This thesis is linked to the author's conception of a close relationship between technological skills and social institutions. But, in any event, a distinction between the two interpretations should be made.

The overriding fact in this domain is the extraordinary number of inventions in the past century and a half which have transformed the conditions of life for mankind. This "technological revolution" has completely overturned man's social life, but it is in various stages of advancement in different countries. The difference between the so-called underdeveloped countries (either those in the process of development or undergoing accelerated development) and the industrialized countries is primarily a difference in the level of their technological development.

We will examine, first, the influence of technological progress on a country's economic and cultural development, and then we will consider its influence on the country's political life, for the latter is largely a function of the former. Technological progress disrupts the economic and cultural structures of political life, and it is this upheaval that transforms political life. The immediate consequences of technological progress upon political life (using television and the mass media for information and propaganda, using electronic machines in making governmental decisions, and so on) are less important than the indirect consequences.

[1] Jacques Ellul, *La technique ou l'enjeu du siècle* (1954) and *L'illusion politique* (1965).

The Transformation of Socioeconomic Structures Through Technological Progress

The technological revolution has brought about an economic revolution, characterized by an increase in the levels of production and of consumption. This economic revolution has itself produced a cultural revolution.

TECHNOLOGICAL PROGRESS AND ECONOMIC GROWTH   Technological progress has given man formidable means of acting upon nature, allowing him to increase production to an unprecedented scale. Thanks to technology, mankind has begun to emerge from poverty. But only those countries that are technologically advanced, namely, the industrial nations, enjoy its benefits, while the others continue to live in poverty.

Technological progress is tending to put an end to a basic phenomenon that has characterized all human societies until now—poverty. From the dawn of mankind until the present day, the world has lived under the law of scarcity, human needs having always exceeded the means available to satisfy them. The term "underdevelopment" appears to suggest an unusual situation when the term "development" is taken as the norm. But just the opposite is true. Before the twentieth century, all human societies were "underdeveloped," everywhere and at all times. By "underdeveloped," we mean that none of the societies had ever succeeded in guaranteeing the minimum basic needs for their entire population—food, housing, and clothing. This situation is barely beginning to change. Industrialized societies now come close to ensuring the minimal essentials for all of their citizens, and the moment is near when they will perhaps be able to provide for everyone's "secondary" needs (comfort, leisure, culture) as well. This is what Western nations mean by the "society of abundance," which they predict will soon arrive (p. 247).

However, even the most technologically advanced societies are still a long way from providing abundance for everyone. Nearly 20 percent of the citizens of the United States fall far below the "American way of life." Two-thirds of the French working class cannot afford to take a vacation away from home. Moreover, industrial nations are still very much in the minority. They account for less than one-third of the human race, and this proportion tends to decrease rather than increase, since population growth is much faster in underdeveloped countries. Some sociologists believe that real social differences no longer exist between classes but between nations, that there are "wealthy nations" and "proletarian nations," between which antagonisms develop.

A Martian visiting the earth would hardly notice the difference between Western countries and socialist countries, but he would be immediately struck by the difference between industrialized nations and underdeveloped nations. To be sure, each group represents two opposite poles with many intermediate stages between them. Japan, for instance, is a nation at the midpoint of industrialization. Latin America, Black Africa, the Middle East, and the Far East are not all underdeveloped to the same degree nor in the same manner. Aside from these superficial differences, underdevelopment presents the same general appearance everywhere: a predominance of agriculture carried on by primitive means, an inadequate food supply, a scarcity of industry and mechanical power, a serious deterioration in the business sector, a low level of national income, outmoded social structures, a great disparity between masses living on a bare subsistence level and a wealthy, privileged few, the absence of any middle classes, a wide gulf between urban and rural ways of life, illiteracy, a high birth rate and a high death rate. All these phenomena are clearly interrelated, although some are occasionally more pronounced than others, depending upon the country. However, the overall picture is quite characteristic and unmistakable. But the level of development is not the only thing that matters; the rate of development is also important. Nations of Asia, Africa, and South America are sometimes described as "underdeveloped" countries and sometimes as countries "in process of accelerated development." The first term places the emphasis on the level of development, the second upon the rate.

Industrialized nations are still a long way from the "society of abundance," although it has been a long time since they experienced famine. Nor are they afflicted with grinding poverty, except in a few special cases. Their working classes began reaching the living standard of the lower middle class a century ago. Thus they are tending to become completely middle class. While all of their basic economic problems have not yet been fully resolved, many have been partially resolved. A lessening of antagonisms has begun to appear in accordance with a process we will describe further on. But proletarian nations, on the contrary, are torn by conflicts engendered by poverty. These conflicts are heightened by increased contacts and communication with others, and by the attempts being made to develop the countries. When the Indians of Latin America and the peasants of the African bush or of the plains of Asia were enclosed in their solitude, more or less isolated from the rest of the world, poverty and inequality were less of a burden to them. But today, radio and television have told them about other civilizations where life is easier. If one lives in a world in which poverty and human misery are regarded as natural phenomena, impossible to avoid, they are more bearable. They become less so when the world begins to move, when it becomes possible to hope for more justice and less misery. The first stages of accelerated development provoke such a change, but the very conditions of this development dash the hopes initially aroused by aggravating, during the transition period, the sufferings that it ultimately seeks to eliminate. We will describe elsewhere the ironic contradictions of the transition period and the antagonisms that are generated (p. 67).

The distinction between wealthy nations and poor nations is based primarily on differences in technological development. Wealthy nations are industrial nations in which production depends mainly upon science and machinery. Poor nations are those in which production still depends upon primitive skills: agriculture is the principal occupation and is carried on by traditional methods, and industry remains in an embryonic stage and is closer to individual craftsmanship than to modern industry. The national per capita income, which measures a country's economic development, is also an important yardstick for measuring the level of technological development.

Technological progress thus seems to cancel out differences in natural geography. Prior to the great technological advances of the Renaissance and the contemporary era, the wealth of nations depended primarily on their agricultural skills, their mineral resources, and the existence of a population large enough to exploit them. Today these natural differences are overshadowed by differences in technological equipment. However, a shortage of natural resources, and special difficulties encountered in exploiting them, have impeded the technological development of certain peoples and retarded their progress in the race for technological equipment. At a certain level, the gap between nations that are technologically equipped and those that are not widens. In this sense, the unequal quality of natural geographical conditions does not diminish with technological advancement, but rather tends to increase. Differences in the state of development between industrialized nations in the temperate zones and nations technologically underdeveloped in the other geographical zones are primarily explained in terms of these facts, and not in terms of differences in racial aptitudes.

TECHNOLOGICAL PROGRESS AND CULTURAL DEVELOPMENT Technological progress favors cultural development in two ways: first, by permitting man to enjoy leisure time that enables him to further his educational and cultural interests and, second, by developing the means of cultural enrichment.

Technological progress favors cultural development, first of all, by freeing man from constant physical labor. Education and instruction require leisure time, which is possible only if men are not always preoccupied with the need to work in order to secure the minimal necessities of physical existence—food, housing, and clothing. Physical labor itself is, of course, a cultural element. Economically poor societies with a low level of technical skills have developed original cultures, based upon the imitation of physical actions and on oral traditions, which may reach a high degree of artistic perfection. But their intellectual progress remains limited. In wealthier societies, certain individuals are more or less spared the need for productive labor and can devote themselves to intellectual and cultural pursuits, thanks to the labors of others who remain culturally deprived. Only in the very wealthiest societies do all men devote a small part of their time to earning a living; the rest is leisure time for self-improvement.

Technological progress alone is responsible for liberating man from the servitude of physical work that was necessary for subsistence. A society without tools, without machinery, and without technological skills is one in which all the members are obliged to work as hard as they can simply to survive, simply to avoid dying. In lands that are technologically underdeveloped, the development of culture is practically impossible: men exist on a subhuman level. Civilization was able to advance only where natural conditions were very favorable and provided greater returns for human effort (the Nile valley, for instance, or easily navigated seacoasts, which made fishing profitable). Art, literature, philosophy, and science were able to develop gradually only because the mass of mankind, deprived of life's necessities, had to work ever harder so that certain individuals could have the free time indispensable for thought, study, and research. As long as "mechanical slaves" did not exist, culture was based upon human slaves. Hence technological progress has brought about man's liberation. The reduction in the length of the standard workday, more time for schooling, the arrival of an "age of leisure"—these conditions culminate in societies in which cultural possibilities are greater and men can develop their inherent talents and capabilities more fully.

There are those, however, who criticize modern culture for being artificial and superficial, and contrast it with the more profound and authentic culture of traditional societies. But modern culture is much more rudimentary, and in time, it will, in all likelihood, gradually penetrate society and develop in depth.

The invention of printing is a typical example of the development of the material means of disseminating culture. One may argue that the Renaissance and the Reformation followed directly from this invention. Before the invention of printing, it was very difficult for men to learn about the ideas of others or about the cultural experience of the past. Afterward, it became much easier to do so. The current development of the inexpensive paperback book has prolonged the printing revolution. The modern mass communications media (press, radio, films, television) are all phenomena in the same category. Certainly, man in the twentieth century, living in industrial societies, is often drowned in a sea of information. In general, it is badly presented with little distinction between what is important and what is unimportant, and this is a hindrance to cultural development. But despite everything, the enormous body of knowledge which men now have at their disposal makes them far better informed than men in traditional societies. The general intellectual level rises at the same time as the material level improves.

Furthermore, technological progress develops culture by greatly increasing communication between men, putting an end to barriers and partitions behind which each little community lived in an isolation that fostered intellectual lethargy. Movies, radio, television, and the press, the mass media in general, put all men in contact with one another, thus encouraging the spread of new ideas and culture. They also develop critical judgment. In seeing other ways of life, other customs, other ways of doing things, other ideas, one acquires a sense of relativity and perspective. "Civilization is first of all a highway," said Kipling, and in a broader sense, civilization is first of all contacts with others. Technological progress alone has permitted the establishment of these contacts by abolishing the physical barrier of distance.

The Political Consequences
of Technological Progress

Technological progress leads to a lessening of social antagonisms, the development of understanding among men, and increased political power. First we will examine the mechanics of these phenomena, then their influence on political regimes (see p. 92) and on the development of social integration (p. 241).

TECHNOLOGICAL PROGRESS AND THE LESSENING OF ANTAGONISMS   Technological progress tends to reduce one of the principal causes of social antagonism, namely, the scarcity of consumer goods. As a general rule, scarcity produces social inequality: a privileged minority lives in abundance, while the population as a whole suffers privation. Often the greater the degree of general poverty, the greater the wealth of the privileged few. In lands where famine is endemic, to be fat is a sign of power. Where the masses of people wear rags and tatters, the privileged few wear gold brocade. Where the masses live in hovels or sleep in the open air, the wealthy build sumptuous palaces. The wealth and luxury of the few, in the midst of general poverty, presents an inherently explosive situation. The gross inequality produces very deep resentments and antagonisms, and the privileged few respond to the hatred of the masses with fear. Politics consists of the violence of the masses in a state of perpetual revolt and of the violence of the elite, protecting themselves from the masses. Moreover, scarcity creates a situation in which exploitation of the masses by the privileged few is the only means of developing civilization. If equality were the rule in underdeveloped societies, everyone would be forced to toil every day just to survive. In this stage of a country's development, science, art, thought, and culture are possible only if certain men enjoy the necessary leisure, which is gained by increasing the burden on others.

Technological progress does not eliminate social inequities, but it weakens their effect. Modern societies are complex societies, where the diversity of occupations and their varying importance entails unequal incomes and working conditions. We must understand this situation clearly. It is possible to present two contrasting views of the evolution of industrialized societies. On the one hand, it can be shown that they are moving in the direction of a complex social stratification, toward a diversification of jobs and occupations; but, on the other hand, we can describe a situation that is just the reverse, the blurring of class lines. Many Americans are fond of saying that the United States presents the picture of a classless society, and as a matter of fact, the similarities in ways of living are quite striking. Economic development tends to reduce the gap between people's living standards and to narrow the range in their incomes. Between a Rockefeller and an American workman, the distance is less great than between a medieval baron and his serf. Industrialized societies seem to be moving toward the elimination of extreme wealth and extreme poverty. They are visibly moving toward a relative equalization in living conditions.

On the other hand, a general rise in living standards, an increase in material well-being and personal comfort, the development of leisure time and its enjoyment—all these factors, which characterize the economic abundance produced by technological progress, tend to reduce the importance attached to social inequities and their resulting antago-nisms. When hungry people, dressed in rags and living in hovels, are splattered by the coaches of wealthy people who live in palaces, the in-justice is deeply resented and the envy is great. But when a workman, driving a small Renault, is passed on the highway by an industrialist in a Jaguar or Mercedes, there is envy, certainly, but it is more superfi-cial, less consequential. Tensions decrease, a certain consensus is estab-lished, the political struggle becomes less violent, social integration de-velops, and democracy becomes possible.

It is interesting that proponents of Western and of Marxist thought agree that technological progress tends to reduce social antagonisms, but they differ as to the rate of this reduction. In the East, as in the West, the idea prevails that technological progress will one day culmi-nate in a society without conflicts and without antagonisms, a com-pletely integrated society. There is a marked similarity, in this connec-tion, between "the final phase of communism," the future paradise of Marxism, and "the society of abundance," the future paradise of the West. But the roads leading to this Eldorado are not the same. For Marxists, the complete disappearance of antagonisms will not be the outcome of their gradual reduction, as technology advances step by step; the new paradise will not be attained bit by bit before it is fin-ally achieved. On the contrary, by altering the means of production and the social relationships involved, technological progress will inten-sify the class struggle, which will grow more desperate through exploi-tation, revolt, and repression, until it culminates in the revolutionary explosion. This will bring the working class to power, but, thereafter, it will be necessary to pass through a long period of dictatorship by the proletariat before the ultimate phase of communism is reached. Thus, the end of social antagonisms will come only after a period of intensification, and it will be generated by this intensification through a dialectical process.

For most Westerners, on the contrary, social antagonisms diminish gradually as technological progress removes the principal cause of these antagonisms—the shortage of consumer goods. The reduction in antagonisms results directly from the progress toward the society of abundance. However, in Western thinking there are certain similari-ties to Marxist theories about the "transition stage" in which conflicts are heightened and exacerbated. They are found in the idea that a rapid, accelerated technological advance temporarily produces an in-tensification of social antagonisms. This leads to the concept of the rate of development.

The rate of development is probably as important as the level of development. Its effect is just the reverse of its intentions: a rapid rate increases social tensions; a slow rate reduces them. Here we find the Marxist idea that technological progress aggravates social antagonisms, but it has been refined. A distinction between stable societies and societies in process of accelerated development is probably as important as the distinction between overdeveloped and underdeveloped societies.

In stable societies, the existing social order represents an almost unanimous consensus, however unjust it may be. People have grown so accustomed to it that they come to regard it as natural. "Natural," from a sociological point of view, is whatever has existed for a long enough time that neither the present generation nor those that preceded it have known anything else. They can hardly conceive of such a traditional order being overturned. They are as used to it as to an old shoe that no longer pinches, even if it did so originally. Injustice and inequality, arbitrary acts and domination by a few, thus become relatively bearable in the course of time, so that there is no need to resort to violence to maintain the status quo. In stable societies, even those with the greatest inequities, social tensions are weakened. The antagonisms remain, but they lie dormant.

Accelerated development has the opposite effect. Sweeping changes in social structures tend to deprive the established order of its natural character. The modifications brought about by industrial development prove that the social order can be changed, for indeed that is precisely what happens. Suddenly the inequities and injustices that were tolerated, simply because they seemed inevitable, become less bearable. Antagonisms between the impoverished masses and the privileged minority increase. Meanwhile, the accelerated development tends to disrupt traditional social structures, uprooting and disorienting many people. To some extent they feel like strangers in their own society, alienated in the true sense of the word. The severance of traditional ties makes them more sensitive to suffering and injustice and more disposed to revolution. Social antagonisms are thus intensified.

The theory that technological progress tends to weaken political antagonisms is very widespread in the West. It is challenged, however, by certain sociologists who base their arguments, to some extent, on psychoanalysis. In their view, technological progress creates a world unsuited to the real needs and the deepest aspirations of man, a world that is increasingly artificial, in which man feels more and more like a stranger. The so-called consumer world satisfies superficial and secondary needs, artificially created by commercial advertising. The deeper and more fundamental needs of man remain unsatisfied, more so, in fact, than in traditional societies. Hence there is a basic conflict between fundamental human desires and a world that is organized, antiseptic, mechanized, and rational—Alphaville—where man is imprisoned by technology. People will, accordingly, resort to violence, producing wars, revolutions, and dictatorships. We will pursue this topic later in studying the psychological factors of political antagonisms.

TECHNOLOGICAL PROGRESS AND THE DEVELOPMENT OF HUMAN UNDERSTANDING   This matter is more in dispute than the preceding one. The basic idea is that technological progress raises man's cultural level, enabling him to understand and deal with his problems. In primitive societies, on the other hand, where the mass of the population is uneducated, illiterate, ignorant, and debilitated by poverty and disease, the average person cannot form a clear idea of basic political problems. He cannot make necessary decisions based on a knowledge of the facts. Someone else must make a choice, must decide for him. Under such conditions, the only possible kind of government is an autocratic regime.

However, technological progress increases the difficulty of problems at the same time that it raises the general level of human comprehension. Some believe that the former is more evident than the latter, that the ability to understand problems actually decreases instead of increasing. Genuine democracy grows weaker. This view is widely held today. "Between the public and the political power, emanating from it, technological demands interpose a zone of obscurity," notes the Club Jean Moulin in its basic text, *L'Etat et le citoyen* (The State and the Citizen). This means that the various options open cannot be presented to the electorate or to their representatives in clear language, but only in technological terms which render them practically unintelligible. In matters of government planning, for instance, a parliament cannot engage in a full-scale discussion of the various alternatives to a plan under consideration. Generally speaking, a technological society makes it so difficult to reach informed decisions about complex matters that it is extremely hard to achieve genuine participation by the nation and its representatives. Decisions must be made by specialists, who alone are capable of understanding them. If this continues, we will end up with a technocracy. A balance between the level of complexity of problems and the level of comprehension on the part of the citizenry appears greater, in certain respects, in traditional, underdeveloped societies than in modern industrial states.

We can cite as an example certain Berber cities of North Africa, which had rather sophisticated election processes, a well-defined separation of powers, and government by an assembly—the *Djemââ.* Before the rise of national states, many small societies were built on similar principles, especially ancient democracies. They were generally agricultural communities, comprised of land-owning peasants (or occasionally communities of fishermen) without great disparities in income. An economic balance was attained, thanks to well-ingrained habits of frugality, which tempered their material needs and kept them exceeding the amount of available goods. A traditional oral culture insures a generally high intellectual level despite the scarcity of reading and writing. The Greek and Roman Republics represented this type of society. The disruption of their material and intellectual balance, following their political expansion and economic development, caused the collapse of their democratic societies and the rise of dictatorships.

Other examples could be drawn from societies even less developed, such as those studied by ethnologists. Very often decisions are made collectively by assemblies of the tribal members. The African *"palabres"* are an example of the discussion process which characterizes democracies. They may be compared to the discussions held in the Greek Agora or the Roman Forum. This "democracy of small units" is based on the fact that the decisions to be taken are fairly simple, owing to the limited size of the community, and can therefore be understood by citizens with little education.

The foregoing examples are not subject to debate. Nor is it questioned that, in modern industrial states, democracy must function largely within the framework of "small units," local units, that is, if democracy is to penetrate the society. Only in small, local units does the level of public understanding truly correspond to the level of complexity of the problems and issues. The correspondence between the two is greater under these circumstances than in the traditional societies we have just described, because the cultural development engendered by technological progress has raised the intellectual level of the average citizen.

Moreover, we must not exaggerate the obscurity and complexity of problems, even on the national level. In the Middle Ages, even though political problems were much simpler and less technical, they were more difficult for the average person to understand than for the citizen of the twentieth century, who is relatively well informed and well educated. The level of difficulty has indeed risen, but the level of man's ability to understand has probably risen even more. We must not forget that very few traditional societies have engendered a well-informed citizenry. Furthermore, we sometimes exaggerate the technical aspects of modern political problems. It may not be possible to explain to a parliament, or to the public at large, the numerous and complicated details involved in the establishment and execution of some comprehensive plan. But it remains possible to formulate very clearly the basic options available and the meaning of each. Citizens and their representatives can thus make a choice and do so with a reasonably clear notion of the issues involved.

TECHNOLOGICAL PROGRESS AND THE INCREASE OF POWER Marxists believe that the state tends to wither away as the class struggle diminishes—a process which depends on technological progress. Westerners in general hold rather different views. Many think that technological progress ultimately strengthens the power of the state in relation to its citizens, on the one hand, by endowing it with a sort of omnipotence, and, on the other, by reducing the individual to the status of a cog in a vast collective organization (concerning the Marxist theory on the withering away of the state, see p. 252).

Technological progress directly reinforces the political power of the state. For example, it enables the central government to extend its authority over the entire country more easily, by eliminating the problem of distance. The centralization which results tends to destroy local autonomy and the freedom such autonomy leaves to the people. In particular, technological progress gives the government irresistible means of force. Formerly, soldiers and policemen were equipped with arms that hardly differed from those of rioters, and the advantage of numbers reestablished equality. Revolutions could succeed, and Praetorian dictatorships were always insecure. Today, as Trotsky said, "people can no longer carry out a revolution against the army." Guerrilla warfare appears to be effective only in underdeveloped countries. Finally, propaganda techniques give those in power the means of exerting pressures that are perhaps even more effective.

Of course, technological progress not only strengthens the state; it also offers new means of resistance to the opposition. The modern state is a powerful machine, but it is complex and fragile and consequently vulnerable. Against its army, resistance from behind barricades is impossible, as was demonstrated in Spain between 1936 and 1938. But a general strike can destroy the power of the military, can turn them into powerless armed monsters in the midst of a people who suddenly stop the life of the community. In Berlin in 1920, it took a few hours for General von Lüttwitz to seize power, but the labor unions forced him to abandon it in forty-eight hours by paralyzing all activity in the city and the nation. Revolutionary cells within the government offer other means of resisting oppression. Nevertheless, it seems undeniable that the state gains far more power from technological progress than the citizenry. In the final analysis, the means of resistance, mentioned above, are of dubious value, and only rarely successful against the enormous power that the state derives from technology.

In other respects, technological progress tends to transform the state and its agencies, as it does private enterprises and agencies, into gigantic organizations which can function smoothly only if their basic components—namely, human beings—are standardized like the parts of a machine. This is why some writers, like Jacques Ellul, use the term "technology" to designate both industrial machines and social organizations. They believe that technological progress forces man to model himself on the machine. This tends to produce a type of man William H. Whyte called "the organization man," an individual who is literally dehumanized. One may hope that each person will fiercely protect his personal liberty behind a mask of outward conformity, like army recruits who inwardly resist military indoctrination in the service, while outwardly complying. But military service is of short duration, whereas the "organization man" is surrounded by his organization throughout his active life. Moreover, during his leisure time he tends to engage in standardized recreations, such as those recommended by the popular press and the mass media. Even then, he does not escape technological influences.

This mechanization of social organizations is reflected at the summit by a transformation of authority, which also becomes dehumanized. There is a tendency to establish abstract and mechanical rules at every level of the hierarchy, so that power becomes something anonymous, both to those who exercise it and those who obey it. The former apply the rules; the latter comply with them. Personal relationships in matters of authority disappear. Citizens obey a machine within a machine—bureaucracy. The "personalization of power," so much discussed in modern societies, is a reaction against this phenomenon. But it remains illusory. The personalized leader, as presented in the public press, radio, and television, is more a myth than a reality. His margin of autonomy in making decisions is very slim. He corrects a few bureaucratic excesses more than he replaces them. We described the consequences of this bureaucratization of power earlier (see p. 39 and pp. 236–37 and 254).

INSTITUTIONS

Human societies are structured; they resemble buildings rather than piles of rock. Institutions, in the strict sense of the word, determine the architecture of these buildings. Robert's dictionary defines them as "the collective forms or basic structures of social organization as established by law or by human tradition." In this sense, institutions have an undeniable influence on political phenomena. Even marital systems, school systems, and social etiquette influence politics. Many sociologists and conservative historians, such as Le Play and Fustel de Coulanges, have tried to explain political life in terms of the family as an institution. Marxists attach a fundamental importance to systems of property, and certain Western writers regard private property as the very cornerstone of democracy. Institutions that are political by definition, those that embody the organization and structure of power, obviously exert a more direct influence on political life.

General Notions About Institutions

First we will study the subject of institutions in general. Then we will examine those that most directly concern the question of power, namely, political institutions.

ELEMENTS INVOLVED IN THE CONCEPT OF "INSTITUTION"   We have already briefly described the concept of "institution" at the beginning of the book. We noted that it is defined by two elements—a structural element and an element of human beliefs and popular images. We must now carry the analysis further.

As stated before, institutions are models of human relationships upon which individual relationships are patterned, thereby acquiring stability, durability, and cohesiveness. Accordingly, they are different from relationships formed outside an institutional framework, which are sporadic, ephemeral, and unstable. In our definition, we have reserved the term "structures" for the institutional models themselves, as distinct from the concrete relationships they engender, although in practice the two elements are inseparable and constitute the very concept of institutions. The structures are systems of relationships, which have no real existence without the relationships themselves. The originality of the latter results from their connections with the structural model.

However, we must distinguish between two types of institutions. Some are simple systems of relationships, based upon a structural model of the kind we have just described. Others have, in addition, a formal technical and material organization: constitutions, local chapters, physical equipment, machines, emblems, letterhead stationery, a staff, an administrative hierarchy, and so forth. So it is with a parliament, a ministry, the office of a chief magistrate, an incorporated group or association. In legal language, the term "institution" is often reserved for this latter group. Jurists, notably those in the field of public jurisprudence, have a tendency to study organizations rather than relationships, under the heading "institutions." For example, a study of "international institutions" is primarily a study of international organizations. The study of "international relations" is a study of relations in the strict sense of the term, when carried out according to the historical method of describing the successive and intermittent relationships between states. It becomes a study of institutions in the broader sense of the term when it seeks to define and classify the different structural models that serve as bases for the various systems of relationships between states. It is noteworthy that the course in political institutions, usually taught in law schools, is primarily a study of political organizations, rather than of systems of relationships.

Actually, the technical and material factors that distinguish "organizations" from simple "systems of relationships" are much less important than the structural models. They, of course, reinforce the cohesiveness, stability, and durability of these structural models by giving them concrete form, a tangible and visible reality. But structural models without physical organizations can be very strong, cohesive, and stable, much more so, in fact, than some organizations with impressive apparatuses. The power of religion's hold on people is not proportionate to the size and number of church buildings. Customs and traditions are often stronger than laws and codes. Organizations are merely the outer layer of institutions, their cover or wrapper, which does not always reflect the inner reality. It is, therefore, much closer to the facts, and certainly far more "operational," to emphasize the unity of the concept of institutions, in the broad sense, as opposed to the simpler, less-frequent relationships not patterned on a structural model, and to relegate to second place the distinction between "organizations" and structural systems without physical organizations. We must reject the narrow concept equating institutions with organizations.

We have repeatedly stressed that the significance of social phenomena is not based solely on their physical reality; it is also on the notions people acquire about them through popular images, ideas, and beliefs, and the value systems that develop about them. These popular images, beliefs, and value systems are a basic element of institutions. It matters little, under the circumstances, whether the public image corresponds to reality or whether it is illusory. The important thing is its acceptance by the entire community.

Every institution is simultaneously a structural model and a collection of widely accepted, more or less standardized images, which is to say, every institution is related, to some extent, to a value system, to a concept of good and evil, of right and wrong, implying a definite stand either "for" or "against." The degree of popular acceptance varies according to the institution. Generally, it is very high for political institutions. Political beliefs are more or less sacrosanct, that is, they are tied to the society's highest system of values.

The notion of "legitimacy" derives from this fact. In any society, people acquire a certain idea about the form, nature, and structure that political power should present in order to be recognized as good and valid in itself (quite apart from the specific actions it takes). Power is legitimate when it conforms to the popular image, to society's system of values. If existing power is considered legitimate, then it is willingly and naturally obeyed. If it is regarded as illegitimate, people tend, on the contrary, to resist it, and it becomes dependent on force. We will touch on this extremely important subject later, especially the question of "consensus" in legitimacy. If certain people in society stand for one system of legitimacy, and others for another, then no power can be legitimate for everyone—which makes all government difficult. It is a revolutionary situation. Such was the case in France, from after the French Revolution until the early years of the twentieth century, when those advocating the legitimacy of the traditional monarchy clashed with partisans of the new democracy.

THE PLACE OF INDIVIDUALS IN SOCIAL INSTITUTIONS: STATUS AND ROLE It is interesting to compare the notion of institutions with those of status and role (a popular topic among social psychologists), for role and status illuminate the basic problem of the individual's relative position within social institutions. As a matter of fact, role and status are themselves institutions, according to one definition of the term. Or more precisely, institutions are embodiments of various types of roles and statuses.

The concepts of role and status were elaborated in 1936 by Ralph Linton in the first edition of *The Study of Man,* and they have since been embraced by most psychologists and sociologists, who have added their own modifications. Today they are generally accepted, although they are still the subject of much controversy, which we will disregard in order to keep the essentials.

Every man holds a great many social positions. For example, one Mr. Dupont is simultaneously a husband, a head of a family, the secretary of a rugby club, a mechanic at the Renault factory, a member of the Communist party, one of a group of friends, and so on. Each of these positions presents the opportunity for a series of social relationships. In the words of the German sociologist Ralf Dahrendorf, it is "a cord that binds together an entire field of social relationships." This field of social relationships is "in principle, something one can think of quite apart from the individual" who occupies the position. Thus, we are dealing with systems of stable relationships that conform to our definition of institutions. In the society in which Mr. Dupont lives, the position of a husband corresponds to a collection of relationships conceived of its members; likewise, the position of the head of a family, or the secretary of a rugby club. If Mr. Dupont should cease being secretary of the club or a mechanic at the Renault plant, he will be replaced by someone else. The social position, thus objectively defined, we call "status." The various kinds of status are just so many models of relationships, which is to say, institutions, in the definition we have adopted.

For every status there are a certain number of behavior patterns expected of the individual holding the position, and, simultaneously, certain attributes he should possess. Thus one expects the Renault factory employee to report regularly for work, to perform his professional duties, to share mutual interests with his fellow employees, to join in their demands addressed to management, and so on. At the same time, the fact that Mr. Dupont is working for Renault implies obligations on his part with respect to attendance, work, and discipline. It also involves salaries, certain social advantages, a measure of respect from friends and neighbors. We designate as "role" the attributes which result from status, and the behavior that other members of society expect of the status holder. In short, role is simply an aspect of status. Stoetzel declares that status is the collective behavior patterns Mr. Dupont can normally expect from others, whereas role is the collective behavior patterns others normally expect from Mr. Dupont.

The term "role" is well chosen because it suggests that each man is an actor in the society in which he lives. Moreover, he is an actor who must play several roles, like certain professional actors who appear in one role at a matinée, in another role at an evening performance, and in still another role on a morning television show. The great difference from the professional actor's role is that a person's social role is not so sharply defined. When an individual assumes one of his social roles, he is not guided, as an actor is, by a script he must adhere to. Instead, he must largely improvise, like the actors in traditional Italian comedy. The roles in the *Commedia del' Arte*—Harlequin, Pierrot, and Columbine—give a fairly good idea of what the social role is like. The idea is even more vividly presented by the Spanish dramatist Pedro Calderón (1600–81) in *The Great World Theatre.*

The purpose of the concept of "role" is to establish the demarcation line between society and the individual. Within his social role, man has a certain margin of freedom. As we have just indicated, he does not follow a written text, but only a general outline. For the most part, he is obliged to improvise. Depending upon his own originality, he may depart, to a greater or lesser degree, from the stereotyped pattern of the role he plays. The personality of an individual and his social role are almost constantly in conflict to some extent; complete integration is seldom achieved. However, status and role are also integrating factors in the formation of personality, helping to create and strengthen it.

Moreover, it should be noted that although the other members of a group expect certain behavior on the part of a status holder—which is what constitutes his role—they sometimes hope, more or less tacitly, that the actor will also "drop out of character" and not do precisely what is expected of him. This hope indicates that the social group is not satisfied with the existing types of role and status and dreams of seeing them modified, at least to some extent. In politics, this is reflected in revolutionary aspirations. The tendency to "personalize" power is also part of this phenomenon: people hope that an exceptional individual, a savior, will break out of the confines of his role in the interest of everyone. The hope for a Messiah is greatest when social institutions are generally found wanting, but it is never entirely absent from any society. Human institutions are too imperfect for men to be entirely satisfied with them.

THE DIFFERENT KINDS OF INSTITUTIONS It is very difficult to classify institutions. Depending upon their objectives, they may be designated as political, religious, economic, family, administrative, and so forth. But we would like to offer here another kind of distinction, one that has the merit of defining the concept of institution, and, in particular, of shedding light on the position of legal institutions.

Certain institutions are produced automatically, almost mechanically, we might say, by the interplay of forces and events. Thus it has been with social classes, levels of income, ways of life, and so forth. They exist even if men are not aware of their existence, though awareness reinforces and transforms them. These institutions do not imply the adoption of a moral judgment about them. Whether one is "for" or "against" them, whether one finds them "good" or "bad," "right" or "wrong," is not a basic reason for their existence, although this kind of evaluation also has a great influence on them. These are "institutions by pure fact"—or so they may be regarded, for this notion is debatable, as we shall see.

Other institutions, on the contrary, are based primarily on an awareness of their existence and on value judgments. As for awareness, people belonging to institutions of this kind know that they exist, and this knowledge is one of the key factors of their existence. As for value judgments, members are not neutral about these institutions; membership implies a commitment. The institutions are basically oriented to a particular system of values (good or bad, right or wrong, proper or improper). A system of values is at the very heart of these institutions.

We will call this second type "institutions by design" or "normative institutions," since they are based upon "norms" (this term comes from the Latin word "norma," meaning "square," which we may take as a synonym for "rule"). These institutions function according to prescribed rules, which stipulate the rules of conduct that members of the group must observe in their actions. Whereas institutions by fact are deterministic in nature—meaning that one experiences their power and influence automatically—institutions by design are "obligatory." It is possible not to conform to the rules they prescribe. No one is physically forced to conform, only "obliged" to do so, in other words, bound by some legal, moral, or social obligation which one cannot shirk without being subject to various kinds of penalties or sanctions. Obedience to these institutions is therefore voluntary. It is also a conscious obedience; whoever is ignorant of the rules cannot conform to the obligations they impose, except by chance.

This distinction between institutions by design and institutions by fact is rather debatable. Do institutions by pure fact really exist, in the meaning we have given to this term? Can there be social institutions without an element of awareness? And as soon as an institution becomes conscious of itself, does it not always reflect a certain degree of self-evaluation, a certain moral judgment concerning itself? And conversely, every institution by design, every one that is consciously established, rests upon a fundamental fact, something that is determined and cannot be disregarded, which serves as its basis. Age groupings become institutions only if we take cognizance of them and deduce certain patterns of behavior from them—which is to say, if we attach a game with rules. In the same manner, Karl Marx emphasized the importance of class consciousness in the institution of social classes. In the absence of any class consciousness, classes may exist in a material sense, but they are of little social importance and it would be difficult to describe them as institutions. On the other hand, certain institutions by design can produce institutions by fact; for example, a system of private property engenders a system of social classes. In the last analysis, the real difference seems to be one of degree, not of kind: in certain institutions, the conscious "construct" is highly developed in relation to the actual fact; in others, the situation is reversed.

The distinction between legal institutions and other kinds of institutions is very important in political sociology, for legal institutions are those that have been established or recognized by political power. Law is thus one of the basic instruments in the exercise of political power.

Legal institutions are institutions by design or "normative," in the sense we have just indicated. Although the concept of normative institutions is not very sharply defined, we can clearly distinguish, within the concept, three types of normative institutions—those based upon law, those based upon moral principles, and those based upon social customs. The distinction rests simultaneously upon the systems of values underlying the "norms," and upon their methods of development and their sanctions. The distinction predicated on value systems is theoretically more fundamental, but in reality it is less precise. Law, ethics, and social customs are all part of value systems, a fact that differentiates the institutions built on them from institutions based on pure fact. But they are distinguishable from one another from this point of view as well. The values that define social customs are based upon "what is done and what is not done." Moral principles are based upon concepts of good and evil, fundamental values considered to be superior to all others. Law is based upon notions of the public good, social order, and the interest of all; but it also entails the concept of justice. The latter—a special aspect of "the good"—is, in fact, a moral value. In this area, law and ethics are not hard to separate, and law borrows the prestige of ethics in order to strengthen institutions.

The technical distinction, according to methods of operation and the application of sanctions, is much more precise. Law is the sum total of rules sanctioned by public authority, and established or recognized by it. Hence we define as legal institutions those that are (1) established by laws, regulations, and, in general, by decisions enacted by governmental power; and (2) those established by social custom or by contracts made by private individuals, but recognized and validated by law, official decrees, or government decisions. Both kinds are sanctioned by governmental power, which utilizes the means of constraint at its disposal (judges, the police, prisons, fines, capital punishment, and so on) to curb violations. In this purely technical definition, we thus consider law to be the entire body of rules established or recognized by those in power (that is, generally, by the state), and which are sanctioned by those in power, this sanction being more general and more precise. A rule of law may or may not be established by those in power, but it is always sanctioned by them. Thus, law may be defined as the sum total of the rules of conduct sanctioned by political power. Morality includes the body of rules tied to religious sanctions (hell, purgatory, and so forth) or to psychological sanctions (remorse), which are either established by religions or are perceived by the human conscience. This definition actually encompasses two concepts of morality, a religious one and a psychological one. The two are not necessarily in conflict, but each raises particular problems we will not discuss at this time. Lastly, mores are rules of conduct developed by social custom whose violation involves various sanctions, unorganized but often severe, such as reprobation, mockery, and ostracism.

Law, morality, and customs do not comprise domains completely separated from social institutions; they tend to overlap one another. Many legal rules are simultaneously moral principles and social customs, and vice versa. However, there are also domains peculiar to each category. There may even be contradictions between them. Conflicts between laws and moral principles are especially serious, for in the hierarchy of values, moral values are deemed superior to juridical values, at least from the standpoint of individual conscience. From the standpoint of community interest, the issues are less clear. The duel between Antigone and Creon is a good illustration of these contradictions, often dramatic in their consequences. While generally less serious and less profound, conflicts between moral principles and social customs, or between customs and laws, are no less acute. Take, for example, Russian resistance to the edicts of Peter the Great, forbidding men to grow beards, and Turkish opposition to the laws of Mustapha Kemal, prohibiting the wearing of the fez.

INSTITUTIONS AND TECHNOLOGY Whether they derive from laws, customs, or any other source, a society's institutions are closely tied to its technological development, as we have already indicated. On this point, Marxists have a tendency to regard institutions merely as a reflection of technology. This view is an oversimplification. Institutions enjoy a certain measure of autonomy with respect to technological developments.

The Marxist position is rigid on the question of the dependency of institutions upon economic and technological development. For Marxism, institutions are the result of a special category of technology, of which they are merely a reflection, an epiphenomenon to some extent:

the technology relating to production. The state of the productive forces, that is, the techniques used in production, determines the methods of production; in other words, the institutions concerned with production, in particular, property. Methods of production determine other institutions—family, religious, political, sexual, and so on. Thus, there are two levels of institutions: the socioeconomic institutions related to production methods and to the class relationships resulting from them, and the other institutions. The latter are a product of the former. Hence both are caused by the state of a society's productive forces. Influences do not all run in the same direction, of course. Institutions on the second level can influence those on the first; superstructures can affect foundations. But such a reaction is secondary by comparison with the influence of the first level upon the second.

Now this concept is much too narrow. Few would deny that institutions depend upon a society's level of economic and technological development, and that socioeconomic institutions dominate the others. But there is by no means a rigid determination, only various degrees of influence. Every type of socioeconomic institution corresponds to a great variety of other possible institutions (family, religious, political, and so forth). Marxists do not deny this plurality of superstructures, but they claim that there is always a correlation between the type of superstructure that is actually established and the nature of its substructure. We will examine later this theory more fully with regard to the connections between political regimes and systems of production. Let us simply note here that the theory is greatly exaggerated.

The conditioning of socioeconomic institutions by the level of production techniques, and of other institutions by the system of production, is much broader in nature. There is a certain autonomy of institutions with respect to economic techniques. The same level of technological development can produce several types of production systems, without a given type being dependent upon a given variation in the level of development. The same system of production can produce a great diversity of family, educational, cultural, political, and religious institutions, but the appearance of one kind of institution rather than another is not necessarily tied to a particular type of production system.

The different school systems in the United States, Great Britain, Germany, and France do not correspond to different production systems any more than do differences in the American presidential system, the British parliamentary system, thé Scandinavian governmental systems, or the Italian and French political systems. Variations in sexual behavior between Catholics and Protestants in the West do not appear to have any connection with variations in systems of production or levels of economic technology. The differences between the flexible two-party system of the United States, the rigid two-party system of Great Britain, the disciplined multiparty system of the Scandinavian countries, and the anarchic multiparty systems in France and Italy are not based on differences in methods of production or the state of the productive forces. We could multiply the number of examples. Institutions have a certain measure of autonomy quite apart from the socioeconomic structures. Within these fairly wide limits, institutions (in and of themselves, and not as proxies) are sources of political antagonisms as well as factors in political integration.

A good example of the autonomy of institutions is furnished by the party systems. No one denies that political antagonisms and integration are profoundly different in a two-party system of the British type and a multiparty system of the French or Italian type. These institutions, which is what political systems are, deeply influence a country's political life, but they remain largely autonomous with respect to socioeconomic structures. To be sure, two-party systems and multiparty systems are largely the result of social and economic factors: parties reflect social classes or social groups in conflict with one another. The historical development, traditions, and circumstances peculiar to each country play a role in this matter; class struggles and conflicts between social groups develop within this cultural context. But another factor intervenes, one that is purely institutional in nature—the electoral system. A majority vote on one ballot, in the Anglo-Saxon type of election, is conducive to a two-party system, while proportional representation or a two-ballot procedure of the French type is conducive to a multiparty system. Electoral systems tend to restrain or else to encourage inherent socioeconomic and cultural factors.

The connections between electoral systems and party systems reveal very clearly the autonomy of institutions. The particular arrangement of one institution (the electoral system) gives to another institution (the party system) a certain configuration which, in turn, influences political antagonisms by intensifying or restraining them. Of course, these institutional arrangements are less influential than other factors causing political unrest or social integration. Yet it is often an important factor. We could cite many similar examples in every area. The changes in family structure in France following the Second World War were due less to a change in methods of production than to a new law that offered material advantages to those increasing the size of their families; this law appears decisive in the changes that occurred in

1944–45. The "sexual revolution" that occurred in the United States and in northern Europe, beginning in 1950, does not appear in any way related to technological developments, but rather to a weakening of religious and moral taboos, and the cause of that needs further exploration.

But keeping within the political domain, we must emphasize one important point. Marxist theories have misunderstood the true nature of power in considering it an outgrowth of techno-economic structures. No one denies that power is conditioned by class struggle. But the view that it depends solely on the class struggle and will disappear along with the social classes (as Marxists claim in their theory of the withering away of the state) seems contrary to the facts. The development of Stalinism demonstrated that the elimination of classes and the arrival of socialism could coincide with the growth of an implacable dictatorship, which cannot be explained away either by the capitalistic encirclement of the USSR or by the resistance of former members of the exploiting classes. Only the concept of institutional autonomy enables us to recognize that political power has a reality of its own, independent of class structures and other influential factors. This reality seems to consist of a natural tendency to expand until it meets effective resistance. We will again encounter this fundamental concept which leads one to believe that power is inherently dangerous and that one must always take precautionary measures in dealing with it, even if the class struggle and other causes of political antagonism have disappeared.

THE PERSISTENCE OF INSTITUTIONS: SOCIAL INERTIA   Even when they are the result of techno-economic structures, institutions retain some autonomy. One characteristic of this autonomy is that, by a kind of social inertia, institutions continue to survive after the factors that produced them have disappeared.

The persistence of institutions is a very common phenomenon. In all countries and at all times, there is a mixture of contemporary institutions, corresponding to current needs, and outmoded institutions, corresponding to needs that have disappeared. These institutions survive because they are based on both material factors—property, personnel, governing bodies, an organization—and on popular images—people are accustomed to their existence and are not fully aware of their obsolescence.

We will note only two very striking examples of this persistence of institutions. The most important one is that of the survival of Roman structures, largely through the church, after the barbarian invasions and the fall of the Roman Empire. They maintained the appearance of a state for centuries, while the economy tended toward a fragmentation of power within small, self-contained, rural communities. The residual structures sparked the reappearance of political centralization at the beginning of the Merovingian dynasty, and especially during the reign of Charlemagne, and they subsequently influenced the formation of the new national states when economic advances permitted the reestablishment of large and durable political groupings.

Political parties offer another example of the persistence of institutions. Let us take the French Radical-Socialist party—an historical relic. Several decades ago, in expressing the opposition of intransigent liberals confronted by moderates and conservatives, the party corresponded to social reality. Yet, although the basic causes of this conflict have virtually disappeared, certain Radical-Socialist organizations persist, together with a certain ideology; the Radical organization continues to survive.

Institutions that survive the factors that produced them tend themselves to become causes of political antagonism or integration. Today the Radical-Socialist party does not exist in response to certain political conflicts; certain political conflicts exist because the Radical-Socialist party survives. Thus, some political struggles no longer have anything but an historical basis. However, it sometimes works the other way: social integration is stronger than it normally would be under new social structures because institutions of common interest, which no longer correspond to present-day reality, still exist.

The persistence of institutions can thus result in the maintenance, or even the revival, of regimes at variance with the socioeconomic structures. The unification efforts of Clovis and Charlemagne, for example, ran contrary to the economic development of the era, that is, to the predominance of an archaic agricultural system that produced small, self-contained communities. The socioeconomic structures favored manors and a feudal society. The persistence of institutions retarded this decentralization of the state and even caused temporary revivals of it. Of course, the rebirths were short-lived, but they were of sufficient duration to change the destiny of many men while they lasted, and to produce long-lasting consequences.

This persistence in the Middle Ages of Roman institutions, which were incongruous with their sociological bases, encouraged social integration rather than social antagonisms: it restrained the development of political conflicts to some extent. Generally speaking, when old institutions are loved and respected, when they seem preferable to those produced by socioeconomic evolution, public opinion supports them and adjusts quite well to their "persistence." But on the other hand, when old institutions are not well supported and when evolution tends to change them, if those with a vested interest try to maintain them despite strong opposition, then social inertia intensifies the conflicts and can produce revolutionary explosions.

Political Institutions: The Classification of Political Regimes

Political institutions are those that are concerned with power, its organization, transmission, exercise, legitimacy, and so forth. Throughout history, these institutions have combined according to different types which we call "political regimes." Political regimes define the specific institutional structures within which political life unfolds, but these structures are themselves part of the overall social framework consisting of the other institutions and the geographical and demographic factors of the society in question. Hence the importance of the problem of classifying political regimes.

Directly or indirectly, all classifications of political regimes refer to a system of values. The classifications of Aristotle and Plato tended to emphasize the virtues of mixed regimes. Montesquieu took the same position, but his concept of "mixed" was different. Western typology, which contrasts democracies with dictatorships, seeks to justify the former and disparge the latter, for the term "dictatorship" has an unfavorable connotation, while "democracy" has a favorable one in contemporary speech. The communist view of capitalist and socialist regimes is of the same nature: "capitalist" is bad and "socialist" is good in the Marxist vocabulary. We shall try to go beyond these subjective classifications to find a more objective typology, one that sheds light on both the similarities and the differences of current political regimes. The historical approach is the best one on this question, since all contemporary classifications are based to some extent on earlier ones.

THE ANCIENT CLASSIFICATIONS   Until the end of the nineteenth century, there was a general acceptance of the classification system inherited from the Greeks, which divided political regimes into monarchies, oligarchies, and democracies.

Monarchy—government by one; oligarchy—government by a few; democracy—government by all: these simple definitions correspond both to a logical classification and to the actual nature of political regimes as they existed in the ancient Hellenic world. The first precise formulation of this distinction is found in Herodotus, and probably dates from the middle of the fifth century B.C., but it appears to derive from an earlier tradition that was solidly established. Moreover, for each type of regime a distinction had already been drawn between the pure, correct form and its "deviations." Aristotle would later provide a famous analysis contrasting corrupt forms of government—tyranny, oligarchy, and democracy—with their corresponding pure forms— monarchy, aristocracy, and "timocracy" (democracy with limited suffrage). Plato had previously expressed similar ideas, adding a theory about the successive appearance of different types of regimes in a constantly recurring cycle.

The trilogy of "monarchy, aristocracy, and democracy" dominates political theory down to the time of Montesquieu, and even later. Each writer added refinements of detail without touching on the essential. The political economist Jean Bodin (1530–96) applied it separately to forms of state and to forms of government, which allowed him to make some bizarre, but often interesting, combinations. A monarchical state, for example, in which sovereignty resides in the hands of the king may still have a democratic government if all citizens have equal opportunity for public office; or a monarchical state may be an aristocratic government if public offices are reserved for the nobility and the wealthy. The Roman principate is a monarchical government in a democratic state, since sovereignty is based on a popular consensus, although exercised by one individual; this last definition can be applied to Bonapartism and to certain modern dictatorships. Clearly, Bodin's typology is not without merit. It demonstrates the possible contradiction between value systems which serve as the basis for a state (which Bodin calls "sovereignty") and the actual organization of the state.

At first glance, Montesquieu seems to depart from traditional typology when he writes: "There are three kinds of governments: republican, monarchical, and despotic." But he soon distinguishes between democracy and aristocracy within the republican form of government; once again we have the old distinction made by Herodotus, and the notion of pure forms and corrupt forms (despotism is a corrupt form of monarchy). However, the linking together of democracy and aristocracy is a fertile idea. The nineteenth century, and even the twentieth, were to bear it out; it is difficult to separate democracy and aristocracy because of the importance of limited suffrage and the role of oligarchies in regimes based on universal suffrage. Likewise, for a modern sociologist, it is essential to distinguish between a monarchy and a dictatorship, as Montesquieu clearly perceived.

CONTEMPORARY LEGAL CLASSIFICATIONS Contemporary jurists still draw upon Montesquieu's ideas, although less upon his theory of the three forms of government than upon his theory of the separation of powers. In practice, they classify political regimes according to the internal relationships between the different "powers," that is, between the different elements comprising the state.

We thus arrive at a new tripartite division of governmental regimes: a regime with a confusion of powers; a regime with a separation of powers; and a parliamentary regime (with a collaboration of powers). A confusion of powers means that all important decisions are taken by one organ of the state. This can work to the advantage of one man or of an assembly. The first case corresponds either to an absolute monarchy or to a dictatorship, the difference between them being determined by the mode of investiture: a king acquires power by heredity; a dictator, by force. The second case corresponds to a "government by assembly" or by convention (since the convention is supposed to have incarnated the government). But this second type is more theoretical than practical, resembling somewhat those false windows of decadent architectural planning, placed there to create an illusion of symmetry. In reality, the convention has submitted to a dictatorship (of the commune or of the committees) more often than it has exercised any authority of its own. In any event, examples of governments by assembly are too brief, too rare, and too unstable to warrant placing them in a category of equal importance with the others.

Within those governments having a separation of powers and those having parliamentary systems, we find the same general subdivision between monarchies and republics. A royalist form of separation of powers is a limited or constitutional monarchy in which a parliament, vested with financial and legislative powers, restrains the authority of the king. The republican form is the presidential system, of which the American example is the most impressive. The linking of royalist and republican types is not artificial; the presidential system was invented by the American colonists, who modeled it after the government of eighteenth-century Britain, which was a limited monarchy. The parliamentary system is characterized by a distinction between the head of state and the head of government: the first fills an honorific position lacking any real powers, while the second assumes exclusive direction of the executive branch within a ministerial cabinet that shares with him responsibility to the parliament. This complex system is the final stage of an evolution from absolute monarchy to democracy, which left the external forms of a traditional system intact but divested them of any substantive power for all practical purposes.

Broadly speaking, European monarchies evolved in three stages, following the pattern established by Great Britain: absolute monarchy, limited monarchy, and parliamentary monarchy. The appearance of a parliament confronting the king—or rather an extension of the powers of this parliament, descended from the assemblage of vassals in a feudal society—effected the transition from the first to the second stage. The development of democratic ideas subsequently obliged the king to pay increased attention to the wishes of parliament. The ministers of state, originally mere secretaries of the king charged with executing his policies, increasingly found they had to secure the confidence of parliament in order to be able to act. At this point, we reach an intermediate stage known as *"parlementarisme orléaniste,"* [2] in which ministers had to gain both the king's confidence and that of the deputies. However, this phase did not last long, because the growing success of democratic principles strengthened the legitimacy of the parliament and of the ministers who supported parliamentary policies, and undermined the power and authority of the king. Thenceforth, the ministry required only the support and confidence of the deputies; the cabinet concentrated all governmental power in its hands, while the king became primarily a figurehead ("The King reigns, but does not govern"). In 1875, France transposed this parliamentary system into a republican framework, and many other states followed suit. Actually, there is only a slight difference between a parliamentary republic and a parliamentary monarchy: whether a king or president, the head of state has virtually no power. It was, however, no small achievement of the parliamentary system to have put an end to the bitter conflict between "monarchists" and "republicans," which divided nineteenth-century Europe, by nullifying its real significance.

MODERN SOCIOLOGICAL CLASSIFICATIONS   The preceding legal classifications do not provide a satisfactory explanation for the differences between contemporary political regimes. The present tendency is to abandon them in favor of another classification, which rests on a basic distinction between pluralistic or democratic regimes, on the one hand, and unitarian or autocratic regimes, on the other.

In pluralistic or democratic regimes, political struggles take place openly and freely, under the glare of the public spotlight. So it is with political parties. There are always several of them, whence the name "pluralistic." Though there may be more than two, there are always at

---

[2] So called because it corresponded in France to the monarchy of Louis-Philippe, former Duc d'Orleans.

least two. The struggle is public and open to the press and other news media. Pluralistic regimes are also liberal regimes, that is, regimes where public freedoms exist, permitting each person to express his opinions orally, in writing, through membership in organizations, by participation in public demonstrations, and so forth. The activities of pressure groups, which try to influence power indirectly, is sometimes more secret; political life always includes twilight zones, but these are kept to a minimum in pluralistic regimes.

In unitarian regimes, on the contrary, political conflict does not officially exist, except in the form of individual struggles to win the favors of a prince. But the prince himself, whether a king, emperor, fuehrer, duce, or dictator, cannot be challenged; his supreme power is above the fray of political battles. This is a basic difference from pluralistic democratic regimes, where the supreme power itself is contested at regular intervals, every four or five years, by the free play of general elections. Those who hold the highest offices wield a precarious kind of power, like tenants whose rights expire with the expiration of a lease, and who must obtain a renewal or else vacate the premises. However, even the most absolute monarch can scarcely escape the influence of his immediate associates, his advisers, his favorites, the principal agencies of the state; a whole series of governmental offices that share in the exercise of authority thus become the object of an intense power struggle. Sometimes the monarch becomes the pawn of certain men or institutions around him, as pharaohs were manipulated by the priests of Ammon, and Merovingian kings became puppets of the *Maire du Palais.*

Within each of these large categories—pluralistic or democratic regimes, and unitarian or autocratic regimes—we can make various subclassifications. In the second category we must distinguish between hereditary monarchies and dictatorships resulting from conquests. More realistic, and less formal, is the government of moderate autocracies, which accept some opposition to the regime and allow certain legal means of expressing political dissent indirectly, and of totalitarian autocracies, which destroy all opposition and force dissenters to resort to clandestine activities.

Concerning pluralistic democracies, the best way to classify them is by combining the legal forms of governmental regimes with the kinds of political parties found in them. When it comes to the structure of political regimes, the distinction between a two-party and a multiparty system is paramount; it determines how a majority is formed in the national assembly, which is fundamental in a parliamentary regime since the government is based on it. In a two-party system, one party holds a majority by the very nature of things; therefore it is homogeneous, it is not paralyzed by internal bickering and disagreements, and it is stable. On the other hand, in a multiparty system no one party holds a majority, which is formed by a coalition of several parties, each looking out for its own interests: a majority so constituted is heterogeneous, divided, and unstable. Moreover, political contests between two parties are altogether different from those involving a large number of parties.

But the number of parties is not the only factor to consider. The stability and cohesiveness of the government in a two-party system depend, above all, on the internal discipline of the majority party. If all its representatives vote the same way, as in Great Britain, the executive has the backing of a parliamentary majority that is truly meaningful and durable. If, however, there is complete freedom to vote as one chooses—as is the case with the "flexible" parties of the United States —then the government has as much difficulty governing and maintaining itself in power as in a multiparty system. Thus the only authentic two-party system is the "rigid" British type in which each party forces its members into line when a question comes up for a vote; the "flexible" American type is actually a "pseudo-two-party system" that produces, in practice, the same results as a multiparty system.

Accordingly, we can recognize three types of pluralistic regimes: (1) presidential regimes which are either pseudo-two-party, as in the United States, or multiparty, as in Latin America, with little real difference between them; (2) parliamentary regimes with a two-party system of the British type; and (3) parliamentary regimes with a multiparty system of the continental European type. On a juridical plane, the last two types are very close to each other and far removed from the first type. On a functional plane, however, the stability and authority of the government in a two-party parliamentary system are more like those of a presidential executive system than those of a multiparty parliamentary government. On the citizens' level and the question of choosing heads of state—an essential factor in any political regime—the resemblance is even greater, as we shall see.

In a parliamentary election, the English citizen is conscious, not only of voting for a deputy, but also—and above all—of selecting the leader responsible for British policy. Because of party discipline, he knows that in casting a vote for the Conservative party or the Labour party, he is putting Mr. X., the Conservative party leader, or Mr. Y., the leader of the Labour party, at the head of the government for four years. His situation is exactly like that of the American voter choosing the presidential electors, who are committed to naming one of the two rival candidates as president. In Great Britain and the United States, despite differences in legal structures, all citizens are aware of registering their own choice in the selection of the real head of government. In Western European countries, however, the multiparty system prevents this direct method of choosing the head of government. Instead, he is chosen by the executive committees of the various parties through political arrangements that are often mystifying to the average citizen.

Thus we can establish a new distinction between "direct" and "indirect" democracies. In the former, the electors themselves actually choose the head of government; in the latter, they designate those who will make the final choice, and who therefore act as intermediaries. In the West, this distinction has tended to become very basic. The executive officer is the focal point of power in modern states; the legislative branch plays a role only in controlling, limiting, or preventing the exercise of power. Accordingly, the direct choice of the head of government by the whole populace is of primary importance. It is much easier to establish mutual confidence between the electorate and those in power in such a system. As a matter of fact, in indirect democratic systems the public feels almost no sense of involvement in the intrigues that take place in political committees, from which a nominee for the head of government emerges. All this comes back to the point that in a "direct" democracy, political competition is more real, more basic, more consciously felt by the citizenry than in an "indirect democracy." The importance of this phenomenon can be measured.

Political Institutions
and Techno-economic Structures

The establishment of this or that political regime in a country is not a matter of chance or of human caprice. As with all institutions, political regimes are determined by a number of factors. There are two major opposing theories on this question. Marxists consider political regimes a reflection of the society's system of production, essentially defined in terms of the property system. By doing this, they deny that political (and other) institutions have any autonomy. Institutions are of secondary importance in the Marxist view. Westerners, on the contrary, who formerly exaggerated the independence of politics in relation to the economy, are now beginning to modify their earlier theories and draw nearer to the Marxist position. But for Western analysts, the essential factor that accounts for the establishment of any given political regime is not the property system, but the level of technological development.

POLITICAL REGIMES AND PROPERTY SYSTEMS We have already given the general outline of the dependency of political regimes upon the production systems and property systems they engender, as in Marxist doctrine.

Marxism distinguishes, first of all, four kinds of states: the slave state of antiquity, the feudal state, the bourgeois state, and the socialist state, each corresponding to a particular mode of production and a particular kind of property system. Each "type" of state is subdivided into several "forms" of state or political regimes: oriental despotism, tyranny, or republic in the slave state; seigniories or centralized monarchies in the feudal state; Western democracies or fascistic regimes in the bourgeois state; and the Soviet system and popular democracies in the socialist state. Thus various political regimes correspond to a given production and property system, but this diversity of regimes itself corresponds to differences within the production system and the property system.

Let us take, as an example, the medieval production system, based on primitive and widely dispersed agricultural techniques, engendering opposition between the landowners and the serfs. The system passed through two broad stages. At the outset, it developed within the framework of a closed economy in which each seigniory was self-contained, providing virtually all the necessities of life for those living on the lands; exchange and commerce were on the simplest levels. Corresponding to this kind of feudal production system was a highly decentralized political regime in which power was parceled up among seigniors, linked to one another by a loosely knit social hierarchy. However, with the development of communications and commerce, the society entered upon a new stage, substituting an exchange economy for a closed economy. The local autonomy of the seigniors gradually disappeared, and a centralized state emerged under the form of the absolute monarchy.

Differences in the forms of the bourgeois state are likewise linked to differences in the capitalistic system of production. When, for example, the capitalistic system began to predominate, but large landed property continued to play an important economic role, the bourgeois state tended to acquire the form of a parliamentary monarchy of the *orléaniste* variety, as it functioned in France under Louis-Philippe (1830–48). But once the capitalistic system of production was shaken by the impact of the worker movements, and the move toward socialism threatened the political regime, the bourgeois state leaned toward violence of a fascist type. Thus parliamentary monarchy appeared to be the form of state corresponding to the first phase of an expanding capitalistic system, and fascism seemed to be the last phase of a declining capitalistic system. In its first, flourishing phase, the capitalistic system produced the Western democratic state, based upon a system of political freedoms, pluralistic political parties, competitive free elections, and so on.

The same correlation between different systems of production and different forms of state can be found in socialism. Marxist theories currently recognize two forms of the socialist state: the Soviet system and people's democracy. Both were "born under different conditions from the standpoint of the disposition of class power." [3] Both forms rely primarily on the working class and on socialistic production. But the Soviet dictatorship is based on a single political party, the elimination of all private ownership of the means of production (except for individual plots of ground belonging to the *kolkhozy,* the collective farms) and the disappearance of the bourgeoisie. People's democracies, on the other hand, have preserved a few forms of private enterprise in certain crafts and small businesses, but especially in agriculture. They also permit, on occasion, the existence of other political parties, but their influence is overshadowed by the dominant Communist party and the practice of forming "National Fronts." Popular democracies rely upon the collaboration of certain elements of the bourgeoisie.

Marxist theories overestimate the influence of production systems and types of property ownership upon political regimes. That this influence exists and is important is undeniable, but political regimes are not a mere reflection or outgrowth of the property and production systems. The correlation between the principal types of states described by the Marxists—slave state, feudal state, bourgeois state, and socialist state—and the principal types of production systems is generally correct. But these "types of state" are poorly defined from a political point of view; we are dealing with very broad categories, encompassing very different kinds of political regimes. And these political differences are sometimes only slightly related to differences in the production system. Let us take the example of fascist regimes. Can we say that the system of production in Germany in 1933 was very different from the system in Great Britain? A Marxist would reply that, unlike the latter, the former had no colonies and that imperialism thus had no other outlet than fascism. This argument is even less convincing when one

[3] *Principles of Marxism-Leninism* (Moscow, 1960).

considers that neither the Scandinavian countries nor the United States had colonies, but they did not succumb to fascism. To be sure, German fascism—like all fascisms—depended upon economic factors, but the part played by the system of production per se does not seem to have been very significant.

The development of Stalinism in the USSR is another good example. The Soviets themselves do not try to explain it in terms of the production system. No doubt it played a part; centralized planning naturally tended toward a dictatorship. But planning was no less centralized at Stalin's death, when the need for liberalization became very clear. The relative economic decentralization that has since taken place in Russia is not the cause of de-Stalinization, but the result of it. To explain the tyranny of Joseph Dzhugashvili in terms of his personal vices and faults of character, as is done officially in the USSR, is not at all Marxist and wholly inadequate. Stalinism was a form of state, a type of political regime, which developed within a socialist system of production; it followed a regime of very different form (Leninism) and preceded another equally different regime (Khrushchevism). The evolution of the production system cannot by itself explain these differences.

The differences between the three great forms of Western political regimes—the American presidential system, the British two-party parliamentary system, and the continental, multiparty parliamentary system—are very important, as we have indicated. It is not possible to correlate them either with differences in production or property systems. The fact that the role of the public sector is much smaller in the production system of the United States than it is in Great Britain or France would seem to have no bearing on the matter. It is an historical and cultural development, unrelated to the system of production, that explains the present differences in political regimes among the major states of the West. Conversely, the transformation of the economic structures of France, Great Britain, and other European nations in the past twenty-five years, which has led to the replacement of the capitalistic system of production by a mixed system—half-capitalistic, half-socialistic, with a very important public sector and a rather advanced level of national economic planning—has failed to produce a political transformation of equal importance. The growth of the executive branch of government is unmistakable, but it is hardly more powerful than in the United States, where economic structures have remained purely capitalistic.

Nevertheless, the opposition of the two major economic structures, as defined in terms of property systems—capitalism and socialism—

correspond, on the whole, to the two major categories of contemporary political regimes—the pluralistic and the unitarian. A capitalistic or semicapitalistic economy is marked by a separation of political power and of economic power; the latter is divided among a number of privately owned firms (and partially, sometimes, by public firms or corporations), all of which are autonomous "centers of decision," more or less independent of the state. Private ownership of the means of production thus leads to a pluralistic social structure, which, in turn, is reflected in the political domain. By contrast, public ownership of all forms of enterprise and a completely planned economy have the effect of concentrating political power and economic power in the same hands—a situation that tends to produce a unitarian regime.

However, the foregoing description needs to be qualified. The separation of political power from economic power is partly an illusion, for the latter has powerful means of influencing the former. In a liberal, capitalistic regime, as it functioned in the nineteenth century, political power had hardly any independent existence; it was little more than a reflection of economic power. The division of the two has acquired significance only in the mixed regimes of today's capitalistic societies. Moreover, the concentration of economic power in the hands of a few powerful corporations belies the notion of a multiplicity of independent "centers of decision." The correlation between regimes based on private ownership of property and those with a pluralistic political system is not as clear as generally believed. The example of the Nazi dictatorship clearly revealed that an extremely totalitarian autocracy can take hold under a capitalistic system. Fascism, moreover, is a phenomenon linked to the evolution of capitalism and its resistance to the establishment of a socialistic or planned economy.

The connection between a socialistic economy and a unitarian regime is equally uncertain. Experiments thus far have been too brief and too few to warrant the drawing of any definite conclusions. The course of capitalistic societies can be traced for more than a hundred years in many countries in Western Europe and North America. But the course of socialistic societies can be traced for only about fifty years and then only in one state, the Soviet Union. In the European people's democracies, where the experiment is less than twenty years old, the history is distorted by the problem of external domination (except in Yugoslavia). In China, where socialism is even more recent, the settlement of a terrible civil war and the extremely low level of technological development make any comparison impossible. The regimes of the socialist states are still too few and too recent to be the subject of valid analyses in political sociology. We must not rule out the possibility that their totalitarian nature and their lack of political pluralism may depend upon their revolutionary status and thus be only a temporary condition. Indeed, this is the picture they themselves offer of their present situation (with the theory of the proletarian dictatorship, which they declare is a transitional phase).

In any event, we can detect within the socialist countries a marked tendency toward economic decentralization, bringing them nearer to the "plurality of centers of decision" which usually characterizes capitalistic societies. Yugoslavia has pursued this policy for a number of years. The USSR and other socialist states of Europe have adopted it in their turn. There is an interesting comparison to be made here with the historical evolution of political decentralization. Under feudalism, decentralization was guaranteed by the hereditary rights of local leaders; in the modern world, it is based upon their popular election. Nowadays, the private ownership of property ensures a fairly effective decentralization of the economy, owing to individual inheritance rights. But one can visualize a similar evolution leading to an economic decentralization based on different, more democratic processes, of the kind envisaged by nineteenth-century socialists.

POLITICAL REGIMES AND PRODUCTION LEVELS   Lastly, the correlation between political regimes and the level of techno-economic development appears as strong as the correlation between political regimes and the systems of ownership of the means of production. We found again here the political consequences of technological progress, which we previously discussed in a general way (see p. 64). Let us now examine them in greater detail, with particular reference to political institutions.

Pluralistic democracy corresponds to a high degree of industrialization. To say that free societies are affluent societies expresses, in a blunt but hardly exaggerated formula, a fundamental truth. Practically speaking, it is impossible to apply a pluralistic system to nations whose populations are largely undernourished, uneducated, and illiterate. Under the guise of adopting modern democratic procedures, old autocratic feudal regimes continue to run the government. Far from changing the established social order, these democratic procedures can be used to camouflage and even prolong it.

An objective study of the different nations of the world seems to confirm the thesis that a high degree of correlation exists between technological development and the development of democracy. If we compare two maps, one showing the developed and the underdeveloped nations, the other showing the democratic and the authoritarian nations, we note that they match almost exactly. The great industrialized zones—North America, Western Europe, Australia, and New Zealand—are also the principal areas of democracy. The underdeveloped zones of Latin America, Asia, and Africa are also the areas of autocracy.

It is possible that the autocratic and unitarian nature of communist regimes is due not only to the concentration of political and economic power but also—and perhaps above all—to the underdeveloped or semideveloped character of the countries where communism was established. The Russia of 1917 and the people's democracies of 1945 [4] have one common characteristic: they were on a lower economic level than the industrial nations of the West. They were not really backward, underdeveloped nations (like Yemen or certain African states); they had reached a kind of intermediate level. We are tempted to say that they constitute the upper fringe of underdeveloped countries, or the lower fringe of technically developed societies. Though these generalizations have no precise meaning, they help us visualize the situation and do, after all, describe rather accurately the situation of countries on the threshold of industrialization, countries forced to make great sacrifices and costly investments, which are all the harder to bear because the living standard is so very low to begin with. An autocratic political regime arises in response to the economic requirements.

Within the world's major political systems, we find the same contrast: liberal democracy is stronger in northern Europe, more highly developed from a technological and economic point of view than in France or Italy; communism is more rigid in China and Albania, the more underdeveloped socialist states, than in the Soviet Union and the rest of Eastern Europe. Historical evolution reveals the same parallel between the growth of production under the influence of technology and the growth of democratic processes. Thus, pluralistic democracy developed in the West during the nineteenth and early twentieth centuries with the growth of industrialization. We will come back to this relationship between industrialization and democratization later. For the moment, we will concentrate on one aspect that is now apparent in the socialist states of Europe.

The "liberalization" that is discernible in the USSR and in the people's democracies corresponds to their economic evolution. The USSR is becoming one of the world's great industrial powers. Its development by socialist means, which has given priority to power over abun-

---

[4] Except the German Democratic Republic and Czechoslovakia (the Bohemian region); but communism was brought in there by the Red Army, and the upheavals of the war made takeover easier.

dance, to technological needs over consumer needs, has delayed the political consequences of this evolution, but political changes are beginning to appear. Like the most highly developed Western nations, the Soviet Union is approaching a state of relative abundance, in which not only man's elemental needs (food, housing, and clothing), but even his secondary needs (comfort, culture, and leisure), are close to being satisfied. A kind of general level of "average satisfaction" will thus be achieved, which tends to relax tensions and diminish antagonisms. Moreover, the functioning of a highly developed industrialized state requires that a significant portion of the population shall have access to a higher cultural level which brings people into contact with foreign ideas and develops their faculties, thus threatening the very foundations of the totalitarian state. Eastern Europe, which was predominantly agricultural until 1945 (except for Czechoslovakia and the German Democratic Republic), has also become industrialized with the same results.

Of course, many factors are delaying this evolution: the actions of politicians and bureaucrats, who are tied to the dictatorship and derive power and prestige from it; the external threat and competition with capitalistic states; the dangers of an internal crisis if liberalization moves too rapidly; the risks of reaction in satellite states; and the technical difficulties inherent in any relaxation of an authoritarian regime. But in spite of all this, it seems that, in the long run, the evolution is irreversible. However, this prospect applies only to industrially developed communist countries (the USSR and the European people's democracies); the underdeveloped communist nations (China, Vietnam, and so on) will probably remain much longer under a system of political dictatorship that corresponds to their level of economic development. It is conceivable that eventually the basic differences will not be between Eastern governments and Western governments, but rather between the political regimes of developed and underdeveloped nations, the economic level of a country proving to be more decisive than its constitution.

On the whole, the theory of the relationship between democracy and technological progress is a valid one. But this general tendency can be upset by other factors that may divert or even reverse it at times. It is an astonishing fact that the most terrible dictatorship of the twentieth century, Nazism, developed within a country that was technologically very advanced, second only to the United States in 1933. We can thus note two kinds of exceptions to the theory of a parallelism between democratic development and technological progress: on the one hand, highly developed countries that are also very authoritarian; on the other hand, underdeveloped countries that are also democratic. We examined this last type earlier in connection with the question of the balance between the level of complexity of social problems and the level of comprehension on the part of the citizenry; we shall not discuss it further here. The best example of the exception to the first type is Hitler's Germany. People have tried to explain it, first, in terms of a particular set of circumstances: a moral crisis after the defeat of 1918, the economic crisis and widespread unemployment, the fear of communism and socialism among the middle classes. To these factors cultural elements are added (an authoritarian tradition, the absence of any democratic spirit, and so on). But all of these explanations remain inadequate.

Some people believe that certain general factors can also account for autocratic tendencies in industrially developed countries. There are two important theories on the question—one psychological, the other sociological. We have already discussed the first one, formulated by psychoanalysts who think that technological progress increases political antagonisms instead of reducing them, because it produces a world that is unsuited to the deeper needs and desires of men, a world that is increasingly artificial. Sociologists, on the other hand, believe that the citizens of highly developed societies are very attached to their material comfort and, at the same time, rather "depoliticized," which is to say, rather indifferent to political issues, insensitive to the dangers of a dictatorship and generally unaware of such a possibility. If a very serious economic crisis arises in such a situation, the possibility of seeing the population throw themselves into the arms of a "savior" is very great. But these general explanations are not very convincing. In many respects they seem less tenable than the preceding explanations based on a particular set of circumstances.

However, another general explanation is much more significant— the one that compares the rate of development with the level of development. We have already indicated the importance of this phenomenon. Its influence seems very great under the circumstances. Dictatorships appear in history during periods of rapid and sweeping social change, and particularly during periods of rapid technological development. At such times, violence serves either to accelerate the rate of change and hasten economic progress (revolutionary dictatorships), or to maintain the traditional social order and impede social evolution (reactionary dictatorships). In the present era, communism is a good example of the first type, and fascism of the second. These phenomena occur at different levels of economic development. In Germany, Hitlerism tended to prevent a highly industrialized society from slipping into socialism. In Spain and Portugal, the object was to check the evolution of an aristocratic society toward a liberal democracy. In China, communism is a means of accelerating the birth of an industrial society and of emerging from economic underdevelopment. In the Soviet Union today, communism tends to serve as the instrument for achieving a very highly industrialized society.

No doubt, the establishment of dictatorships is always easier and occurs more frequently in underdeveloped societies than in highly developed ones. It has even been possible to show that there is a certain incompatibility between a high level of development and dictatorship. In very advanced countries, the entire social edifice rests on the shoulders of scientists, technicians, and intellectuals, who can only work in an atmosphere of freedom. (In causing an exodus of scientists, by its oppression of the human spirit, Hitler's Germany undermined the very basis of its power.) Moreover, in societies of this high economic level, freedom in all its forms is part of the everyday comfort that citizens take for granted. Its absence is keenly felt and provokes a deep unrest; freedom is always fragile. But the fact remains that the level of development is less important in this matter than the rate of development.

CULTURES

By contrast with "techniques" and "institutions," the term "culture" refers to the beliefs, ideologies, and myths, that is, the collective images and ideas of a community, which are in a way its spiritual and psychological elements; technology and institutions constitute a community's material aspects. But we must emphasize once again that all such classifications are artificial. Collective beliefs and images are intermingled with all of the material factors—with traditional habits and behavior patterns, with other institutions, with technology, and even with geography and demography. Moreover, collective ideas and images reflect to a great extent the material elements of the group. When we consider culture in this first sense, we are only indicating that we want to examine separately the elements of a community which are primarily the collective views, without pretending to isolate them completely from the overall picture that includes the material factors.

The term "culture" is often used in a broader sense, one that refers to unique forms around which all the elements comprising a social group combine—collective images, beliefs, ideologies, institutions, technology, and even geographical and demographic factors. A sociologist uses these factors to develop abstract syntheses that enable him to define different kinds of societies—capitalistic societies, socialistic societies, feudal societies, tribal societies, and so forth. But these general syntheses are reflected in reality by a variety of forms, each of which has its own unique characteristics; and this is what cultures are. In the real world there is not a capitalistic society or a socialistic society, but a particular capitalistic society or a particular socialistic society, dated and situated in the unique way history produced it, and in the unique way it differs from other societies. Each of these societies constitutes a culture.

To avoid any confusion, we will call cultures in the broad sense of the term "cultural entities," whereas strictly cultural elements of a social group, as opposed to institutions and techniques—in other words, cultures in the narrow sense of the term—we will call "beliefs." We will examine "beliefs" first and then "cultural entities," because an analysis of the latter will enable us to synthesize the various elements described in this first part of the book, "Political Structures."

Beliefs: Ideologies and Myths

In a certain sense, society is the sum total of the ideas and images its members have formed of it. But among these collective ideas, some correspond to external realities that have an objective, physical existence—the earth, nature, men, tools and machines, an army, a parliament, and so on. Other ideas are only states of mind, apart from the material expression they acquire—books, photographs, symbols. These are the ideas that we are going to examine here. We call them "beliefs" because they are based not on an objective knowledge of facts but on subjective opinions.

DIFFERENT KINDS OF BELIEFS It is virtually impossible to classify the many different kinds of beliefs. We propose to establish two principal categories: ideologies, which are more rational, formulated beliefs; and irrational beliefs, which are more spontaneous and which we will call "myths." But myths are often given an elaborate rationale, while ideologies are not always rational. Sometimes the two categories become interwoven in an inextricable manner; a striking example is the case of religions.

Ideologies are collections of rationalized and systematized beliefs, reflecting the situation of the society in which they originate. Marxists claim that they are nothing more than the reflection of the class situation. But the personal action of those who create ideologies—

thinkers, philosophers, system-builders, and "ideologists"—remains important. Without Marx, there would no doubt have been a socialist ideology, but it would not have been exactly the same and perhaps not had the same capacity for penetration and expansion. The combination of social factors and individual creativity is not fundamentally different in terms of means and general invention in ideological and artistic matters. On the one hand, the creator of ideas, forms, and techniques acts under the pressure of a social need, but, on the other, the fate of his work depends on its reception by society. Between the two there intervenes the mysterious alchemy of the individual creation.

To some extent, the ideologist expresses his own psychological tendencies and his inner conflicts in the doctrine he expounds.[5] But he also feels within himself the concerns, aspirations, and passions of the society in which he lives. Social forces are expressed through him; he is able to express common experiences better than other men, because his talent and profession give him more effective means of expression. Montesquieu, Adam Smith, and Karl Marx were, like Victor Hugo, "sonorous echos" who reflected the cries of their generation. They were in a way the instruments, the agents of social forces. The doctrines they formulated, the systems they erected, did not spring from their minds by spontaneous generation; the substance of their systems came from a society whose needs they translated.

The role of a system-builder is not simply that of a tape recorder or a loudspeaker. Society provides him with the building blocks; he constructs the edifice. His function is rather like that of an architect. In this respect, the influence of his personal genius, and especially his aptitude for synthesizing facts, is extremely important. Many ideologies have suffered for lack of a first-rate thinker who could coordinate the scattered facts and data and convert them into a solid construction, a system in which all the pieces fit firmly together. Neither fascism nor Christian democracy, for example, has ever had a spokesman of Marx's stature, a fact that has certainly impeded their development. The strengthening of conservative ideologies in France between 1900 and 1940 was largely due to the intellectual power of Charles Maurras. Forceful expression is as important in this respect as the aptitude for synthesis: many ideologies have been handicapped by the lack of a writer of genius who could give them vivid and memorable expression.

After being carefully worked out by individuals who are under the same pressure of social needs as other men, ideologies are then sub-

[5] On this point, see our analysis of the psychological factors of political antagonism, pp. 122–32.

jected to society's reaction. Some are rejected and soon forgotten or attract only a small group of followers without influence. Others are "accepted," so to speak. Men recognize themselves in the new ideologies and use them to express their aspirations and demands, and to define the basic objectives of their political action. Around these ideas they form parties and organizations serving the same purposes. The acceptance or rejection of an ideological system depends primarily upon the extent to which it reflects the needs of the community and the social forces within it. No doubt other factors play a part; the dissemination of a new ideology can be hastened or retarded by the position of its author, the persuasiveness of his thinking, and especially the means at his disposal for publicizing his views, above all, the availability of the communications media. Propaganda and publicity can assist in the social acceptance of ideologies, but in the long run they cannot assure the success of an ideology that fails to correspond to the needs of the times. On the contrary, an ideology that is relevant eventually asserts itself. The greater the need for a particular ideology, the more intellectuals it will have to crusade for it, and the more likely it is to find a thinker capable of translating it into a logical and coherent system.

Once it has been "accepted" by society, the new ideology will begin living its own life, independent of its creator. And the longer it lives, the more its original thought will undergo transformations. Present-day Marxism is far removed from the theories elaborated by Karl Marx a century ago. And today's liberalism is even further removed from the thinking of Adam Smith or Benjamin Constant. If the author of the doctrine is still revered, his works furnish an arsenal of quotations which, lifted out of context, permit the justification of current interpretations without regard for authenticity. Thus, through a process of constant change, of a collective and more or less unconscious nature, ideologies adapt themselves to the evolution of social forces and structures. Their original content is of little interest to anyone except specialists in the history of ideas, unless their opponents use it to support their charges of heresy and heterodoxy.

By "myths" we mean beliefs that are vaguer, less rational, less carefully thought out than ideologies. This rather imprecise definition includes, in reality, two quite different things: myths we may call traditional and those we may call myths of action.

Traditional myths are more or less fabled depictions of nature, the world, man, and society, which have been strongly accepted (meaning that they have assumed the character of a primary good or evil), and thus serve to inspire the life of a social group. Original sin, a lost Paradise, a golden age, the value of virginity, incest taboos, the fear of snakes and spiders, the nutritive power of blood, royalty, universal suffrage—these are a few examples of myths intentionally drawn from very different domains. Anything may become a myth through the dual process of transforming it into a fable, which removes it from tangible reality, and assigning it a moral value, placing it in a category of good or evil. But this process is not voluntary and deliberate, like the elaboration of an ideological system; it resembles instead the development of ·customs in relation to the establishment of laws. To be sure, deliberate and concerted interventions can occur in this phenomenon: modern methods of publicity and propaganda create and develop myths through the press and the mass media. But they become genuine myths only when they enter the traditional structures of human belief or replace previously accepted myths.

The basic problem concerns the origin of traditional myths. Materialistic theories view them as the result of deliberate action by certain men and certain social classes, who use the myths to camouflage their exploitation of other men and other classes. Thus Marxists explain ancient mythologies, religions, and the development of modern myths. In the same way, sociologists explain the process of making and idolizing celebrities and the creation of myths in the film world, the theater, and political life. These explanations are partially true, but they fail to take into account certain aspects of traditional myths, some of the strange and bizarre characteristics they often assume, and the profound fascination these cause. Psychoanalysis has renewed the approach to this problem by regarding many myths as the fablelike transposition of deep-seated psychological conflicts formed during childhood. Its explanations of the Oedipus myth and the Virgin Birth—common to many religions—as well as the myth of the Golden Age and of lost Paradise, can be mentioned as typical examples. Jung developed an even more original theory about a collective unconscious he called "archetypes," which is the reservoir of humanity's great myths.

Early in the twentieth century, French journalist Georges Sorel developed another notion about myths—"myths of action." Sorel believed that one of the most effective ways of influencing a community is to give it concise and uncomplicated images of a fictitious future or a fabled past, which will polarize its passions and lead to action. It is only to the extent that one can create myths, accepted by the masses, that one can succeed in arousing them to action: "We can talk indefinitely about revolt, without producing a revolutionary movement as long as there are no myths accepted by the masses," Sorel stated in the Introduction to his *Réflexions sur la violence* (1907). Defined in this way, myths are simplified ideologies, or rather ideologies reduced to brief and brutal themes or images. To the extent that these artificial myths can be poured into the molds of traditional myths, they acquire an even greater power and intensity. These action myths can provoke revolutionary movements, as Sorel believed, as readily as they can contribute to maintaining the social order (compare, for example, the current myth of the "society of abundance," which anesthetizes popular demands by confusing a future, allegedly at hand but as yet unrealized, with a present that is altogether different).

THE POLITICAL INFLUENCE OF POPULAR BELIEFS Marxists hold that popular beliefs play only a secondary role in political life, merely reflecting socioeconomic structures, and especially the relationships between social classes, which constitute the fundamental reality. Certain Westerners, on the other hand, think, in the words of critic Albert Thibaudet, that "politics is ideas." We will explore these notions, both of which are too categorical, too absolute, although the Marxist theory is closer to the truth. For the moment, we will examine only the forms of political influence produced by popular beliefs, not their importance.

Myths and ideologies play roughly the same role in political life: they mobilize the citizenry, either in opposition to power or in support of it. This mobilization often assumes the character of a "camouflage," which is to say that beliefs can serve to conceal reality in order to win its acceptance. Myths and ideologies are effective, and frequently used, instruments of camouflage. But they can also reflect reality: myths do so in a short, simplified manner, making the reality more vivid and accessible; ideologies do so in a more precise and detailed manner. Like the tongues in Aesop's fable, myths and ideologies can be made to lie or tell the truth. We will confine ourselves to pointing out certain essential characteristics of their behavior.

In the first place, myths and ideologies define systems of value. Every society is based on definitions of good and evil, right and wrong, which together constitute a system of values. These definitions are themselves subjective beliefs, for the ideas of good and evil, right and wrong, do not come from experience, but from faith and voluntary acceptance. Thus they are ideological or mythical. Actually, every ideology is, to some extent, a system of values, even those that claim to be totally objective. Myths are such by their very nature, as we have noted. Not every phenomenon or every social activity is tied to a value system, but many are. In certain areas, value judgments are more general and more deeply rooted than in others—especially in the religious, family, and sexual domains, and, of course, in politics. In passing from the level of what is useful or harmful, agreeable or disagreeable, to that of what is right or wrong, good or bad, political antagonisms grow much stronger and more obdurate. Thus myths and ideologies tend to reinforce political conflicts.

Yet they can also serve to reduce tensions. If, in fact, each social class or social group forges its own ideology and its own myths in the political struggle, power also develops myths and ideologies of its own, which tend to alleviate conflicts and bring about social integration. All the members of a given society share certain beliefs and value judgments, which constitute a unifying ideology that is at variance with the partial and conflicting ideologies of the various groups fighting each other. The question of legitimacy has considerable bearing on this aspect of the problem.

Legitimacy itself is, in the last analysis, a question of belief, depending strictly upon the ideologies and myths prevalent in the society. Every ideology seeks to depict the image of an ideal government; governments that resemble this image are considered legitimate and those that do not are regarded as illegitimate.

The ideology thus determines a type of legitimacy—whether monarchical, democratic, communist, or whatever. Legitimacy is not defined in the abstract, in terms of an ideal type of government with an absolute value, but concretely, in terms of each of the historic concepts of the ideal type of government, that is, each of the political ideologies. In this sense, we describe as legitimate the government which—at a given moment, in a given country—corresponds to the idea that the general populace has about legitimate government, in other words, the popular beliefs about legitimacy. Thus, monarchy was legitimate in seventeenth-century France, democracy is legitimate in contemporary France, liberal government is legitimate in the United States, and a socialist system is legitimate in the USSR.

These theories of legitimate government reflect, more or less, the social structures and especially the class situations: they tend to justify a type of government that meets the requirements of those running the government. They transform a temporary and relative social situation into something permanent by giving it an absolute and eternal character. Belief in the legitimacy of a government tends to place the latter in the category of the "sacred," the equivalent of mythical absolutes. If the governed believe that their rulers are legitimate, they are inclined to obey them spontaneously; they recognize that obedience is due them. A legitimate government is one which people feel an obligation to obey, whereas no such obligation is felt toward governments considered illegitimate.

As G. Ferrero has said, legitimacy is "the invisible genius of the city" that maintains the state and the social order by securing the obedience of the citizenry. To some extent, citizens naturally obey a legitimate government; threats and constraints play only a minor role, used to control a few recalcitrants or in exceptional circumstances. But when confronted with a government they consider illegitimate, people are naturally inclined to refuse to obey it; compliance is achieved only through force and constraint. Threats and violence thus become the only bases of power, and power is much more fragile than appearances suggest. Consequently, illegitimate governments become very harsh and authoritarian, which accounts for the violence of dictatorships— illegitimate regimes.

There is "consensus" in a society when we can observe among its members a fairly general agreement on the form of government regarded as legitimate. We say "fairly general" and not "absolutely unanimous"—the idea being that those opposed to the dominant view of legitimacy are very much in the minority and have little influence (like, for example, the monarchists in present-day France). The existence of such a consensus proves that political antagonisms are relatively moderate: there is conflict within a regime, without putting the regime itself in jeopardy (concerning the difference between a struggle within a regime and a struggle over a regime, see pp. 172–73).

But it sometimes happens that an ideology ceases to be accepted by the majority of citizens without being fully replaced by another. Several ideologies and several legitimate systems of government then coexist within the country. There is a break in the consensus. In such a situation, no one government can be legitimate in the eyes of the great majority. A legitimate government in the eyes of some is illegitimate in the eyes of others, and vice versa. This means that any government is based only on force and violence in the opinion of a large portion of the population. Such, for example, was the situation in France in the nineteenth century, when advocates of monarchical legitimacy and those of democratic legitimacy were almost evenly divided.

Such a situation is revolutionary. It reveals a crisis in the social structure, which is thrown into doubt by an important segment of the population. A new political ideology, and the new myths that accompany it, oppose the previous system of legitimacy and express the desire of new social classes or new social forces to play a greater role in governing the state. At the same time, the breakdown of consensus intensifies the revolutionary situation, compounding the material crisis with a moral and intellectual crisis, a crisis of belief. It makes the old political system more vulnerable by desanctifying it for many of the citizens and by taking away the mythical attributes it had previously enjoyed.

Political awareness concerns ideologies almost exclusively, not popular myths. Public opinion polls, in France and elsewhere, indicate that five principal factors play a significant role in determining people's choices and attitudes: (1) the standard of living, the condition of being salaried or nonsalaried, a sense of social belonging in general; (2) age group and sex; (3) the level of education; (4) religion; and (5) sympathy for a political party. The last three factors are ideological; parties are based on political ideologies, more or less tied to religious doctrines, and the level of education affects the possibility of mutual understanding.

By integrating each of these specific behavior patterns into a comprehensive political program, ideologies can influence their course of action. The influence is greater when the ideology is more complex, more precise and systematized, and when the citizen is more familiar with it and supports it more fully. The concept of "political awareness" clearly indicates the role of ideologies. Each particular political attitude is simultaneously a response to a concrete situation arising in society, and the manifestation of an overall vision of power, its relationship to the individual citizen, and the conflicts in which power is the central issue—a universal vision that constitutes, in effect, political awareness. The higher the degree of political awareness, the greater its influence, and the less each attitude is dictated by the circumstances of a particular situation. Political awareness is the product of numerous factors—education, environment, experience, and the like—but ideology generally occupies first place. First of all, ideologies develop the political awareness of the people, thus serving as the basis for ideological groups.

Cultural Entities

All of the elements comprising a community—geographical, demographic, and technological elements; institutions; popular beliefs and images—are intermingled in actual situations, forming distinct combinations we may call "cultural entities." Every individual community belongs to a cultural entity or is itself a cultural entity. Cultural entities synthesize all the factors studied in this chapter; we are not speaking of abstract syntheses, but of concrete syntheses, corresponding to the different aspects of reality.

THE CONCEPT OF CULTURAL ENTITIES   Every social group is in some way
a cultural entity. A family, an organization, a group of adolescents
have their own myths, their own collective beliefs and images, their institutions, technical skills, population, and geographical area, which
are not exactly like those of other families, other organizations, and
other youth groups. However, the degree of originality within these
entities is limited. Most groups virtually borrow the greater part of
their characteristics from larger groups, which are more clearly typed
and defined. It is for these larger groups that we reserve the term "cultural entities." The most important ones are nations or groups of nations belonging to the same civilization.

Cultural entities are essentially formed by history, then reinforced
by education in the broad sense of the term.

On the whole, all peoples follow the same general outline of historical development. In this sense, a political scientist can describe the
evolution from feudalism to capitalism, the various stages of the latter,
and so on, just as a biologist can describe the different phases of a
human being's childhood, adolescence, adult years, and old age. But
what distinguishes the personality of each individual, what accounts
for its uniqueness, is the particular context in which this general evolution takes place. By the same token, what differentiates nations or civilizations from one another is the uniqueness of the historical development of a people or of a group of peoples. This uniqueness results,
first of all, from particular events that have occurred, each producing a
certain effect, which eventually influences the sociological development
of the community. It results also from the fact that certain aspects of a
society's evolution occurred earlier or later, or more or less completely,
than elsewhere, owing to natural circumstances or to particular reactions of the population.

The order of appearance of the different general factors in social
evolution, and their respective development, vary from country to
country and from civilization to civilization. Thus, the same general
socioeconomic development presents a somewhat different picture in
each case, and the difference itself affects subsequent development. For
example, the transition from a closed feudal economy to a freer, more
open economic system was a general phenomenon caused by sociological factors common to all European countries beginning in the tenth
century. Situations and circumstances led it to culminate in France in
an absolute and centralized monarchy; in northern Italy, the Netherlands, and Germany in the appearance of numerous principalities or
city states; and in Great Britain in the development of parliamentary
rights. These different institutions then forced future developments to

move in different directions, just as they, too, had resulted from earlier national differences. We could find similar examples on the level of national groups with a common civilization.

Cultures, as they are formed by the unique historical development of each people or group of peoples, are transmitted through the mechanisms of education in the broadest sense of the term. No doubt some of their elements operate in a physical way without people being aware of it (for example, the centralization of government in France, the proliferation of clubs and organizations in Anglo-Saxon countries, and so on). But most elements operate by means of conscious phenomena, through collective beliefs, images, and attitudes, that are transmitted from generation to generation by the process of education. The education of children is designed not only to provide new generations with useful skills but also to give them a cultural outlook. The same is true of information media intended for adults: the press, radio, television, and so forth, do not merely disseminate news, information, and propaganda; they also supplement and complete the adult's cultural education. And this sometimes happens without the originators realizing it. The messages they transmit to the public have no real chance of being understood unless they are adapted to the community's cultural context. In doing this, they tend to strengthen the particular culture.

Cultural entities vary according to periods of history and geographical locations. At one time, tribes or small ethnic groups formed the basic cultural entity; in other eras, it was cities or city-states; today it is the world's nations. Thus there appears to be a correlation between the nature of cultural entities and the character of the social groups having the strongest organization of political power. Today a nation is simultaneously the principal cultural entity and the structure of the state, in other words, the strongest political organization. However, there is always more than one category of cultural entities. Tribes, ethnic groups, cities, and nations continually regroup within much larger cultural entities, generally called "civilizations."

The nation is a very complex phenomenon. Depending on whether we stress one component factor or another, we end up with very different definitions of what constitutes a nation. There are those who define a nation in terms of its soil, its geographical setting, and its influence on men; the theories of natural frontiers and of climatic influences derive from this point of view. Others define a nation in terms of its language, the fundamental instrument of communication, which gives a human group its cohesiveness. Still others define a nation in terms of race: some interpret the word to have a basic biological reality (see pp. 153–54 on racial theories); others use the word to designate what we might call a "sociological" race, consisting of a series of fusions of primitive racial elements in the course of history and culminating, not in a pure race, but in a mixture of races of almost constant proportions (a theory still based on the racist notion of the importance of biological characteristics).

In contrast to these "materialistic" definitions of a nation, those based on material criteria, there are definitions of a "spiritual" nature. Some define a nation in terms of a doctrine or an ideology which the nation affirms and propagates: thus many Moslems speak of the "Arab nation," which they interpret as the community of all Moslems, the *"oumna"* of the prophet; and many liberal Frenchmen tend to define France as "the country of the Rights of Man," believing that France would no longer be the same if it stopped defending and promoting human rights. Still others define the nation as a common will to live together, as a community with a destiny, so to speak. The definition of a nation as a cultural entity is probably both broader and more precise. Every national culture presents a marked degree of originality. Generally speaking, nations are the most important and the best defined of cultural entities. However, some nations do not correspond to a single culture, but are instead the geometrical location of several cultures (Switzerland, for example, where Germanic and French cultures coexist). Still, the very manner in which the coexistence of cultures is organized defines in a certain way an original cultural entity.

Lastly, and above all, several neighboring nations often belong to the same cultural entity, which we generally call "civilization." Thus we may speak of a European civilization, a Western civilization, a Latin American civilization, an Asiatic civilization, and so forth. Clearly, if we pursue our analysis of each civilization, we are obliged to differentiate between the various national forms each one presents. The problem of knowing which is the basic distinction—that of "civilizations" containing a collection of national cultures or that of "nations" which can then be regrouped into civilizations—has very little significance. Sometimes differences are greater between two national cultures within the same civilization, and sometimes the differences are greater between two civilizations. In the political sphere, national entities are more important because nations are the seat of the fundamental organization of power—the state. But this difference is institutional, not cultural.

THE POLITICAL INFLUENCE OF CULTURAL ENTITIES   We must not overestimate the political importance of cultural entities, as conservatives do, nor should we underestimate it, as Marxists do. They are very important politically, but not as important as socioeconomic structures.

A few examples will make their importance easy to understand. Let us consider first the present tendency toward liberalization in the people's democracies, which seems to be the result, in a general way, of economic development and the rise in living standards. Consequently, liberalization should be all the stronger as the country becomes more industrialized and its production system is modernized. This is true in general; the contrast is quite noticeable between the more liberal communism of developed countries (the USSR and the European people's democracies) and the more rigid communism of underdeveloped countries (China and Albania). But it is true only in broad outline. When we examine specific situations, the parallelism between the degree of economic development and the degree of political liberalization is far from absolute.

The case of Poland, Hungary, and Yugoslavia is particularly interesting in this respect. In these three countries, "liberalization" is more advanced than in the Soviet Union; they are the most "liberal" countries in the communist world. However, Poland, Hungary, and Yugoslavia are far less economically developed and far less industrialized than the USSR. The disparity between economic evolution and political evolution seems to be explained by cultural factors. Those three countries have an old tradition of fighting for their freedom, which has doubtless nourished a desire for freedom among the general population; their political leaders were, in many instances, educated in Western universities, where they received a liberal orientation.

Another example of the importance of cultural factors in political competition is provided by an analysis of European party systems. In the nineteenth century, socioeconomic evolution first produced the conservative and liberal parties and then the socialist parties; subsequently, the twentieth-century communist parties, fascistic movements, and Christian-Democratic parties appeared. But over this general pattern, common to all countries, cultural factors have worked different designs for each one. In France, the succession of political regimes before 1875 complicated the situation, intermingling the conflicts over the constitution and the great debates between conservatives and liberals; there were thus several conservative tendencies and several liberal tendencies, and the separation between them at the center was never very clear. In the Netherlands, religious problems were intertwined with political questions, with the conservatives splitting into two parties, the conservative Catholics and the conservative Protestants, before the latter also subdivided into two factions ("antirevolutionaries" and "historical Christians"). In Scandinavia, a liberal tendency developed in the rural areas, distinct from the liberal parties in the cities; later on, it moved toward the political right, but it never joined forces with the real conservatives.

In these examples we can see exactly how cultural factors affect political life. They occupy a secondary position with respect to socioeconomic factors, which are the primary elements. In the first place, they generally act not as motivating forces, but as brakes or accelerators. In Poland, Hungary, and Yugoslavia, for example, cultural factors accelerated "liberalization," in comparison to the level of economic development, so that the former is ahead of the latter. In Germany, cultural factors retarded the evolution toward Western democracy in the nineteenth century and at the beginning of the twentieth, although the economic level of capitalism should have brought it to that political stage much sooner, long before the post-World War II period. In France, on the contrary, cultural factors hastened the movement toward a liberal democracy.

In other respects, cultural factors determine the details of political regimes. As we noted above, they weave the designs on the loom constructed by a country's socioeconomic evolution. The latter determines the architecture, or more precisely, the skeletal framework, while national factors apply the decoration. They also define the style of a regime and its political life, and that is extremely important in the final analysis. British democracy depends on a certain style of parliamentary life, of relations between the government and the deputies, of discussions and debates, as much as it depends upon constitutional rules, party structures, and balances between the various pressure groups. The style of northern European assemblies, and that of assemblies in Paris or Rome, are profoundly different, and this difference is very significant in the functioning of parliamentary systems.

PART II

The Causes of Political Antagonisms

ANTAGONISMS are the most important element in politics; because they exist, an effort must be made to eliminate them or at least to reduce them in order to achieve social integration. The first problem is to determine the causes of these political antagonisms. At first glance, they appear to be many and varied. Every political doctrine emphasizes one cause or another. For traditional conservatives, the struggle for power sets the "elites"—those capable of exercising power—against the "masses"—those who refuse to acknowledge the natural superiority of the elites and their right to govern. Some people also maintain that there are superior races, destined to dominate, and inferior races, which can participate in the process of civilization only under the guidance of superior races, but who more or less refuse to recognize this.

Liberals reject these notions of natural inequality among social groups or races. They view the political struggle as something like the economic struggle. In a society in which there are not enough consumer goods to satisfy the public demand, there is constant competition among men, with everyone trying to win maximum advantages for himself at the expense of others. Holding a position of power gives one a considerable advantage. Hence *homo politicus* is not unlike *homo economicus:* political battles have the same motives as economic competition. Both are forms of the "struggle for life," which basically sets one species against another and the individuals within a given species against each other, in the manner of Darwin's biology.

For Marxists, political antagonisms are also of an economic nature, but they depend more on the production system than on a rivalry for consumer goods. The state of technology determines the modes of production (ancient agriculture, feudal agriculture, and modern industrialized agriculture, for example) which, in turn, produce social classes; some classes possess the instruments of production and are therefore dominant, while others have only their ability to work and must sell their services to the former. The class comprised of property owners uses the state to maintain its domination over the nonpropertied class, which naturally resists this oppression. Consequently, the political struggle is caused by the class struggle.

Marxist doctrines relegate political conflicts between social groups other than classes (communities, regions, nations, religions, ideologies, and so forth) to a secondary level. Marxists consider them only a reflection of the class struggle. This single all-encompassing explanation does not appear warranted. "Sociocultural" factors, in which history, traditions, and education play a prominent part alongside material factors, seem to make their own contribution to political antagonisms and cannot always be attributed to the class struggle.

Lastly, contemporary theories of psychoanalysis cast light on the psychological motivations of political battles. Inner conflicts, for example, produce frustrations which develop into tendencies toward aggression and domination. One of the virtues of analyses of this kind is to show that *homo politicus* is very complex, that the desire for the material advantages of power is not always the principal motive driving him to acquire it. In truth, there is no more a *homo politicus* than a *homo economicus;* rather, it is the whole man who is engaged in the life of society in all its different aspects.

We can group these different causes of political antagonisms into two main categories. Some operate on the individual level, such as individual aptitudes and psychological factors; while others are collective, such as racial factors, differences in social classes, and sociocultural factors. Each category corresponds to a form of political struggle. Struggles that revolve around power occur between individuals, on the one hand, and between groups, on the other. The struggle for power sets in opposition individuals who are competing for a ministerial portfolio, a parliamentary seat, the post of prefect, the stars of a general, a cardinal's hat, and so on. In large human collectivities, these individual conflicts are compounded by conflicts between groups within the universal society—races, classes, local communities, corporations, nations, and so forth. The two kinds of struggles become intermingled. Their respective importance is interpreted differently by the various political ideologies: liberal ideologies consider primarily the individual conflicts and neglect the collective conflicts; socialist ideologies and conservative ideologies do just the opposite, the former emphasizing class conflicts, and the latter, conflicts among races or "horizontal groups" (nations, religions, and the like).

3

Individual Causes

We can distinguish two kinds of individual causes in political struggles. On the one hand, the difference in natural aptitudes among men means that some men are more gifted than others and tend to get the upper hand, in other words, to secure possession of power. On the other hand, depending upon their psychological tendencies, certain individuals are more inclined than others toward domination or obedience: the former seek to command the latter, and the latter more or less accept their state of subjection.

INDIVIDUAL APTITUDES

Theories explaining political struggles in terms of differences in individual aptitudes derive, more or less, from the biological concepts of Charles Darwin on the "struggle for life." According to the author of *Origin of Species* (1859), every individual has to contend against others in order to survive, and only the ablest succeed. This process of natural selection guarantees the preservation of the species as well as its improvement. Darwin's theory is the biological equivalent of the bourgeois philosophy, whose doctrine of free competition is the economic manifestation; the struggle for existence is thus transformed into the struggle for satisfying human needs. In the political arena, it becomes the "struggle for preeminence" (G. Mosca), and this serves as the basis for theories of the elite: from the competition for power emerge the best, the ablest, and those most capable of governing.

It is well to point out that contemporary biology no longer accepts Darwin's doctrines. However, the study of animal societies is very interesting for political sociology, illuminating as it does certain aspects of theories pertaining to natural aptitudes, considered as primary factors in political conflicts.

Theories on Individual Aptitudes

Theories that regard individual differences in aptitudes as the primary factor in political conflicts vary considerably. But they all have one point in common, namely, that some individuals are more gifted than others, that these individuals use their talents to acquire and exercise power, and that the less gifted try to prevent their rise. In liberal doctrines, this competition is based essentially on economic motives and selfish desires. In the conservative view, the most gifted individuals are motivated more by altruistic than by economic considerations.

LIBERAL THEORIES: ECONOMIC COMPETITION AND POLITICAL COMPETITION   Liberals conceive of political struggle in terms of economic competition, the first being no more than a form of the second.

The basic fact about all human societies, from the very beginning to the present day, is economic scarcity—that is, the insufficiency of available goods compared to the needs demanding satisfaction. With every man trying to satisfy his own needs, a permanent competition results between consumers, who are too numerous, for products, which are too scarce; each one tries to secure the greatest possible portion of a production output that is too small to provide for all. We have already mentioned these theories in noting that technological progress tends to reduce political antagonisms by raising general living standards, which makes the competition for consumer goods less fierce.

In this competition, those holding political power have an important advantage. History reveals that the individuals, groups, and social classes who exercise political power always assure for themselves great economic privileges, and obtaining these privileges in the main reason for the political struggle. People do not seek power for its own sake, but for its benefits. Moreover, these benefits strengthen the position of those holding power. The more political power one has, the greater one's share of the economic wealth; but conversely, the greater one's share of the economic wealth, the greater one's share of the political power as well.

In the political struggle, as in economic competition, the best contestants win, that is, those who are the most qualified by their intelligence, their courage, their strength, their cunning, and their capacity for work. This victory of the ablest assures the satisfaction of the general interest through the interplay of private interests.

Self-interest is the principal motive in political struggles, as it is in economic competition. Power is sought for its personal advantages, not because of dedication to public service. In the same manner, products are manufactured and sold for the profits to be made, not to please the consumer. But since success goes to the most capable, the interest of the general public is automatically satisfied. Economic competition places the best entrepreneurs at the head of production; the less talented are eliminated. Political battles place in power those most capable of exercising it, and, by the same token, remove less-capable contenders. The privileges of those who govern, like the profits of private enterprise, are as limited as possible in relation to the services that are rendered to the entire community. Thus, in the liberal view, political integration is produced by the political struggle itself, just as "economic harmony," says economist Claude Bastiat (1801–50), is produced by competition.

CONSERVATIVE THEORIES: THE "ELITES"   As with liberal theories, conservative theories regard individual differences in aptitudes as the primary factor in political struggles. But conservatives believe the most talented persons are motivated less by economic than by altruistic considerations.

For conservatives, the most capable are not the strongest, the most intelligent, the most cunning, and the most daring; rather, they are the "best" persons. There is more than a nuance of difference between the two ideas. The former implies simply material effectiveness; the latter denotes, in addition, a moral quality, a value judgment.

Conservative theories are based on the notion that men are naturally evil, motivated by base instincts and impulses, and always ready to revert to a state of primitive savagery. Only a few individuals, endowed with great moral strength, succeed in surmounting these instinctive tendencies. All civilization has been achieved by these "elite groups" despite the opposition and the envy of the blind and brutal "masses." Civilization is primarily maintained through the use of force, exercised by the political power held by the elite. Without such constraints, societies would fall into anarchy and revert to a savage state. The political struggle is a struggle by the masses, who do not accept an established authority in the general interest, against the elite, who exercise this authority to the advantage of the entire community.

In this rivalry, the elite are not moved primarily by selfish interests. To be sure, no man is perfect, and the advantages of power—wealth and prestige—are not insignificant. But the elite are motivated even more by a sense of "service," an awareness that their social obligation is to act in the interest of all.

Conservatives believe that purely economic and selfish motives are crude and unworthy, and that civilization tends to replace them with loftier, more altruistic motives, motives that appeal to the sensitivities of the best people. Education and traditions reinforce their sense of service. Accordingly, in conservative doctrine, it is not merely innate aptitudes which account for the distinction between "elites" and "masses"; it is also social training, which develops good instincts and restrains bad ones. Those individuals belong to the elite who best succeed, thanks to their education, in rising above their native savagery and egoism to become truly civilized men. Since education is essentially based on the family, heredity tends to preserve the elite—less in a biological than in a social sense.

INDIVIDUAL APTITUDES AND THE FORMATION OF SOCIAL CLASSES   In principle, the struggle between the elite and the masses, or between the most gifted and the less gifted, is an individual struggle. It is the personal qualities of an individual which make him part of the elite and more likely to succeed in the competition. However, certain factors tend to transform these personal qualities into hereditary privileges, which constitute social classes in the sense we will explain later.

Conservative theories tend to confuse the "elites"—made up of superior individuals—with the aristocracy—an hereditary caste. Arguing from the premise that education is a fundamental factor enabling men to overcome their natural, evil instincts and to develop altruistic tendencies, conservatives are led to conclude that aristocracies tend to be the framework in which elites develop. For education is not only the result of schooling, but even more so of family and surroundings. It depends not only upon abstract principles but also on a style of living and on a kind of "conditioning" provided by one's environment, by its traditions and examples.

In conservative doctrine, elite groups can exist outside the aristocracy, and some aristocrats do not belong to the elite; but both cases are exceptions to the rule. Normally, aristocracy and elite coincide. Civilization thus rests on the formation in society of an elite with a sense of community interest, honor, and service, which it transmits to its descendants in the midst of a "mass" motivated only by selfish desires and instincts. Individual aptitudes yield to collective education, which is primarily guaranteed by the family, in an hereditary social structure. More precisely, collective education, based on family and heredity, develops individual aptitudes.

The Theory of the "Movement of Elites"

This conservative doctrine gives a very idealized picture of reality. Much closer to the facts is the theory of Italian sociologist Vilfredo Pareto on the "movement of elites," which clearly reveals the permanent conflict between the interplay of individual aptitudes and the tendency to form social classes or hereditary castes.

Pareto begins with a definition of elites based on individual aptitudes. For him, elites are the most capable individuals in every branch of human activity. These elites struggle against the masses—against the less gifted, the less capable—to reach positions of power. But, in this effort, they are blocked by the tendency of the elites who are in power to form self-perpetuating, hereditary oligarchies. This tendency restricts the movement of the elites, that is, the unimpeded advance up the social ladder of the best and the most gifted. Pareto's theory has the virtue of disclosing one of the mechanisms by which social classes are formed—the tendency toward the hereditary transmission of privileges.

It also sheds light on one of the causes of political struggle, namely, the extremely important conflict between individual capabilities and social groups based on heredity (classes, castes, "orders," and so on). When social classes or castes are very rigid and tightly closed, the talented individuals from lower classes or castes have no opportunity to rise to supervisory positions commensurate with their abilities. Consequently, they align themselves against the existing social order, with a greater or lesser degree of violence, to try to overthrow it; for that, they rely on the masses whom they assist in formulating their own grievances. If, on the contrary, the ruling classes are more open and accessible, then highly gifted individuals from the lower classes can gain admittance, thus reducing social tension. But it is quite possible for ideologies and value systems to make it appear treasonable for the elite of the lower classes to abandon their peers. The lower classes can also be very closed and rigid, sometimes becoming so in reaction to the exclusiveness and rigidity of the upper classes.

The Experience of Animal Societies

Theories which consider differences in individual aptitudes to be the primary factor in political struggles find some confirmation in the study of animal societies. In certain ones, as a matter of fact, we discover phenomena that seem to be truly political: power and a struggle for power both exist. But this struggle is entirely individual and seems to be caused by individual differences in ability. Among animals there are no castes or classes with hereditary privileges.

TWO TYPES OF ANIMAL SOCIETIES   Along with certain partial or limited social phenomena (such as temporary groupings, parasitism, commensalism), we also find genuine communities in the animal kingdom— some small ones of a family nature, other quite large ones, made up of a great many individuals· of the same species. Certain communities have a very complex and highly developed organization. Animal societies have been known for a long time, and for a long time men have been comparing them with human societies. The beehive, the anthill, and the termites' nest have furnished materials for innumerable dissertations. In this connection, it is interesting to note an "anthropocentric" tendency. Comparisons with animal societies are more or less favorable or unfavorable depending upon the usefulness or harmfulness to man of the animals under study. To compare a human group to a hive (comprised of useful bees) is flattering; to compare it to a nest of termites (made up of harmful insects) is depreciatory; to compare it with an anthill (consisting of rather indifferent creatures) is neutral or ambivalent.

The appearance of social phenomena in the evolution of animals is something sporadic and unusual. They occur in certain species, whereas others, very closely related, show no evidence whatever of comparable behavior. There is no correlation with zoological classifications. Social animals are neither more nor less highly evolved than solitary animals. Some animals that are only slightly evolved biologically are highly evolved socially (certain insects, for example), whereas other animals that are biologically very advanced have no social organization (certain mammals). By the same token, there is no correlation between social evolution and organic evolution. Although termites are biologically much simpler organisms than bees and ants, termites' nests are much more highly organized than beehives or anthills. It seems that "socialization" results from a process in the evolution of the species that is quite different from the process of organic evolution. Everything suggests that, at all levels of biological evolution, certain species embark on the road of "socialization"—for unknown reasons—and find there another possibility for evolution, which has sometimes led to a high degree of perfection.

Insect societies, such as the beehive, the anthill, and the termites' nest, have long fascinated sociologists and political scientists and furnished them with examples for the study of human societies. It would appear that such comparisons are of no value, since insect societies have special characteristics, very different from those of human societies or societies of the higher vertebrates. Only the latter can be compared to our own. E. Marais, an observer of termites, has written: "The termites' nest is a composite animal that has reached a certain level in its development; only the absence of automobility distinguishes it from other animals of the same type." Termites in their nests, ants in their anthills, and bees in their beehives resemble cells that comprise a human organism or the organism of higher animals more than they resemble the citizens of a state, or the beavers of a beaver community.

The grouping of insects in a termites' nest, an anthill, or a beehive seems to result primarily from material, physical, and organic stimuli (tropisms and reflexes based on form, movement, contact, and so forth). The differentiation among the members of the insect society assigned to perform specialized tasks is also organic in origin: "kings" and "queens," "workers," "soldiers," and "drones"—all have physical characteristics as different from one another as the muscle, bone, and nerve cells of vertebrate animals. The coordination and control of the group are assured in almost automatic fashion. If the queen bee dies or disappears, workers proceed to feed and care for certain larvae to turn them into queens and insure the replacement of the old queen. It has been shown that this behavior is dictated, not by the fact that the workers have noted the death or the disappearance of the queen, but by the absence of an "external hormone" secreted by the latter. In a hive in which the queen bee, alive and visible, was isolated by a transparent envelope, the workers began to pay special attention to the larvae, as if there were no queen; in a hive from which the queen had disappeared but a bit of cloth impregnated with her "external hormone" had been introduced, the workers did not begin feeding the larvae and behaved exactly as if the queen were still there. Likewise, in the human organism and that of the vertebrates, internal hormones assure the regulation and coordination of cells and body organs.

However, we must not exaggerate this characteristic of the "collective organism" of insect societies. In the first place, the mechanisms for automatic regulation are less rigid than in the organism of man or the vertebrates. In the hive it often happens that, in spite of the presence of the queen and her "external hormone," the workers cause additional queens to appear, leading to conflicts of a social nature. Moreover, and above all, the basic elements of this "collective organism," that is, the individual insects, have an infinitely more complex autonomous structure than the cells of the human body—a fact that gives the whole organism an entirely different character. Actually, these "collective organisms" are in an intermediate stage, between real organisms and genuine societies, those of vertebrates.

In the last century, the Englishman Herbert Spencer (1820–1903) sought to prove that the laws of evolution for biological organisms were applicable to human societies (growth in size, increasing integration, shift from the homogeneous to the heterogeneous, and so on). His disciples pushed the analogy still further: the Russian scientist Lilienfeld studied human society as a "real organism"; the Belgian scientist De Greef described it as a "hyperorganism." This theory which confuses "society" with "organism" is known as "organicism." It works very well with insect societies, but not with human or upper vertebrate societies, which appear to be very different in nature.

To be sure, in these societies there are automatic responses and biological factors, as there are in insect societies. But these are not the only factors: in addition, there are psychic elements that are not automatic and are very important. When hierarchies arise, they are psychological, not physiological, in nature. Certain vertebrates at the bottom of the social scale, deprived in fact of any opportunity to reproduce become, so to speak, psychologically castrated, bound to a condition of forced continence. But there is a basic difference between them and the workers and soldiers of insect societies; the latter are physiologically sexless.

Likewise, though certain regulatory phenomena in a social group seem to have a mechanical and automatic nature, they are unimportant compared with the psychosocial regulation provided by the existence of "leaders," whom the whole group obeys. In the termites' nest, beehive, or anthill, there are no "leaders": the anthropomorphic terms of "kings" and "queens" are misleading in this respect. The component elements of this "composite animal," of this organism, obey no one; the very notion of obedience has no meaning for them, no more than for the cells of the human organism (cancerous cells are not "disobedient"; an automatic regulatory mechanism has malfunctioned, that is all).

There is probably no solution of continuity between the two types of animal societies. No doubt certain psychic elements begin to appear in insect societies, just as certain automatic elements remain in vertebrate societies. Nonetheless, the two categories are clearly differentiated. Above all, the difference is greater than that separating higher vertebrate societies from human societies. In the latter, the collective images are much richer and more complex, the phenomena of knowledge and, especially, of beliefs are much more important. On the contrary, collective images, knowledge, and beliefs are embryonic in higher vertebrate societies. However, like human societies, these are basically psychic rather than organic and mechanical like insect societies.

POLITICAL PHENOMENA IN ANIMAL SOCIETIES The distinction between insect societies and vertebrate societies is fundamental in this connection. Indeed, we can speak of political phenomena only in vertebrate societies, not in insect societies, except by misusing the word or by superficial and false comparisons.

A basic political phenomenon—the distinction between those who govern and those who are governed—exists in animal societies. But we must not confuse simple hierarchies with genuine leaders.

In higher vertebrate societies, this political phenomenon appears in its most elementary form with the establishment of hierarchies. Usually, they are linear in structure: a dominates all the others; b dominates the others except a; y dominates the others, except for a and b; and so on. Sometimes the arrangement is triangular: a dominates b, who dominates y, who dominates a. In general, the hierarchies are useful only to those who occupy the top positions; they do not appear to serve the collective interest of the group. However, among certain fish, the unfortunate one in the lowest position plays an important social role, like a scapegoat or a whipping boy. The attacks of the others are all directed against him, which diminishes tensions within the group. Meek and humble, hiding behind a rock or the thermostat in the aquarium, he often dies as a result of this ostracism. Sometimes, however (among the jackdaws of the crow family, for example), high-ranking individuals intervene to defend the weakest when they are attacked; the "powerful" protect the "weak" and thus maintain the social order. At this point we have progressed to the notion of leaders, properly speaking.

In certain animal societies, the leader is not only preeminent in the hierarchy, with advantages over the others; he is also a ruler who commands the entire group in the general interest. Sometimes he may be the leader of a flock or herd who leads the group to food, brings it back, and acts as its guide. Sometimes he may be a warrior chief who directs the strategies of defense and offense. Occasionally, a leader appears only during the mating season, generally among the males, to become the head of a veritable harem. In certain family societies, male and female are the leaders with respect to the children, but neither one actually dominates the other: there is simply a division of labor. In some societies, the governmental organization is more complex, with various animals serving as scouts, flanking guards, border guards, and so forth.

Hierarchies bring great advantages to the animals at the top. Genuine leaders enjoy equivalent advantages. These privileges are very much like those that accompany power in human societies. Sometimes it is merely a question of having the right to attack others, to rough them up, bully them, peck at them, or claw or strike them. Sometimes this extends to territorial rights: among certain fish in an aquarium, number one occupies a large space into which others do not intrude; number two has a smaller space; and so forth. In other cases, the hierarchy concerns food privileges, the top few keeping the best morsels for themselves and reducing those at the bottom to a meager share, or nothing at all. Often the hierarchy controls sexual relationships. Studies of Wyoming roosters revealed that the ruling cock performed 74 percent of the sexual acts; his "seconds" together accounted for 13 percent; his "guards" (he has from three to six) totaled 3 percent; roosters of inferior rank were forced to observe an involuntary continence, which visibly affected them. Many animal leaders have a genuine harem, unlike other members of the group.

The hierarchy or power arrangement is never based on birth in higher vertebrate societies. Sometimes they depend upon age (the oldest animal becomes the head of the flock or herd), sometimes upon sex (the males occupy the top positions, but the reverse is possible). Sometimes the male and female hierarchies are separate, in which case the coupling of a female with a male of high position confers on the female a comparable rank in the society of her own sex (among the jackdaws, certain rabbits, and certain hens). Most of the time, access to power and the higher positions results from a contest between several candidates, in which the means of combat are similar to those of human societies—force, energy, cunning, audacity, and often bluffing (those who scream the loudest or rush around the most gain the coveted positions). This struggle for power is constant. Hierarchies are often challenged; leaders are often toppled from power. "Social mobility" is high among animals, and the political struggle is lively.

We must not push the analogies with human societies too far. In the latter, collective images and ideas are infinitely richer and far more complex; the phenomena of knowledge and beliefs are much more important. In animal societies, even among the highest vertebrates, there is only the most rudimentary kind of collective images or knowledge. Summarizing the observations on animal societies, four essential facts stand out. First, a distinction between the rulers and those who are ruled, between leaders and members of the group, does exist in certain animal societies (as does the notion of territorial rights). Thus, political phenomena preceded the appearance of man in the evolution of species. Second, animal leaders derive personal advantages from power, which makes it an object of permanent and lively competition. Third, in certain animal societies, power plays a role in integration to the benefit of the common good, though not in all societies; some hierarchies secure advantages only for the individuals at the top. Finally, the acquisition of power or of a high position in the hierarchy depends solely upon individual ability in animal societies; birth plays no part in it. In the last analysis, this is the most important conclusion the political scientist can draw from the study of animal societies. Classes are not a natural phenomenon, but a creation of man. There are no classes in animal societies, nor is there an aristocracy, or anything that resembles hereditary rights and privileges.

PSYCHOLOGICAL CAUSES

Individual abilities and psychological temperaments are not two separate causes of political antagonisms, but simply two aspects of the same phenomenon. Aptitudes are the external aspect; psychological analysis defines its inner nature. We have already made a psychological analysis by contrasting liberal doctrines, which regard personal interest and especially economic interest as the motivating force in social activity, with conservative doctrines, which stress the development of altruistic sentiments among the elites. But our psychological analysis was brief and general. Equally brief and general was the reference to medieval doctrine that attributed political struggles to an instinct for domination, regarded as a fundamental human tendency. Moreover, this doctrine had a moral character. Theologians viewed the instinct for domination as a form of "concupiscence," driving men toward evil actions. They therefore denounced the threefold concupiscence of the flesh, of the spirit, and of power: this last—*concupiscentia dominandi,* the desire to dominate—they considered the primary cause of political struggles.

The development of modern psychology has enabled us to make a more thorough analysis of individual motivations in political struggles. Psychoanalytical theories, in particular, have brought to light certain fundamental phenomena, although sometimes they have been exaggerated, especially in the United States, for ideological reasons. Certain people wanted to make Freud serve as an antidote to Marx: hence the attempt to make "frustrations," rather than the class struggle, the cause of all political conflicts. A healthy reaction against such excesses is beginning to develop. In any event, Freudian theories are very significant politically. Rather than having them oppose Marxist theories, they should be allowed to complement one another.

Psychoanalysis and Politics

We can do no more here than give a summary, schematic, and hence distorted, notion of psychoanalytical explanations for political antagonisms. In this domain, as in so many others, the conclusions of psychoanalysis are complex, involved, and vary from one writer to another. We will present only the principal and best-established conclusions. Their sometimes strange or paradoxical nature should not be surprising: in attempting to penetrate to the very heart of the human mystery, psychoanalysis must necessarily avoid false simplifications.

THE PSYCHOLOGICAL BASES FOR POLITICAL ANTAGONISMS   For psychoanalysis, political antagonisms are primarily the result of psychological frustrations more or less related to conflicts of early childhood that lie buried in the unconscious.

One of the tenets of psychoanalysis is that the experiences of early childhood have a decisive bearing on an individual's subsequent psychological development. In early childhood, parents play an essential role; a person first defines himself with respect to society through them. Thereafter, parental relationships unconsciously influence all of his other social relationships, particularly those having to do with authority.

These theories about the importance of early childhood have a physiological foundation which Freud does not seem to have emphasized. In the words of Aldous Huxley, man is an "embryonic ape": the human baby is born at a much less advanced stage of development than any other mammal. Therefore, instead of remaining enclosed in the maternal womb, he receives external stimuli sooner, and he must use his intelligence at an earlier stage. He also becomes a social animal much sooner. Mother-child relationships are social relationships among the human species, whereas among other animals they remain purely physiological and mechanical relationships for a far longer time. Whatever the consequences of this premature birth of the human fetus, we must keep in mind the extreme importance psychoanalysis attaches to the first years, even to the first months, of life.

In the first stage of his existence, a child lives in a state dominated by pleasure and freedom. His whole life is based on the pursuit of pleasure. Freud has given a good description of what he calls infantile sexuality, diffuse, not centered on any particular organs of the body, "polymorphous," and expressed in many different ways. In a child, this search for pleasure encounters no restraints. Although he cannot always oblige others to give him pleasure—to suckle him, carry him, rock him, caress him—he cannot be forced to renounce the pleasures available to him—crying, moving about, sleeping, screaming, evacuating whenever he wishes. Thus the life of an infant is dominated by the "pleasure principle." Man will always retain a nostalgia for this lost paradise (psychoanalysts believe that the myth of the Golden Age and Paradise Lost, found in so many societies, expresses this yearning for one's earliest childhood).

But man is eventually forced to leave this paradise, and this produces the first shock, the first "traumatic experience" of his existence, which will mark him for life. To integrate with society, he must replace the pleasure principle with the "reality principle," which is to say, he must give up pleasure or limit it very severely. He is obliged to comply with a whole series of constraining rules, obligations, and prohibitions. He must learn to stop following his instincts, his impulses, his preferences, and his desires. But the need for pleasure is too strong to simply disappear. It continues to exist. The conflict between society's demands and this desire for pleasure produces "frustrations," which are the fundamental cause of social antagonisms. Either the need for pleasure, the "libido," is buried in the unconscious, where it generates dreams and neuroses, or it is transformed into a craving of a different kind through displacement, substitution, or sublimation. Unable to satisfy his sexual desires, for example, an individual plunges into economic competition, competitive sports, political contests, and creative activity.

Certain psychoanalysts believe, therefore, that an industrial civilization, which tends to erect a rational, mechanized, moral, antiseptic universe, is diametrically opposed to the instinctive tendencies and the deeper desires of man. The reality principle tends to stifle the pleasure principle completely. This inhuman social structure leads to the development of aggressiveness and violence by way of compensation. As Norman O. Brown has said: "Aggression results from the revolt of disappointed instincts against a desexualized and inadequate world." This theory is directly opposed to the view that technological development, with its resulting rise in living standards, diminishes social tension and fosters integration. In the psychoanalytical view, technological progress, by constructing a world in which human instincts have no place, tends to cause an increase in aggressiveness, in the desire to dominate, in violence, and consequently in the intensification of antagonisms and conflicts.

The theory of frustration remains a basic part of the psychoanalytical explanation for political antagonisms. But it was considered inadequate by Freud himself, who completed it with other theories. In the later years of his life, he believed that aggression and particularly violence were based on a "death wish",which he described as an instinct in conflict with the libido. The struggle between Eros and Thanatos in each man's soul is one of the most grandiose but also most disconcerting and obscure—and least verified—aspects of psychoanalytical doctrines. Every person is simultaneously driven by a will to live through the pleasure instinct, and by a will to seek his own destruction, as if seized by vertigo. Yet no one dares to look death in the face: it repels at the same time as it attracts. Accordingly, the individual redirects his desire for self-destruction to others. Aggressiveness, that is, the tendency to destroy others, is seen as a transfer of the death wish in the people it controls, with Thanatos tending to repress Eros.

Aggresiveness, violence, domination, authoritarianism—obvious factors in political antagonisms—can also be the product of compensatory phenomena. Psychoanalysis lays great stress on the ambivalence of human feelings and attitudes, on their contradictory nature. It holds that a propensity for erotic behavior can be the result either of a strong sexual potency or, on the contrary, of an impotency that drives its victims to continual efforts at self-reassurance in order to conceal and compensate for their inadequacies. Likewise, the desire to dominate and an authoritarian attitude may result from either the genuine "will to power" of a strong and energetic individual, or from a psychological weakness, an inner confusion, an inability to win the respect of others, hidden behind just the opposite attitude. In this connection, the investigation conducted in the United States in 1950 by Theodore Adorno on the "authoritarian personality" is quite interesting. It indicated that the conservative attitude in politics is linked to a certain type of psychological structure. The authoritarian personality is defined by rigorous conformity, by blind submission to traditional value systems, by unquestioning obedience to authority, by a simplified vision of the social and moral universe divided into clear-cut categories (good and bad, right and wrong, black and white), in which everything is neatly defined, regulated, and delimited—a universe in which the powerful deserve to rule because they are the best, the weak deserve their subordinate place because from every point of view they are inferior, and the value of people is determined solely by external criteria, based on the social condition.

In general, this authoritarian personality is characteristic of individuals who are unsure of themselves, who have never succeeded in establishing their own personality and stabilizing it, who distrust themselves and have doubts about their own identity. They cling to external forms because they have nothing within themselves to cling to. The stability of the social order thus becomes the basis for the stability of their own personalities, which might disintegrate without it. Accordingly, when they defend the social order, it is themselves, the foundation of their own beings and their psychological equilibrium, that they are defending. This accounts for their aggressiveness and their hatred of those who do not agree with them, especially of "others," the "different" ones, whose way of life and system of values challenge the existing social order, those who question its foundations and general principles. Authoritarian personalities support conservative parties in calm times when the social order is not threatened. If a threat does arise, their aggressiveness naturally increases and drives them toward fascistic movements. Thus, people who are the least stable internally affect the greatest outward appearance of stability; political parties founded on force are primarily comprised of weak individuals.

Authoritarianism, domination, and violence find still other psychological explanations. Sometimes they are compensations for individual disappointments and setbacks. People take revenge on others for not liking them, for making fun of them, for treating them as inferior. Hence the weak, the stupid, and the unsuccessful try to bolster their egos by humiliating those who are superior to them, by endeavoring to drag them down and keep them in a state of subjection. A dissident psychoanalyst, Alfred Adler, noted that brutality and despotism are often an overcompensation for the pain that people of small stature or with a physical deformity experience (most dictators have been small men—Caesar, Napoleon, Hitler, Stalin, Mussolini, and Franco). Adler considered authoritarian tendencies a fundamental element in the human psyche. For him, the instinct to dominate is the mainspring of human behavior, replacing the libido—the pleasure instinct—in the Freudian conception. It is interesting to compare this theory with the old medieval concept of *concupiscentia dominandi.*

PSYCHOANALYSIS AND THE TWO FACES OF JANUS Psychoanalysis does more than shed light on the problems of antagonisms. It also provides an interesting explanation for the two aspects, conflict and integration, that men have always recognized in politics. These two faces of power —simultaneously oppressor and benefactor, exploiter and creator of order—reflect the ambivalence of a child's feelings with respect to his parents.

Many historians and sociologists regard the family as the cell, the basic unit of all human societies, and believe that the latter are all modeled on the family pattern; Le Play, Fustel de Coulanges, Charles Maurras, and many others could be mentioned here. It is noteworthy that they are nearly always conservatives. Sociologically, their theory is very questionable: several primitive societies have never known the family, as we think of it; the ties between family structures and other social structures are not as important as generally believed, and so on. However, Freud reconciled these traditional ideas on the psychological plane, by considering, in effect, that parental authority served as a model to some extent, as a prototype for other forms of authority.

Power is always based in some measure, within the unconscious mind of man, on images of the father and the mother, a phenomenon reflected in everyday speech. A colonel is referred to as the "father of the regiment"; we speak of "paternalism" (*pater* being the Latin word for "father"); a pope is referred to as the "father of the faithful"; the word "metropolis" derives from the Greek word for "mother"; there is a respectful attitude toward "patricians"; the head of a business enterprise in France is called the *patron;* and so forth. Likewise, patriotism is based on a transposition of the parent-child relationship. For Frenchmen, the *patrie* is not only the land of their ancestors but also the land of their "fathers"; it is thought of as a parental entity. France is the *mère,* and the head of state, who embodies the country, is the *père.* Every political ideology and every belief relating to power thus preserve traces of paternalism.

In the first painful experience in human life, in the difficult transition from the pleasure principle to the reality principle, parents play a decisive role. It is they who formulate the rules, obligations, and prohibitions with which the child must comply. They are the archangel with the flaming sword driving man from his earthy paradise and forbidding him to reenter it, after having been the angel who guided him into the paradise and made him taste its fruits. This change of role by his parents creates a conflict in the heart of the child with respect to them. Until then, he had received from them, and especially from his mother, only joy and pleasure. Now they are going to be an obstacle to his pleasure, while, at the same time, he needs them and remains dependent upon them because of his weakness. This situation generates strongly ambivalent emotions in the child toward his parents—simultaneously love and hate, gratitude and resentment.

The ambivalence toward all authority—felt simultaneously as protective and unbearable, beneficent and oppressive—comes not merely from experience, which reveals that power is both useful and irritating, necessary and constraining; it also has deeper causes, more difficult to discern. It reflects unconsciously, to a greater or lesser degree, the child's ambivalent feelings toward his parents, feelings born of the conflicts between the reality principle and the pleasure principle. But some kinds of authority appear to be unrelated to the unconscious memories of parental authority—for example, "bureaucratic" authority, in the sense described by Max Weber, that is, authority based on competence, effectiveness, and technical skill. Studies of leadership in small groups also suggest that there is very little connection between leadership and paternal images.

Political Temperaments

Adorno's studies brought to light the concept of political temperament. Psychological temperaments are categories that serve to classify individuals according to their overall behavior and attitudes. Controversy arose over the nature of the component elements of these different psychological types. For some, they are innate, biological; for others, they are primarily acquired through psychosocial relationships. Actually, these factors are so inextricably intermingled that it is impossible to separate them or to determine their respective proportions.

Nevertheless, the concept of political temperament implies the predominance of factors connected to individuals, not to social structures. In this sense, it is distinct from the concept of social classes or that of roles, which tends to define human attitudes and behavioral patterns in terms of social structures. The notion of temperament seeks to explain social antagonisms in terms of individual dispositions, which are more or less congenital. Thus, certain types of people are driven by their personal tendencies toward a particular political attitude, which brings them into conflict with other types of people whose personal proclivities lead them toward the opposite political attitude. The concept remains within the framework of individual causes for political antagonisms.

GENERAL CLASSIFICATIONS OF POLITICAL TEMPERAMENTS AND ATTITUDES' The attempt was first made to find possible correlations between political attitudes and general types of temperaments. Unfortunately, the classification of these general types has not met with widespread agreement among psychologists. Certain classifications have gained greater acceptance than others, but none without reservations. And the reservations are even more emphatic when the classifications concern the political domain.

Some believe they have succeeded in finding correlations between political attitudes and the characterological classification of Heymans and Wierzma, popularized in France by René Le Senne and Gaston Berger. The classification depends on three basic criteria: emotivity; activity; and "reverberation," that is, the length of time an idea or image persists in a person's mind. With respect to reverberations, a distinction is made between the "primaries," who live in the present and the future, but not in the past, and the "secondaries," in whom the "reverberations" continue for a long time. In politics, the "amorphs" (unemotive, inactive, primary) and the "phlegmatics" (unemotive, inactive, secondary) are naturally indifferent to struggle or conflict, disinclined to seek power, respectful of other people's freedom, and are hence moderate and conciliatory in political antagonisms. On the contrary, "passionate" individuals (emotive, active, secondary) and "choleric" individuals (emotive, active, primary) are attracted by political battles and the struggle for power; the former are naturally authoritarian leaders, and the latter are more likely to be molders of public opinion, orators and journalists, disinclined, in the last analysis, to exercise dictatorial power (Danton, Jaurès, for example). "Nervous" people (emotive, inactive, primary) and "sentimental" people (emotive, inactive, secondary) are naturally revolutionaries, the former somewhat anarchical, the latter not always reluctant to use authoritarian methods (Robespierre). "Apathetic" individuals (unemotive, inactive, secondary) are naturally conservative, and "sanguine" individuals (unemotive, active, primary) tend to be opportunists (Talleyrand). All of this remains quite vague and superficial.

The classification of Ernest Kretschmer, which is used by some members of the medical profession, modernizes some very old ideas that go back to the time of Hippocrates. On one hand, it is primarily based on physical morphology, and on the other, on mental illnesses, which are regarded as distortions of tendencies inherent in a certain type of character. Kretschmer distinguishes three principle human types: (1) the ·"pyknic" type, individuals with a "predominance of transverse measurements," in other words, rather wide in comparison with their height; psychologically they are predisposed to manic-depressive states; (2) the "leptosome" type, individuals with a "predominance of vertical measurements," which is to say, tall and slender; pathologically, they are predisposed to schizophrenia; (3) the "athletic" type, characterized by a sturdiness of bones and muscles, whose nature "associates a quiet state of the body fluids with a certain explosiveness"; pathologically, they have a tendency toward epilepsy.

Emmanuel Mounier noted a correlation between this classification and political attitudes. French revolutionist Mirabeau, alternately docile and impetuous, brilliant and common, would thus provide a perfect example of the "pyknic" and cyclothymic politician. Schizoidal leptosomes, on the other hand, would either be the unscrupulous, abstract, calculating type of politician or else partisan idealists and insensitive tyrants "to whom any human compromise or middle ground is completely alien." Correlations of this sort appear even more fragile than the Kretschmer classification.

Lastly, we must mention the classification of the Swiss psychoanalyst Carl Gustav Jung (1875–1961), which is so often referred to in popular conversation. It is based primarily on the relationship between the individual and the external world. Jung thus distinguished two principal character types—the *extravert* and the *introvert*. The introvert is turned inward upon himself, toward an inner world, toward ideas. He is little concerned with the opinions of others, is naturally a nonconformist, and tends to be unsociable. The extravert, on the other hand, is primarily interested in externals, in everything around him, in wealth, prestige, social approval, and conformity. He is fond of activity, change, variety, and so on. The democratic politician, the representative, the town councillor, the prominent citizen in the community generally correspond to the extraverted type; the technocrat or the Jacobin corresponds to the introverted type.

EYSENCK'S THEORIES ON POLITICAL TEMPERAMENTS   The English psycho-sociologist H. J. Eysenck established a classification of political temperaments which is interesting for both its content and its analytical method. For one thing, it goes beyond the purely descriptive stage and tends to explain certain fundamental differences in political attitudes, particularly the opposition of "right" and "left." In addition, Eysenck's classification is not based on abstract reasoning, but on a very thorough mathematical analysis of the answers to a questionnaire on political attitudes (a factorial analysis).

Before Eysenck, most classifications of political temperaments were "one-dimensional," that is, they concluded by distributing individuals along a single axis, such as the "right-left" or the "authoritarian-democratic" axis. Eysenck's principal contribution to political sociology is the replacement of one-dimensional classifications with a multidimensional classification, using two axes: one a "radical-conservative" axis ("radical" being used in the English sense of the word, meaning an advocate of change, which is to say, a "progressive"), the other a "hard-soft" axis. The first roughly corresponds to the traditional distinction between the "right" and the "left." The second takes into account the fact that within both of these groups very different attitudes coexist: that of the conservatives, properly speaking, and the fascists on the political right; that of democratic socialists and the communists on the left. For Eysenck, these differences are explained by a second axis of coordinates: fascists and communists, on the one hand, and traditional conservatives and social democrats, on the other, are located at the two ends of this axis. The intersection of the two axes, one an "x" axis, the other a "y" axis, enables us to depict the various types of political temperaments as follows:

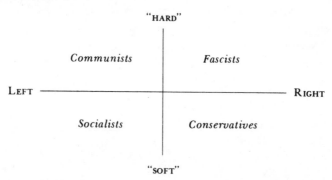

We must keep in mind that Eysenck's classifications are based on factorial analyses. These analyses have revealed the existence of two basic factors in political attitudes, but they do not enable us to identify the factors in question. By themselves they are only mathematical expressions. One can never determine precisely to what element of reality the "factors" in a factorial analysis correspond. The identification of one of them with the "radical-conservative" opposition, namely, the "left-right" axis, seems very plausible. The identification of the other is more dubious. In some respects it resembles the opposition of "theoretical" and "practical" as much as that of "hard" and "soft." Eysenck even hesitates on his designation: he likens it to William James's classification between the "tender-minded" and the "tough-minded," but this is not very clear.

When we take a close look at the questions Eysenck used to identify the "hard" and the "soft," we have the impression we are dealing with a moral as well as a political distinction. "Hardness" can be equated, to some extent, with what we call a "strong spirit," with a lack of concern for traditional ethics; "tender-mindedness," on the other hand, is a religious and moral outlook, but within the Protestant concept, strongly individualistic, based on the will of each person to perform his duty without external pressure. The "soft" spirit corresponds to faith in God and religion, to strict sexual morality, to a belief in the equality of men, to gentleness and nonviolence, Christian charity, and the freedom of each individual vis-à-vis the state (but not with respect to religion and morality). It is not possible to equate the "hard-soft" and the "authoritarian-democratic" axes, as is so often attempted. The concepts of "hard" and "soft" are quite different and hardly seem applicable outside an Anglo-Saxon context.

4

Collective Causes

We have said that political struggles have two aspects. On the one hand, they pit against each other individuals competing for power or the favor of those holding power. On the other hand, they set various groups, collectivities, and social elements against one another. Liberals stress the first aspect; socialists and conservatives, the second.

According to socialists, the struggle between classes is the main cause of political conflicts; in the conservative view, political conflicts reflect struggles between races, rivalries among nations, provinces, and other territorial communities, competitions between organized groups, and battles between religious or ideological collectivities. We shall examine here these different collective causes of political struggles—classes, races, and "horizontal" groups (territorial, corporative, and ideological).

THE CLASS STRUGGLE

"The history of every society down to the present has been merely the history of the class struggle": this famous statement which introduces the *Communist Manifesto* of 1848 does not express as new an idea as people have thought. Before Marx, many believed that political antagonisms were caused by inequality among social groups—these unequal social groups comprising social classes, in the broadest sense of the term. Marx's originality lies in having made the class struggle the fundamental and almost the only cause of political conflicts, and in having given a new definition to social classes.

Today, whenever we speak of social classes and class struggles, we think of Marx, consciously or unconsciously. It is therefore natural to take the Marxist doctrine as our starting point in analyzing the notion of classes and the influence of the class struggle on political conflicts. This, of course, does not imply a bias in favor of Marxism. It simply means that we recognize that Marxism is, at the present time, the dominant doctrine in this area, the one to which all other doctrines refer in one way or another.

The Notion of Class

Before Marx, the notion of class was based more or less on the old contrast between the rich and the poor, the "have's" and the "have not's," the privileged groups and the exploited groups. Contemporary American sociologies have readopted this concept in their theories on social "strata," determined by differences in the standard of living. Marxism rejects this distinction, or, to be more precise, assigns it a subordinate role. The problem, in fact, is not to state that there are poor people and rich people, but to determine what causes the wealth of some and the poverty of others. If wealth and poverty depended only on the individual abilities of a person—on his intelligence, courage, and capacity for work—there would be no classes. The concept of classes is based on the idea that differences in social status do not depend simply upon individuals, but are imposed upon them in a particular manner. A social class is defined not only by wealth or privilege, poverty or exploitation, but also by the fact that this wealth and privilege, this poverty and exploitation are, at least in part, the result of birth and thus have an hereditary character.

THE MARXIST NOTION OF CLASSES   If the Marxist concept of social classes is fairly clear and rigid, it was never given a precise formulation by its authors. Nowhere in Marx's writings do we find a definition of classes. He describes in concrete terms the class struggle, the oppression by the bourgeoisie, its conflict with the proletariat, and so on, but he does not give an abstract definition of social classes. In "The Great Initiative," a brochure published in 1919, Lenin offers the following definition: "What we call classes are vast groups of people distinguished by the position they hold in a system historically defined by social production, by their relationship (generally fixed and consecrated by law) to the means of production, by their role in the social organization of work, and hence by the means of procurement and the portion of social wealth which they have at their disposal. Classes are groups of men, one of which can appropriate to itself the work performed by others, as a result of the differences in the position they hold in a regime determined by the social economy." [1] Although this definition is not particularly well written or expressed, it clearly reveals the complexity of the Marxist concept of classes.

The central idea of Marxism is that social classes are defined by their position vis-à-vis the means of production. These have varied throughout history, and their variation consequently modified social relationships: "Social relationships are intimately tied to the productive forces. With the acquisition of new productive forces, men change their mode of production, the manner in which they earn a living; they change all their social relationships. A mill operated by hand will give you a society with a feudal lord; a mill operated by steam power will produce a society with industrial capitalism." [2] Social classes are defined in relation to a type of fixed social relationships, which is itself produced by a certain state of the "productive forces" (that is, technical skills).

"Classes exist only at historical periods determined by the development of society," declares the *Petit Dictionnaire philosophique soviétique*: "The birth of social classes is due to the appearance and development of the social division of labor, to the appearance of private ownership of the means of production." This last point is extremely important. Marxists believe that humanity originally experienced a primitive form of communism, in which all goods were collectively owned and classes did not exist; such is the situation among groups of people who live by hunting, fishing, or the gathering of fruits and berries. With the creation of the first agricultural techniques, private ownership of property appeared, and it will not disappear until the arrival of the socialist states in the twentieth century.

Private ownership of the means of production is the primary basis for the division of society into classes. Every society organized on this basis produces two classes in conflict with each other: the class that owns the means of production and the class that depends solely on its ability to work in order to live. The former exploit the latter by taking advantage of the "plus value" of labor. Marx believed that there is a creative element in human labor, that is, through his work, man

[1] Quoted in *Petit Dictionnaire philosophique soviétique*, 1955 edition.
[2] Karl Marx, *The Poverty of Philosophy* (1847).

adds something to whatever is produced. When we remove from an object manufactured by man everything that is used to produce it (raw materials, the liquidation of the cost of machines and materiel, all that is needed to keep the worker alive, including the "amortization" of his youth, his old age, his leisure time, and the risk of accidents, illness, and so forth), something still remains—namely, what the man has created with his labors. Marx called this something the "plus value" of human labor. In Marx's view, the capitalist, that is, the private owner of the means of production, confiscates this plus value of labor and gives the worker no more than is required to keep him alive.

Consequently, for Marx, there are always two primary classes in opposition to each other in any given society: one that controls the instruments of production and another that has only the ability to work. But, according to the nature of the "productive forces," which is to say, the state of technological development, the means of production acquire different forms, and the status of their ownership also changes. Thus we can distinguish the property system of antiquity, the property system of the feudal society, and the capitalistic property system. To each of these systems correspond two kinds of antagonistic classes: masters and slaves in ancient society, land-owning seigniors and serfs in feudal society, and bourgeois owners of factories and businesses and the proletariat in capitalistic society.

But a production system and its corresponding property system do not appear or disappear all at once. New systems develop slowly within the framework of existing systems; the latter die out gradually and continue for a long time alongside the systems replacing them. Thus, at a given moment, several types of antagonistic classes coexist. But together with the principal classes, there are secondary classes which either are just emerging—the bourgeoisie in the feudal society —or are about to disappear—feudal elements or peasants in the industrial society (Marxism, incidentally, has never defined the position of the peasants very clearly).

Lastly, Marxists distinguish classes and social "strata." No class is completely homogeneous, except in very underdeveloped societies. In feudal society there were the *grands seigneurs* and the *petits seigneurs,* the *nobles d'épée* [aristocracy of military origin] and the *nobles de robe* [lesser aristocracy of ennobled bourgeois, often in the legal profession]. And there were many categories of serfs. There are even more varieties within the bourgeoisie (upper and lower, industrial and commercial, and so forth) and within the proletariat ("blue collar" and "white collar" workers, various groups of craftsmen, technicians, civil servants, and administrative personnel). These subdivisions within a class constitute social "strata." The various strata of the same class do not have exactly the same interests; there are inconsistencies among them. Each class, in the class struggle, exploits the contradictions among the strata of the other classes in order to weaken them: the bourgeoisie stirs up the conflicts within the proletariat in order to maintain its power; the proletariat takes advantage of the contradictions in the bourgeoisie to hasten the advent of socialism. But Marxism carefully distinguishes between the "contradictions" among the strata of one class (considered relatively unimportant) and the "antagonisms" between classes (considered fundamental).

OTHER CONCEPTS OF SOCIAL CLASSES   Apart from the Marxist theories, there are other concepts of social classes, which overlap one another and sometimes overlap the Marxist concept. The principal ones are defined in terms of living standards, way of life, and prestige.

The definition in terms of living standards is the clearest one at first glance: it systematizes the traditional opposition of the "rich" and the "poor" by marking off vertical strata in a society according to an average income. The most common distinction on this basis is that of upper, middle, and lower classes. But this notion of class distinction has been criticized for two reasons. First, it is very difficult to establish the lines separating these different classes; any choice is strictly arbitrary, like setting the boundaries of various age groups.

Second, and more important, social strata.established on the basis of income do not constitute genuine social groups, felt as such by their members; they are simply a series of "pigeon holes" into which individuals are arbitrarily placed. To have a genuine social class, the great majority of the individuals assigned to a particular category must be conscious of a special solidarity among themselves, and of a distinctness from other categories. In answer to this argument, proponents of the theory reply that this is precisely the case: the members of the middle class, for example, are aware of such a solidarity, as are members of the upper and lower classes. To a certain extent this is true. Yet, if we push the analysis a little further, we discover that this solidarity, when it does exist, is not determined by living standards. Low-paid wage earners regard themselves as middle class, but skilled laborers, with higher salaries, have no feeling of solidarity with them. The middle class is defined by its way of life or its prestige, far more thàn by its standard of living—unless we are dealing only with a political myth intended to establish an artificial bond between social groups whose interests are opposed for the benefit of one of them.

Marxists are firmly opposed to this definition of classes based on income or on standard of living. "A crude kind of reasoning transforms the distinction between classes into the size of one's wallet. The size of the wallet is a purely quantitative difference, by which one can always create a conflict between two members of the same social class," Marx wrote in *The Holy Family*. This is an apparent contradiction of Lenin's definition, quoted above, which spoke of "the portion of social wealth" the classes have at their disposal. Nevertheless, Marxist theory remains clear on this point: the oppression of the proletariat is not a consequence of its living standard; it results from the fact that the private owner of the means of production confiscates the plus value of the labor of the salaried worker. But in general, this obviously leads to high living standards for the owners and low ones for the salaried workers.

The notion of "way of life," which serves as the basis for another concept of social classes, is singularly vague. The expression designates an entire complex of social behavior, habits, traditions, and mentality whereby one social category is distinguished from another. Farm workers offer the best example of a class defined by its way of life. Its position in relationship to private ownership is secondary here: farmers, farm operators, cultivators, tenant farmers, even hired hands (with certain reservations) have similar ways of life. Likewise, the standard of living is less important. Aside from large landowners (who are not farmers and do not engage in farm work themselves), differences in income do not change the fact that all who work on the land have a similar way of life. And we are speaking now of a genuine social class, not of a simple, artificial category. Farmers are very conscious of being farmers; they are aware that they comprise a different community from urban dwellers.

Marx himself was struck by this truth about the agricultural class, as evidenced by a very interesting passage in his *German Ideology*: "The greatest division between physical labor and spiritual labor is the separation between town and country. The distinction between cities and rural areas began with the transition from barbarism to civilization, from the tribal system to the state, from the locality to the nation; it is encountered throughout the entire history of civilization down to the present time. . . . It is here that we first discover a division of the population into two large classes, based directly on the division of labor and the means of production." Marx does not define farm workers here by their "way of life," which is a vague and derivative element, but by their manner of work, by their relationship to the instruments of production, which conforms to the Marxist theory of social classes.

The way of life is seen as a consequence of the method of production; farm life results from working conditions on the land.

It is noteworthy that Marx makes no reference to the ownership system of the means of production. Can the methods of production define social classes, independently of the property system? Personally, I think so, but that is not the Marxist view. Such a concept of classes could lead to many significant developments, such as explaining the differences between "white collar" and "blue collar" workers, between employees in automated industries and in traditional industries, and so forth. It could also explain why workers feel no change in their class status when the industry they work for becomes nationalized. But we must not exaggerate the significance of this point: private ownership of the means of production remains an essential factor, especially where it concerns the exploitation of certain classes by other classes and the ensuing political conflicts. But it remains important to consider the possibility of defining certain social classes by the technical methods of production, which produce certain ways of life irrespective of the property system.

French sociologists of the Durkheim school, impressed by the importance of popular beliefs and images and by the phenomena of awareness in social life, have a tendency to define classes by criteria of this kind. In their view, social classes are defined primarily by the fact that the members of a society decide for themselves that they are divided into several categories, to which different degrees and forms of prestige correspond. In 1925, E. Goblot studied in this manner the "boundary" and the "level" of different classes. Maurice Halbwachs constructed a comprehensive theory of classes considered as a "phenomenon of collective psychology." This subjective theory of social classes has been adopted by a large number of American sociologists.

After conducting a very extensive and detailed study of an average American city, which they called "Middletown," Robert and Helen Lynd determined that there were six different social classes according to criteria established by the townspeople themselves. This amounted to subdividing each of the three traditional classes—the upper class, the middle class, and the lower class—into upper and lower levels. Thus, there was (1) "an upper upper-class," (2) "a lower upper-class," (3) "an upper middle-class," (4) "a lower middle-class," (5) "an upper lower-class," (6) and "a lower lower-class." This classification has more merit than the simplistic terminology suggests. The essential problem with this definition based on "collective ideas and images," as with definitions based on "ways of life," consists in seeking out explanations for the differences in behavior and prestige, the differences in ways of life or popular images. The advantage of objective theories of class differences—such as the method of production or the standard of living—is that they endeavor to get to the basic causes of class divisions.

FACTORS IN THE CONCEPT OF CLASS   The Marxist concept of classes and other class conceptions are not contradictory. In some respects, they are complementary. The position on the ownership of the means of production leads to differences in the standard of living, which in turn produce differences in ways of life, which leads to differences in popular notions regarding social status and prestige. The real difference between the Marxist concept and others is the importance attached to the private ownership of the means of production. For Marxists, it is the essential element in the differentiation of classes, the one from which all other distinctions derive; for non-Marxists, it is just one factor among others. Thus we can come to a generalization on the notion of classes. The concept is based, finally, on two factors: the collective inequality of social conditions and the hereditary transmission of privileges.

The class concept is directly opposed to the concept of elites, as set forth by Pareto. The concept of elites is based on the idea of a competition between individuals, with the most gifted reaching the higher levels of the social scale and the less gifted remaining in the lower levels. The class concept is based on the fact that discrimination of a collective nature interferes with the free interplay of individual competition; certain individuals, even very gifted ones, cannot reach the upper levels of society because they belong to a group which society keeps collectively on lower social levels; conversely, other individuals, even those without talent or ability, find themselves on an upper social level to begin with because they belong to a group endowed with privileged status.

The notion of social level, as used here, is intentionally vague. It concerns the question of both income levels and levels of social prestige. Even the "way of life" can have inequitable aspects—certain ways of life being judged superior to others because of their material benefits or the social prestige they enjoy. For this reason, farmers are often considered inferior to urban dwellers, laborers to "white collar" workers, and so on. The concept of classes presupposes, first of all, that a society is subdivided into unequal groups, each with a fairly strong sense of internal solidarity. The feeling of belonging to a class—"class consciousness," as the Marxists call it—is the feeling of being a part of one of these unequal groups, and of finding it difficult to escape from the group by relying on one's personal abilities. Classes have a certain rigidity which is opposed to the free movement of elites, and this rigidity is based primarily on the hereditary transmission of social privileges.

Belonging to a privileged or to an underprivileged class is a result of one's birth. The hereditary transmission of privileges or inequalities is the fundamental basis of the class concept. Thus we can arrive at a definition of social classes that is both more general and more "operational" than the Marxist definition or the other definitions we have reviewed. In fact, this definition encompasses all the others.

Private ownership of the means of production is a form of the hereditary transmission of privileges. Other forms have existed in the past. In aristocratic societies, the hereditary transmission of privileges also involved legal statutes: to be born a nobleman in France under the *ancien régime* gave one the right to be an officer in the army, to receive an ecclesiastical benefice or to fill an important position in the church, to be presented at court, to enjoy certain prerogatives, to receive gifts or pensions, to collect feudal taxes, to exercise seignorial powers, and so on. In ancient societies, the attributes of a citizen, a foreigner, a transient, a slave, and an emancipated slave were all passed on by heredity and determined a variety of statutes, of which the caste system in India is but an extreme example.

Therefore, a class is a category of people whose conditions at birth are comparable to, but different from and unequal to, the conditions of birth in other categories. Social classes result from the unequal opportunities society gives its members at birth, and from the fact that these inequalities determine certain important types of basic situations. Classes may be defined by the level of wealth, by the type of property system, by legal privileges, by cultural advantages, and so on. The forms of social inequalities at birth are unimportant: what matters is that there are social inequalities at birth, and these are divided into categories which men are keenly aware of and which produce various ways of life and feelings of social identification.

Capitalism has made some progress toward equality. For in this system, through his work, intelligence, and capabilities, an individual can freely acquire privileges and advantages and can subsequently transmit them to his children, even if he received none from his own parents—something that was far more difficult, even impossible, in aristocratic societies or caste systems. An untouchable cannot become a Brahmin; a slave could not easily become a citizen; a peasant could not easily enter the ranks of the nobility. In the nineteenth century, it was easier, in Europe or America, to acquire wealth. The myth of the "self-made man" or François Guizot's *"enrichissez-vous"* had a basis in fact, however exaggerated such notions were. Still, the accumulation of capital in the hands of certain individuals has produced many hereditary inequalities.

The importance of the latter is decreasing in the more technologically developed societies of the West. But other inequities are arising there, inequities that also exist in the socialist regimes. Apart from all private ownership of the means of production, inequities in salaries and social positions are not without hereditary consequences. The son of an important government official, of a famous doctor, of a renowned lawyer, or of a wealthy business executive has more opportunities from the beginning than does the son of a laborer, a farmer, or a craftsman. This is so because he has more material means of furthering his education, because he absorbs an important education from his environment, and also because his parental connections will help him a great deal in getting ahead. Phenomena of this kind also play a role in socialist countries, where certain types of classes are re-created.

But such factors are far more limited in scope than the discriminatory practices of the past. In the first place, a more equitable arrangement of the educational systems and of the means of recruiting and promoting personnel for careers of various kinds can greatly reduce the effects of privilege and favoritism. Moreover, the hereditary transmission of privileges is more restricted in extent and duration. A nobleman passed on his nobility to his son, intact; the owner of a business transmits his enterprise to his son, intact. But a man earning a high salary does not transmit his high salary to his son; he merely transmits better educational opportunities, social connections, and certain indirect material advantages through the inheritance of traditional goods and property. If the transmission of goods and property is restricted, as in socialist countries, the formation of social classes and the resulting inequalities are reduced.

We must not confuse the natural inequalities of birth with the social inequalities that create classes. From a certain point of view, the difference is not very great: to be born intelligent or to be born an aristocrat is to enjoy an innate advantage. Mentally deficient individuals also bear the weight of an original act of chance. The same reasoning applies to physical strength or weakness, health or sickness, beauty or ugliness, talent or mediocrity. But, sociologically speaking, the inequalities of birth that are due to differences in individual abilities are less shocking than inequalities of birth that derive from a social situation which divides men into antagonistic classes: for the former situation is unavoidable to a certain extent, whereas the latter is not. To adjust to natural injustices is something quite different from creating additional injustices, which do not exist in nature. To be sure, we must also seek to reduce natural inequalities. Socialist theoreticians believe that we must pass from a distribution of wealth based upon ability to a distribution based upon needs.

But this belief assumes that men will act largely from altruistic rather than selfish motives. To establish an absolute equality of incomes, regardless of the work done and the results it gives, is not possible unless people feel motivated to work on behalf of the entire community with the same zeal they apply to improving their own personal situation. Otherwise, there will be a considerable drop in production which will make for social regression, as was the case in the USSR after the October Revolution. The substitution of altruistic motives for selfish motives is a great hope, but it remains a remote prospect, if indeed it can ever be achieved (it has, however, been realized in some small, closely integrated communities such as monasteries and kibbutzim). In the meantime, it is extremely important that the most capable, gifted, and intelligent should be the most successful. From the standpoint of absolute justice, this principle is shocking since it seeks to perpetuate natural inequalities. Yet it is far less shocking than the creation of new inequalities by society. This is why social inequalities have produced deeper and more violent antagonisms than natural ones.

Class Antagonisms and Political Conflicts

Few people deny that class antagonisms are a source of political conflict. The real disagreement lies in the fact that Marxists believe all political conflicts derive more or less directly from class antagonisms and contradictions, whereas non-Marxists regard class antagonisms as one factor among others, and the importance of this factor is variously interpreted.

THE MARXIST THEORY OF THE CLASS STRUGGLE For Marxists, political antagonisms are a reflection of the class struggle, which in turn is determined by the production system and property system, both of which are a consequence of the state of technology (or "productive forces").

The dependency of political phenomena on systems of production can be outlined as follows: technology (productive forces) → systems of production and a system of property ownership → social classes → the struggle between classes → political antagonisms. Accordingly, primitive skills and techniques produced the production and property systems of antiquity, with its accompanying struggle between masters and slaves and the existence of the slave state; medieval agricultural methods produced the feudal systems of production and property ownership, with the struggle between seigniors and serfs, and the state of the *ancien régime;* industrial technology has produced the capitalist production and property systems, with the struggle between the bourgeoisie and the proletariat, and a democratic state of the Western type. The very evolution of industrial technology tends toward the elimination of private property, the basis of previous systems of production, and toward the socialist system of production, which puts an end to the class struggles (according to Marxist doctrine) and culminates in the withering away of the state, after an intermediate phase of dictatorship by the proletariat.

Every production system (or property system) produces several kinds of political regimes, which is to say, several forms of the class struggle. We must refer again, in this connection, to some ideas discussed earlier (pp. 88–89). Contemporary Marxist theoreticians make a distinction between what they call "types of state" and "forms of state." Types of state correspond to a definite class system, such as the slave state, the feudal state, the bourgeois state, and the socialist state. Within each type, several forms of state exist, which is to say, several forms of political regimes. The slave state of antiquity might be a despotism of the Egyptian or Persian type, a tyranny such as developed in the Greek city-states at certain periods, a democracy of the Hellenic type, or an empire of the Roman type. The feudal state evolved from a process of decentralization, based on fiefs that were very independent of one another, and moved toward a centralized monarchy of the Louis XIV type. The bourgeois state is at times a Western-style democracy, at other times a fascist regime. In the socialist state based on the dictatorship of the proletariat, we can distinguish between the Soviet regime and the regimes of the people's democracies.

For Marxists, the principal source of antagonism remains constant within each type of state. In the ancient state, the primary struggle was between masters and slaves; in the capitalist state, it is between the bourgeoisie and the proletariat. In every case, the adversaries in the conflict are the private owners of the means of production and those whose only asset is their ability to work, but this basic struggle takes on different appearances according to the forms of state, within each type of state. Thus, in the medieval state, serfs struggled by themselves against their feudal lord, usually without assistance, within each separate fief; in the centralized monarchical state, they sometimes won support from the bourgeoisie in the towns or from the king, adversary of the powerful seigniors; they were also able to develop general conflicts on a larger scale. In the capitalist state, the struggle between bourgeois and proletarians does not assume the same forms in Western democracies, where the conflict is expressed through political parties in which workers can freely develop their organizations, and in fascist regimes, where the domination of the bourgeoisie is violent and implacable and resistance by the working class becomes clandestine and brutal.

In addition, secondary antagonisms (or "contradictions") compound the fundamental antagonism, based on the class struggle. For the latter is never simply a conflict between two classes; the pure type never corresponds to concrete reality. As we have already indicated, alongside the two main classes, which correspond to the existing system of production, classes corresponding to an earlier production system, which has not entirely disappeared, still persist. Thus we find aristocratic landowners and peasants in a capitalistic regime. We can also find social classes corresponding to future systems of production, the first signs of which appear very gradually (thus a bourgeoisie was already arising in feudal society). Classes on the rise and classes on the decline play varied games of alliances with the principal classes, uniting first with one, then with the other, depending on their special interests. Moreover, no class is absolutely homogeneous, each being comprised of diverse elements that are often in conflict with one another: small businessmen against big businessmen, industrialists against bankers, "white collar" workers against "blue collar" workers, and so on. Extremely varied patterns and designs are woven on the loom of the class struggle.

AN EVALUATION OF THE MARXIST THEORY   The Marxist theory has the virtue of demonstrating that the class struggle is an essential factor in political antagonisms. Its weakness lies in its claim that this factor is, at all times and in all places, predominant, and that other factors are secondary to and always derive from the class struggle. The Marxist theory more or less corresponds to the actual situation during certain periods of history but not all.

In the nineteenth century (that is, at the time when Marx developed his theory), and at the beginning of the twentieth century in the most advanced societies of Western Europe, political conflicts were first of all class conflicts in the Marxist sense of the term. The antagonism between conservatives and liberals (political) was primarily an antagonism between the aristocracy and the bourgeoisie, the peasantry serving as a "supporting class" for the aristocracy. The antagonism between the liberals (economic) and the socialists was the antagonism of the bourgeoisie (which had then formed an alliance with the declining aristocracy) and the proletariat. To be sure, other factors intervened —religious, national, racial, and so on. But they were of secondary importance to the class factor, serving as a camouflage, in part at least, for class interests. At the time Marx was writing, at the time his doctrine was developed, it described the basic movement of political struggles accurately enough. It is less certain, however, that the doctrine can be applied as rigorously to all other periods of history.

Even in the nineteenth and the early twentieth centuries, when the class struggle was predominant, it was not the only cause of political antagonisms. National rivalries, religious and ideological differences, and other factors played important roles, as we have just noted. Marxism does not deny this fact, but it claims that these other sources of antagonism are themselves derived from the class struggle. Religions and ideologies are used to conceal class interests, and the same is true of national and racial rivalries. This analysis is only partially correct. Although, to some extent, religion is the "opiate of the masses," serving the privileged minority by persuading the oppressed majority to bear their burdens patiently, it is also something else. The yearning for a "hereafter" is not merely the reflection of class conflicts. And although patriotism serves to establish an artificial sense of solidarity between the oppressed and the oppressors within a given nation, it is also a natural feeling of attachment to one's homeland.

Elements of the class struggle are to be found in all periods of history, but their importance varies. Class struggle does not always play as great a role as it did in the political conflicts of the nineteenth and early twentieth centuries.

As a rule, prior to the nineteenth century, the mass of the population were excluded from political life. Although exploited, they had neither the intellectual capacity to realize this situation or to imagine the possibility of escaping from it; nor did they have the material means to combat their exploitation. Political struggles occurred within the confines of a limited group, an elite that was not generally concerned about class differences. Rivalries between clans and factions competing for power were not based on class differences: national or dynastic rivalries, ideological or religious conflicts, feuds between clans or politically powerful families, and personal rivalries were more important than the class struggle. There was only a very tenuous connection, as, for example, when certain warring clans tried to enlist popular support from the masses to defeat other clans, or when the masses

plunged into violent revolts, usually without achieving any lasting results. Accordingly, class conflicts seem to have been less general and
less open in political life prior to the nineteenth century.

With the general rise in living standards, characteristic of twentieth-
century industrial societies, class conflicts have lost their intensity.
They have not disappeared, as some maintain. But present-day Western industrial societies appear to be less unequal than those of 1866.
Yet many inequities remain. The range of incomes is smaller in the
USSR than in the capitalist countries. The inequality of classes has
not disappeared in the West. The thesis of the absolute pauperization
of wage earners is scarcely tenable in modern capitalism. Yet, a relative
pauperization appears to have been established: the percentage of the
total national income that is received by salaried workers (taking into
account the increase in their numbers) is tending to decrease rather
than increase. In addition, inequalities of opportunity persist. Sociological studies reveal that birth or marriage are the principal roads to
capitalism. A fairly closed social class continues to dominate political
and economic life. Private enterprises in the West remain dominated
by the principal owners of capital. The latter always wield great influence in the state, but they are no longer its absolute masters: universal
suffrage, freedom of the press, popular political parties, and trade unions limit their political power. Yet their power remains very great.
The inequality between capitalists and noncapitalists—and the domination of the latter by the former—still constitutes the basic foundation of Western states. The class struggle continues; but is expressed in
less violent forms.

RACIAL CONFLICTS

Certain political antagonisms are caused by conflicts between races,
such as the violent tribal warfare in a number of African states. We
must differentiate these genuine racial conflicts from racist theories
which allege that inequalities among races are the basic cause of political antagonisms.

The Various Racist Theories

From a zoological point of view, man forms a unique species—*homo
sapiens*—but this species, like so many others, is divided into several
stable varieties with certain hereditary physical characteristics. Racist
theories maintain that the different races of mankind have dissimilar

and unequal social and intellectual aptitudes. They regard some races as biologically inferior to others, for instance, as incapable of organizing and maintaining modern societies at an advanced level. But the "inferior" races refuse to acknowledge their inadequacies. Consequently, there is a struggle between inferior and "superior" races for the acquisition and exercise of political power. According to racist theories, only the superior races are capable of governing in the interest of everyone and thus advance civilization. Inferior races cannot do so, but will not admit their inferiority. Therefore, they struggle against the superior races to try to prevent their domination. This conflict resembles that of the elites and the masses in the conservative concept, but transposed to a collective plane: the superior races correspond to the elites; the inferior races, to the masses.

THEORIES ON THE INFERIORITY OF THE COLORED RACES   The theory of the superiority of the white race over the colored races is the most predominant form of racism, and it is expressed in a variety of ways.

The one point these theories have in common is the assumption of the superiority of the white race and the inferiority of the other races. But there are degrees of inferiority, according to the nature of the color, and these degrees vary from one country to another. Generally speaking, racists believe that blacks find it very difficult to move beyond primitive tribal social structures. Yellow people can rise to the point of achieving complex states and societies, but are unable to give them a democratic form; at best, they can only reach the level of European nations of the seventeenth or eighteenth centuries.

In the United States, Indians occupy the highest place among the "colored." If it is disgraceful to have "black blood" in one's veins, Indian ancestry is something to be prized, somewhat like European titles of nobility that date back to the Crusades—it is almost like having "blue blood." But this opinion is held only in certain localities. As a general rule, racists put yellow-skinned people at the top of the colored races. This view no doubt reflects the fact that Chinese civilization, in particular, has been known for a very long time, and its highly developed character is hard to deny. But by way of compensation, white people often dwell on the faults they regard as inherent in the yellow races—cruelty, deceit, and so on.

The yellow and black races have been known to European peoples since antiquity. However, white racism is a relatively recent phenomenon, born and developed at the same time as the colonial conquests and the exploitation of colonies. One of the first racist theorists appears to have been the Spaniard Juan Gines de Sepulveda, who, in

1550, described "the inferiority and natural perversity of indigenous Americans," declaring that they "are not rational beings" and concluding that they "are as different from Spaniards as monkeys are from men." Black racism increased when Africans were enslaved to develop the American colonies (the slave trade sent 50 million Africans across the Atlantic, half of whom died during the crossing). Slavery was defended by certain Anglican clergymen, notably the Reverend Thomson, who stated in 1772 that "commerce in black slaves on the coast of Africa respects the principles of humanity and the laws of revealed religion," and the Reverend J. Priest, who published in 1852 *A Bible Defence of Slavery*.

Racism was revived again in the nineteenth century with the second wave of colonial conquests, and in the twentieth century, there has been another upsurge with the wars of decolonization. Racism is strongest today in multiracial countries, where a white minority in control of the government is afraid of being overthrown by the colored majority. The southern states of the United States, on the one hand, and South Africa, on the other, are the most racist states in the world today. Of course, this antiblack or antiyellow racism generates a counterracist reaction among colored peoples, once they have achieved independence. The poet-playwright Jean Genet effectively expressed these feelings in his play *The Blacks*.

THE THEORY OF THE INFERIORITY OF THE JEWS   Anti-Semitism is the second most conspicuous form of racism, one that has produced the greatest excesses, since 6 million Jews were slaughtered by the Nazis in Germany between 1933 and 1945. Moreover, National Socialist theories had adopted a particular type of anti-Semitism based on the notion of an "Aryan" race, superior to all other races, the Jews being the anti-Aryans par excellence.

It appears that anti-Semitism was born in the Middle Ages, probably as a result of religious fanaticism: the Jews were considered responsible for the death of Christ and were therefore a people with a curse upon them. These popular notions, inculcated by the teachings of the church, were used and exploited by kings and princes to justify their seizure of Jewish goods and property. Inasmuch as medieval Christian doctrine forbade the making of loans at interest, only non-Christians could engage in banking; Jews naturally filled this social function, which became increasingly important with economic developments at the end of the Middle Ages.

In its first form, anti-Semitism was more religious than racial; conversion could bring Jews into the category of Christians. French anti-

Semitism at the end of the nineteenth century and the beginning of the twentieth (the Dreyfus affair) was not strictly racist. By defining the Jews as a people half assimilated, half refractory, French writer Charles Maurras explains anti-Semitism as much in terms of what he calls civilization, which is to say, social and historical factors, as in terms of biological factors. The racist theory of anti-Semitism was developed primarily during the present era by German National Socialism, and it is tied to another racial theory—Aryanism.

The theories we have examined thus far, however false they may be (as we shall show further on), are based upon certain facts: there is a white race, a black race, and a yellow race, which are all recognizable; there is a Jewish religion, which imparts certain habits and certain traditions. Theories about an Aryan race, on the contrary, are fevered imaginings: no one has ever seen this Aryan race or has even succeeded in defining it.

In 1788, a linguist named Jones, struck by the resemblance between Sanskrit, Greek, Latin, German, and Celtic, concluded that all these languages derive from a single mother tongue, which is totally unknown to us. In 1813, Thomas Young called this mother tongue "Indo-European," and in 1861, F. Max Mueller referred to the people who spoke it as "Aryan." But Mueller later explained that this definition of the Aryan people was purely linguistic: "In my opinion," he wrote, "an ethnologist who speaks of an "Aryan race," of "Aryan blood," or of "Aryan eyes and hair" is guilty of as serious an offense as a linguist speaking of a "dolichocephalic dictionary" or a "brachycephalic grammar." But it was too late: the idea had been set in motion.

There was endless speculation as to the geographical location of this Aryan race. Merely to list the many hypotheses is proof of their absurdity. In 1840, August Pott concluded that the Aryans came from the Indian valleys of the Amu-Daria and the Syr-Daria; in 1868, Theodore Benfey had them coming from the north of the Black Sea, between the Danube and the Caspian; in 1871, J.C. Cunok found their origin between the North Sea and the Urals; in 1890, D.C. Brinton surmised that they came from North Africa; in 1892, V. Gordon Childe located them in southern Russia; in the early twentieth century, K.F. Johannson discovered their birthplace on the shores of the Baltic; in 1921, Gustaf Kossinna, less specific on the location, simply placed them in northern Europe; in 1922, Peter Giles had them originate in Hungary; and so on.

Two writers were to popularize these myths about the Aryan race, drawing from them very different conclusions. The first one, Arthur de Gobineau (1816–82), was a Frenchman of legitimist, antiliberal, antidemocratic persuasion, whom the liberal Alexis de Tocqueville included in his cabinet when he was minister of foreign affairs during the Second Republic. Gobineau was later a diplomat. His basic work, *Essai sur l'inégalité des races humaines* (1853–55), utilizes the Aryan myth to justify social inequality—within each nation there is a racial difference between the aristocracy and the common people. European aristocracies all descend from "Aryans," the dominant race by nature and the creative race of civilization. Disciples of Gobineau, Vacher de Lapouge and Ammon, tried to verify these theories scientifically by establishing statistics based on the measurement of human skulls. This was the origin of the alleged sociological law of Ammon, which maintained that dolichocephalics, those with relatively long heads (associated with Aryans), were more numerous in cities than in rural areas; this law was later shown to be false.

The second founder of Aryanism was the Englishman Houston Stewart Chamberlain (1855–1927), son of a British admiral and a friend and later son-in-law of composer Richard Wagner. Chamberlain was a neurotic individual with a passionate admiration for the Teutonic peoples (he became a naturalized German citizen in 1916, in the midst of World War I). In his *Foundations of the Nineteenth Century* (1899), an enormous work of 1,200 pages, he uses the myth of the Aryan people in order to glorify the Germans. Instead of identifying the Aryans with a social class—the aristocracy—as Gobineau had done, he identified them with a nation—Germany. "The Teuton," he wrote, "is the soul of our civilization. The importance of any nation, insofar as it is a living power today, is in direct proportion to the genuine Teutonic blood in its population." Chamberlain tried, furthermore, to prove that all the great geniuses of humanity were of Teutonic blood, including Julius Caesar, Alexander the Great, Giotto, Leonardo da Vinci, Galileo, Voltaire, and Lavoisier. For Chamberlain, even Jesus Christ was a Teuton: "Anyone who has claimed that Jesus was a Jew has either demonstrated his own stupidity, or else he has lied.. . . Jesus was not Jewish."

The Germans enthusiastically adopted Chamberlain's theories, which justified their expansionist aims. Kaiser Wilhelm II invited the author to Potsdam on several occasions, wrote to him frequently, and awarded him the Iron Cross. Adolf Hitler visited the aging Chamberlain in 1923—shortly before writing *Mein Kampf*—and was the only political figure to attend his funeral in 1927. Chamberlain's theses became a basic part of the doctrine of National Socialism.

However, the Nazis gradually transformed his theories into anti-Semitism pure and simple. Chamberlain called anti-Semitism "stupid and revolting"; he considered the Jews not as inferior to the Teutons but as different from them. Nevertheless, he expressed crude insults regarding the Jews. In any event, he did not put them at the heart of his doctrine. However, when Hitler wanted to adopt Chamberlain's theories, he found it could not be done. It was impossible to claim that all Germans were "Aryans" in the racist sense of the term—that is, dolichocephalic, tall, with blond hair and blue eyes. This definition was cruel to the Nazi leaders themselves, for none of them conformed to the Aryan type. In the final analysis, they settled on defining Aryans as non-Jews, and they conceived of history as a struggle between these two races. Thus it was that the myth of the Aryan race served to revive anti-Semitic theories.

OTHER RACIST THEORIES   Other racial theories have created less stir and, fortunately, have had fewer dire consequences. We will mention only a few, developed in France and Britain.

The violence of political hostilities in France in the nineteenth century (when the partisans of the French Revolution and those of the monarchy of the *ancien régime* fought each other so fiercely) led certain sociological historians to believe that two opposing races were at war with one another in the country. François Guizot accepted the theory formulated by Augustin Thierry in his *Lettres sur l'histoire de France* (1827). Thierry held that a struggle between two races—the Gallo-Romans, original occupiers of the territory, and the Franks, Germanic conquerors—had been going on for centuries in France. The former were found mainly among the peasantry and the Third Estate; the latter, among the aristocracy. The fierce struggle between liberals and conservatives since 1789 was thus simply another manifestation of this ancient rivalry; the Gallo-Romans being more naturally imbued with the spirit of freedom and democracy, and the Franks more attached to authoritarian and corporate systems of a Germanic nature. It is clear that this theory was one of the sources of Gobineau's thought.

Theories of the Celtic race were developed in France after the defeat of 1871 as an anti-German reaction, and in Great Britain by the Welsh and Scottish peoples as an anti-English reaction. A. de Quatrefages, a naturalist, explained in 1872 that the Prussians "are not Aryans, but rather Mongols." Biologist Paul Broca maintained in 1871 that France is a "Celtic" nation and that the Celtic race is superior to the Germanic race. Taking the opposite view from Aryan theories, he claimed that brachycephalics (those with wide, almost round skulls) are biologically more advanced than dolichocephalics, which is no more absurd than the contrary view. He deduced from his theory the supremacy of the Celts ("proud Gauls with round heads"). In Great Britain, the Celtists were in a quandary, for the Welsh tend to be rather brachyce-phalic and dark-complected, while the Scots are rather dolichocephalic and fair-complected. John Widney declared therefore, in 1907, that the "true" Celts were dolichocephalic and fair-complected; he, of course, was himself a Scotsman.

A Criticism of Racist Theories

Racist theories are scientifically false. Biologically speaking, there are no inferior races or superior races. Having said that, racism requires sociological and psychological explanation; for it is social conditions and psychological tendencies that encourage belief in racist theories.

THE ABSENCE OF SCIENTIFIC BASES FOR RACISM   To be sure, different races exist and are defined biologically by the statistical predominance, among those comprising a particular race, of certain genetic factors, such as skin color, hair texture, and blood types, which are determined by the genes of the reproductive cells.

Everyone acknowledges the existence of five major races, determined by the relative frequency of certain genes (usually eight): (1) the Euro-pean or Caucasoid race; (2) the African or Negroid race; (3) the Amer-indian race; (4) the Asiatic or Mongoloid race; and (5) the Australoid race. Certain biologists believe, in addition, that these five principal races can be divided into smaller ones, still based on genetic frequen-cies; some argue that it is possible in this manner to establish as many as thirty races. But this view has been challenged. For our purposes, the debate is unimportant. Whether one does or does not recognize the "subraces" or accepts only the five "major races," the conclusions are the same for a critical examination of racist theories.

In some cases, these theories seem to be valid, because they concern genuine races. These races are not biologically inferior (as we shall presently show), but they do exist as races. There is a black race, a yel-low race, and a white race. On the other hand, certain racist theories do not even have this semblance of truth, because they concern races that are nonexistent. The example of the Aryan race is typical: it is a purely imaginery race found only in books. No one has ever met an Aryan in the street or excavated an Aryan skeleton. The case of the al-leged Jewish race is more interesting because it concerns a race that appears to exist. Actually, the Jews are a religious and cultural com-munity, but they do not constitute a race.

No serious biologist will speak of a Jewish race. It has been shown in careful scientific studies that genetic characteristics of the Jews and non-Jews of a single nation are more similar than those of the Jews of two different nations. The Jews of Asia are generally brachycephalic like other Asians, the Jews of Africa are, for the most part, dolichocephalic like other Africans, and the European Jews are distributed among the two categories like other Europeans. In certain groups, a convex nasal profile is found in 44 percent of the cases; a straight nose in 40 percent; in Poland, 49 percent of the Jews have blond hair and 51 percent have black hair. Like most "subraces," the original Jewish race has intermarried with other racial strains over the centuries, and its interbreeding has probably been more varied than other "subraces," because it has been more widely dispersed.

As for the authentic races (black, yellow, white, and so on), the only differences that science recognizes among them are of a biological order—such as pigmentation, color of eyes and hair, stature, shape of the skull, and blood type. No one has ever been able to establish that differences in intellectual aptitudes or in social and political capabilities result from these genetic differences. Certain sociologists have claimed to use mental tests (intelligence tests, aptitude tests) to prove the superiority of the white race over the colored races, but it has been shown that the tests in question were constructed within the framework of the white man's civilization. Hence it is not surprising that individuals raised in another civilization do not do as well on such tests as white persons. In 1931, some American scholars used tests on infants that were not directed toward intellectual factors, and they revealed a certain measure of superiority on the part of whites of the same age. But it was pointed out that the black babies who were tested were poorer than the whites and not as well nourished—a fact involving a considerable difference of development at that very early age. Experiments conducted during World War II on babies of both races, fed the same diet, confirmed the foregoing hypothesis experimentally, since the tests gave identical results for both races.

Arguments drawn from differences in the degree of social and economic development are no more valid. Certain yellow, Amerindian, and black civilizations were superior to the white civilizations of their time. Differences in development and behavior stem from living conditions (material and sociological), not an alleged inferiority or biological difference. The slower technological development of the colored races in comparison with the white race is due to the inequality of basic geographical conditions, as we have already noted (p. 34).

The derogatory character traits racists ascribe to Negroes are exactly the same as those attributed to the European proletariat fifty years ago —laziness, shiftlessness, deceitfulness, and so forth. They are associated with economic underdevelopment, and, we observe, they gradually disappear among black workers whose standard of living improves, just as they do among white workers. It is not something of a genetic nature that accounts for the attitude of American Negroes or of the Negroes of South Africa, but the fact that they have always been treated as different beings from whites, as inferior to whites, and this treatment has given them inferiority complexes (which the blacks have more or less associated with the color of their skin) and caused deep resentments. Likewise, the way in which the Jews were treated for centuries, the physical or spiritual ghetto in which they were confined, the feeling of persecution that developed—all of that explains why their behavior is different from that of non-Jews.

THE MEANING OF RACISM   Racist theories have no scientific value. Their recourse to science is in reality an attempt at justification, a more or less unconscious cover for socially unacceptable reasons. It is to be noted, moreover, that before making their appeal to biology, the various racisms invoked religion, at a time when religion enjoyed more prestige than science. At first, anti-Semites justified their hatred of the Jews because of a divine curse upon the people who killed Christ. White racists also invoked a Biblical curse upon "the race of Canaan," identified with the black race (we find the argument current among certain white Protestants of South Africa). The truth of the matter is that racism finds its explanation in social and psychological factors.

In general, racism serves to justify some form of domination or exploitation. It is said that the theory of black inferiority developed with the slave trade along the coasts of Africa and with colonial exploitation. The situation of the slave, the forced laborer or subproletarian —so shocking in a social system proclaiming the equality of all men— becomes acceptable if the people subjected to such treatment are not regarded as men like the others, but as "inferior brothers." In the southern states of the United States, an economy based on the production of cotton, which was impossible without slave labor, gave rise to the development of racist theories. The entire economy of South Africa is based today on keeping the blacks in a state of underdevelopment. Likewise, anti-Semitism first served to justify the pillaging of Jewish banks by Christian kings and princes, and the plundering of Jewish shops by mobs in Poland, Russia, and the Middle East.

Nowadays, it tends to serve as a diversionary political tactic. Anti-Semitism increased in Europe at the end of the nineteenth century in reaction to the rising tide of socialism among the masses of the population; the bourgeoisie sought to direct the proletariat's resentment against them toward the Jews. By denouncing Jewish bankers, Jewish industrialists, and Jewish merchants, Christian bankers, Christian industrialists, and Christian merchants hoped to divert public attention from capitalist exploitation, which they practiced in the same manner as the Jews. Moreover, they were partially successful during the early phase, when they were dealing with a very backward and uninformed proletariat. In other countries, anti-Semitism enabled the government to blame the Jews for errors the government had committed, making them serve as scapegoats—just as Roman emperors had persecuted the Christians to make the populace forget the faults of the government.

It has been noted that anti-Negro racism in the colonies and in the American South is deeper and more militant among the poor whites than among the better-educated whites who hold responsible positions. There is a simple reason for this: the fact that there are "niggers" beneath them gives these unfortunate whites a feeling of superiority. Thanks to the blacks, they enjoy a modicum of importance, a bit of prestige, and are not at the bottom of the social ladder. Should racial inferiority disappear, they would become what they really are —and they really know this themselves—poor unfortunate and hopeless failures.

Psychoanalysts also explain racism in terms of fear and hatred of the "other," of the foreign, the unfamiliar, the "different"—feelings that are very strong in people whose personalities have never become integrated, who have never succeeded in establishing a firm sense of self, who are insecure about their own identities. Such people cling to external social structures: they desperately need to conform, to feel part of an ordered, stable, hierarchical world (see p. 128). People of other races, whose way of life is different, upset this strict order of things, and even introduce questions and doubts about it. In order to reestablish this external order, which is basic to their inner equilibrium, they must regard people of other races as backward, primitive, and inferior.

Psychoanalytical theories also tend to indicate that racists secretly envy, in the race they scorn, people who live according to principles which they themselves have rejected and unconsciously regret having done so. Negroes are especially hated by individuals who have adopted rigid mores, an organized existence, a rational and mechanized way of life, who lack freedom and the satisfaction of their instincts, which they see—or think they see—in the race they despise. Anti-Semitism is based on a similar situation, but one that is just the reverse: efficiency, organization, a sense of determination, a readiness to help one another —characteristics for which Jewish businessmen are criticized—are secretly envied by those who are disorganized, inefficient, impractical, and individualistic.

It is likely that racism also has sexual bases. In every instance, we find very strong opinions on this subject voiced by racists with regard to the race they hold in contempt. In the southern states of the United States and in colonial territories, it seems undeniable that white men entertain a secret fear of black men, who are considered more impressive than whites in sexual performance (the myth of the sexual power of blacks is very widespread). Among white women, a feeling of repressed attraction to Negroes is doubtless mingled with a certain sense of fear and remorse. As with any psychoanalytical theories, we must not exaggerate the significance of these explanations, but we cannot afford to neglect them either.

The Existence of Racial Conflicts

The fact that racist theories are false does not prevent the occurrence of racial conflicts. But they are not what racists believe them to be, that is, conflicts between inferior races and superior races; rather, they are conflicts between different races.

THE DIFFERENT TYPES OF RACIAL CONFLICTS   Basically, we must distinguish "vertical" racial conflicts from "horizontal" racial conflicts.

"Vertical" racial conflicts occur between a dominant racial group, situated high on the social scale, and a dominated racial group, situated beneath it. Such is the conflict between white people and colored people in colonies or in pseudocolonial states, like the American South or the Republic of South Africa. Such was the conflict between non-Jews and Jews in anti-Semitic states, and such are the conflicts between certain racial minorities and the dominant race in "polyethnic" nations.

Racist theories are offered in an attempt to justify these conflicts by contending that the politically dominant race is the one with the moral right to dominate because it is superior. The falsity of racial theories ruins this effort to conceal the truth, but it does not eliminate the conflicts. It is not enough to prove that racism has no scientific validity to put an end to the domination of certain races over other races. Nevertheless, this domination is a little more difficult to maintain when deprived of moral justifications.

In racial conflicts we describe as "horizontal," the two races confronting each other are not in a dominant-subordinate relationship, placed at different degrees on the same social scale, as, for example, social classes. They are located at approximately the same social level, on the same horizontal plane, like two individuals or two nations. The best example is seen in conflicts between tribes in certain African states today.

But do conflicts between nations also have racial overtones? Many think so and speak of the German race, the French race, the Spanish race, and so on. Actually, it is not a question of true races in a biological sense, but of pseudoraces, which are cultural entities rather than distinct biological groups. This leads us to a second distinction.

TRUE AND FALSE RACIAL CONFLICTS   Certain conflicts are confrontations between genuine races. In others, the word "race" is used improperly to designate a community that is not defined by biological characteristics.

Conflicts between whites and blacks in colonies, or among different African tribes, are genuine racial conflicts. By this we mean that the adversaries belong to races defined by their biological characteristics. In the case of whites and blacks—or whites and yellows—we are dealing with the "major races" in the sense biologists have given the term (in the sense we have previously defined). In the case of African tribes, we are dealing with "subraces" or racial variants within one of the major races. In highly developed societies, these subraces have intermingled and intermarried for a long time. In less-advanced societies, where the communication between groups is less frequent, endogamy is practiced in a very strict manner, thus maintaining the separateness of each group. Racial purity is characteristic of underdeveloped societies, not of advanced societies—a fact that also contradicts racist theories.

Conflicts between Jews and non-Jews, or between Germans and Frenchmen, or between "Nordics" and "Mediterraneans" are not genuine racial conflicts. None of these contending groups presents homogeneous biological characteristics capable of defining a race in the correct sense of the word. They have practiced exogamy for so long—*de facto* and *de jure*—that they have achieved very extensive cross-breeding. We are no longer dealing with groups defined by their biological characteristics, but by their sociocultural characteristics. Once again we come to the notion of "basic personality," proposed by A. Kardiner, who defined it as "a particular psychological pattern peculiar to the members of a given society, and which is reflected in a certain style of living upon which individuals model their own distinctive variations." All societies thus engender—by their history, their way of life, their customs, and their educational system—a kind of basic personality.

CONFLICTS BETWEEN "HORIZONTAL" GROUPS

We have just seen that certain racial conflicts are not "vertical"— between groups placed one above the other on the social scale—but "horizontal"—between groups on the same plane, such as families, tribes, and provinces. Actually, it is difficult to distinguish vertical from horizontal groups. In conflicts between horizontal groups, each one tries to dominate the other in some manner; in conflicts between vertical groups, lower groups aspire to social equality, which is to say, a "horizontal" division of society. We will simply designate as horizontal groups those that, in principle, are not unequal to other groups, even though certain inequalities may actually exist. This classification includes territorial groups (nations, provinces, districts, *communes*), corporate groups (professions, associations, unions), and ideological groups (political parties, religions).

Among these horizontal groups, antagonisms develop, many of which are of a political nature, that is, their object is to win power or the advantages resulting from power. Certain antagonisms among horizontal groups are more or less a coverup for antagonisms of another sort, such as class conflicts. But others have a reality of their own. Conflicts among horizontal groups play an important part in the development of political antagonisms; this is the case with international conflicts.

Conflicts Between Territorial Groups

Most human communities are subdivided into territorial groups: nations within international society; provinces, regions and districts within nations; and sections or committees within associations. Although these territorial groups are unequal in size and power, they are generally equal from a legal or theoretical point of view, thus constituting horizontal groups. Rivalries between these territorial groups contribute greatly to political antagonisms; sometimes, they partially conceal rivalries of a different nature, but they always have some reality in themselves.

THE FORMATION OF TERRITORIAL GROUPS   Territorial groups are based, it would seem, on an extension of what Durkheim called "solidarity through similarity." This he contrasted with "solidarity through the division of labor," which served as a basis for corporate groups. We might designate as "solidarity through proximity" this form of solidarity through similarity.

People who live close together naturally feel more interdependent than people who live far apart. The Christian notion of "neighbor" is a good illustration of this natural phenomenon. We do not become directly acquainted with individuals geographically distant from us, except at rare moments. We come to know them better indirectly through hearsay (books, magazines, newspapers, and so forth), or through pictures. Indirect contacts are quite different from direct contacts, and the results are accordingly quite different. The parceling up and partitioning of space, ·because of geographical conditions, produces groups of people whose members feel interdependent with one another and in competition with other groups.

This "solidarity through proximity" is a variant of "solidarity through similarity." Considered by itself, proximity constitutes a resemblance, with its similar living conditions. In addition, it produces other resemblances, some depending on similar geographical conditions (which lead to resemblances in morphology, mores, and ways of life), others resulting simply from the direct relations caused by proximity (similarities in language, phenomena of imitation). From this last point of view, however, we must not confuse cause and effect. More precisely, we must observe the reciprocal nature of certain interactions; proximity produces resemblances, but it can also be the result of preexisting resemblances.

Certain territorial groups appear, in this connection, to result from the extension of natural, undifferentiated groups, founded on blood relationships, either real or imaginary. The first natural communities, tribes and clans, appear to be based exclusively on kinship—whether of an actual physical consanguinity traced back to a common ancestor, or of a mythical kinship linking the group to a common pseudoancestor who never really existed. In the nomadic stage, based on hunting, fishing, and the gathering of fruits and berries, the concept of territory is relatively unimportant (even though it is already a feature of certain animal societies). When agriculture appears, groups attach themselves to fixed areas, and territory becomes an important element of solidarity. The community based on soil tends to replace the community based on blood. But, of course, the former favors the continuance of the latter so long as the group lives in a closed agricultural economy based on small units of production. Intermarriage inevitably occurs within the villages, and everyone becomes a cousin, to some degree, of his neighbor.

These small territorial groups tend to merge with one another as technological advances occur and exchanges develop; in this way they pass from villages and towns into states. But then the increasing need for administration and organization necessitates subdividing large territorial complexes, so local districts and various regional units are created for administrative purposes. Accordingly, we can distinguish two categories of territorial groups within a given society: those which predated it and contributed in some degree to its formation, and those which are the result of the society's development and which the society itself has created. From the point of view of political sociology, this distinction is not without value; antagonisms between groups in the first category are generally deeper, because they are more firmly rooted in history than antagonisms between groups in the second category. But it is difficult to apply this kind of distinction because the territorial division among groups in the first category usually serves as a basis for the establishment of groups in the second category.

THE DIFFERENT TERRITORIAL GROUPS We cannot then use this distinction between "natural" and "artificial" groups as a basis for classifying territorial groups. Let us note simply that conservatives generally attach great importance to it because they believe "natural" groups should play an important role in governing the state. We will use a more accurate classification, based on the fact that, in the pyramid of groups overlapping and interlocking with each other, one category is of fundamental importance in the world of today—nations. It is in terms of this category that we will define the others.

In the second half of the twentieth century, nations still constitute the basic territorial entities. Both in law and in fact, the earth is divided above all else into nations. Other divisions are secondary in comparison with this one. This situation is relative to a moment in history. In ancient times, tribal groups and then cities comprised the principal horizontal groupings. Occasionally, vast communities developed, somewhat similar to modern nations, and these were called empires (Egyptian, Assyrian, Persian, Roman). Some people believe that contemporary nations will one day fuse into larger collectivities; this federalist movement is especially noticeable in Western Europe where it has given rise to various international communities. But nationalism still remains a more powerful force than federalism.

We will not reexamine at this point the concept of "nation," but will refer the reader to the earlier section where we discussed a nation as a "cultural entity" (p. 106). We will simply note that a nation is defined as a horizontal group, because of the intense solidarity that nations generate, as compared with the feelings that develop toward the entity to which nations belong—international society. There are antagonisms between nations because national loyalties prevail over international loyalties. Conflicts between nations are especially important for two reasons. First, national solidarity is generally the deepest of all, and antagonisms which develop between nations are therefore difficult to alleviate. Second, national political institutions—which together constitute the state—are the most highly organized of all political institutions. Accordingly, the state has more powerful means of coercion at its disposal than any other community (including the international community), and it is difficult to impose any limitations upon its use of these means, since the state can reject such restrictions by resorting to force.

Conflicts between nations are, therefore, the most serious and important of all political conflicts. There is nothing in modern times that approaches the violence of international warfare. This is so not only because of the importance of national feelings of solidarity and the powerful organization of the state, but also because international societies have weak political organizations compared to other social groups. As a rule, international power does not have the material means of enforcing national compliance with its decisions. In the international community, antagonisms therefore tend to prevail over integration. Hence, conflicts between nations tend to be settled either by force (war) or by purely contractual procedures (treaties, diplomatic agreements), when there is no arbitration of political power. The study of international relations is very interesting for political sociology because the importance of power in social integration can be measured by observing what happens in its absence.

It is within the national framework that political power reaches its maximum development. This does not mean—as we have said heretofore—that the power exercised by a nation is different in nature from the power exercised in other communities, or that national power is the only kind that can be described as "political" (see Introduction). It simply means that there is a difference in intensity and complexity. In another sense, nations in and of themselves are "universal societies," which is to say, ensembles of communities in which general feelings of solidarity develop (on the notion of "universal society," see Introduction). Certainly, they are not the only universal societies, but they are the most important ones.

Most territorial groups, in the sense we have given the term, exist within nations. Some are smaller "universal societies," which comprise subdivisions of the nation, such as communes, regions, and provinces. Others are local subdivisions of particular societies also constituted within the nation, such as local chapters of various associations, unions, and societies; from the latter point of view, divisions of territorial groups and those of corporative groups combine with one another. Antagonisms among territorial groups within nations are more or less developed depending upon the degree of national integration. They can sometimes jeopardize the very existence of the national society, with each territorial group tending to split off and form a new nation, not unlike the process of cell division among simple biological forms. But even in the most highly integrated nations, antagonisms among territorial groups always exist.

There are also territorial groups outside national groupings, some of which are subdivisions of the international society. Some nations may organize into more or less coherent blocks—for example, NATO, the Eastern bloc, the European Community, and the Organization of American States. International politics are then based not only on antagonisms between nations but also on antagonisms between blocs of nations. Moreover, certain territorial groups coincide with national frontiers, but are also divisions within larger communities. For instance, within the Roman Catholic church, we find the Catholic church of France, the Catholic church of Spain, and the Catholic church of the United States. With respect to political conflicts within a nation, these groups are ideological groups (which we will examine later); with respect to conflicts within the community of the Catholic church, they are territorial groups.

ANTAGONISMS BETWEEN TERRITORIAL GROUPS   Behind the antagonisms between territorial groups, we find factors similar to those we have discovered in antagonisms between individuals, between social classes, and between races. However, certain characteristics deserve special attention.

The distribution of territory among human groups results in inequalities, like the distribution of land ownership (and ownership of the means of production in general) among individuals. Consequently, a natural antagonism develops between groups that are well off and groups that are at a disadvantage. The struggle between wealthy nations and poor nations is one of the basic causes of international conflicts. Rivalry between wealthy regions and impoverished regions within a given nation can also be very intense. This material aspect of

conflicts between territorial groups is sometimes concealed behind ideologies and myths, which make the controversy appear more idealistic,
less materialistic; but the material factor is present nonetheless.

However, it would be absurd to regard this competition for wealth
as the sole basis for antagonisms between territorial groups. Man's natural distrust of "the other," the "foreigner," the one who does not belong to the group, is a contributory cause. The sense of solidarity, arising from similarity and proximity, generally has as its corollary a
natural hostility toward those who are different and geographically remote. This phenomenon is naturally exploited by those who have an
interest in strengthening the unity of the group, and so they encourage
hostility toward the "outsider." Polarizing the aggressiveness of a group
by directing it toward an external "enemy" is an effective way of rein-
forcing internal unity. "Hereditary enemies" have always played a
great role in developing feelings of national, provincial, and local solidarity.

Along with these real elements, antagonisms between territorial
groups are often a cover-up, at least in part, for conflicts of a different
sort—such as class antagonisms. Nationalism is a means of masking
the hostility between the privileged and the oppressed of one country
with the sense of solidarity which comes from belonging to the same
territorial community. To the communist slogan "Workers of the
world, unite!" nationalism offers a counterslogan: "Oppressors and oppressed of the same nation, unite!" In smaller territorial frameworks,
the same process applies. In certain respects, territorial solidarities are
archaic, based on a past they are trying to preserve, whereas class solidarities are a more recent phenomenon. It is not by chance that right-
wing politics is nationalistic, as well as "provincial," and "communal-
ist."

But we must avoid generalizing about such phenomena. The
camouflage varies according to circumstances and social structures.
Originally, the concept of "nation" opposed the common interest of all
citizens to the aristocracy or the monarch, as the source of sovereign
power; its first meaning was revolutionary. Throughout the nineteenth
century in Europe, nationalism was an ideology of the political left before it was adopted by the conservatives who had had little use for it
until then. In 1793, the term "nation" was the rallying cry of the partisans of the French Revolution; today it is often used by the descendants of the émigrés of Coblenz.[3] However, in the current resistance to

[3] A German city on the Rhine, which was a rallying point for French émigrés in
1793.

American hegemony, nationalism has once again become a force in the European political left. Likewise, movements for provincial or regional autonomy sometimes have a progressive meaning, especially when the goal is to liberate a more advanced territory from the domination of reactionary national authorities (the Catalan movement in modern Spain, for example, or the Paris Commune of 1871).

In certain cases, however, national factors play a fundamental role in political struggles. At such times, they are the motivation behind change, more so than socioeconomic structures. This is particularly true of countries that are in the process of winning—or have recently won—their national independence. National problems and problems of independence are then at the heart of political competition. They dominate all other considerations. They temporarily override class conflicts and socioeconomic antagonisms. Wars of independence often produce political parties and governmental regimes far beyond the evolution of socioeconomic structures. Present-day China and Algeria clearly illustrate this situation, and there were many similar instances in nineteenth-century Europe. And it often happens that the evolution of socioeconomic structures, in and of itself, plays a prominent role in the heightened awareness of national realities, so that national realities are partly a consequence of socioeconomic factors. But this does not prevent the predominance of nationalistic elements in the crises of independence. When long-established nations are engaged in wars that threaten their existence as a community, we note the same temporary predominance of national antagonisms.

THE CONFLICT BETWEEN WEALTHY NATIONS AND POOR NATIONS   Earlier in the book, we discussed briefly the distinction between rich nations and poor nations (see p. 58). Some people wonder whether the conflict between them will not become increasingly serious, whether this class struggle on the national scale will not supersede the class struggle within nations at the end of the twentieth century and in the twenty-first century.

Two worlds now confront each other—one, rich; the other, poor. While the former sees on the horizon the dawn of a society of abundance, the latter remains close to the Middle Ages, with its famines, epidemics, and human misery. The national income per capita is ten times higher in Western Europe and North America than in Asia and Africa. The amount of mechanization per individual worker is ten to thirty times greater. On the other hand, the infant mortality rate is ten times lower. In industrialized nations only 3 percent to 4 percent of the population is illiterate; in certain Asiatic and African countries, the illiteracy rate runs as high as 90 percent. The gap between today's bourgeois and proletarian nations is as great as the gap between the bourgeoisie and the proletariat of a single nation in nineteenth-century Europe.

This gap is widening instead of decreasing. We speak of the nations of Africa, Asia, and Latin America as being in a state of accelerated development. That is true by comparison with their very slow rates of progress during the previous centuries, but it is untrue by comparison with the progress achieved in industrial nations, which are developing much more rapidly. By and large, the rate of annual increase in national income is higher in Europe and North America than in the Third World, where the rich grow richer and the poor grow poorer. The share of the world's riches enjoyed by industrial nations increases, while that of underdeveloped countries decreases. As social antagonisms gradually diminish in industrial societies, the class struggle tends to move from the national level to the international level. The fact that rich societies become richer and poor societies become poorer naturally aligns the latter against the former.

The antagonism is further intensified by the fact that wealthy countries exploit the poor ones, just as the bourgeoisie exploits the proletariat in capitalistic societies. Technical assistance, however useful it is, is not unlike the kind of charity that was practiced in Charles Dickens' England. In a few special cases, for political reasons, certain affluent nations give certain poor nations more than they receive in return, sometimes a great deal more; such is the case with France in Africa. Generally, however, throughout the world, the sacrifice wealthy nations make to help underdeveloped nations is less than the benefits they gain from the low cost of raw materials purchased in these same countries. Industrial societies exploit agricultural societies by taking advantage of their economic weakness.

Good intentions are no more effective in eliminating this exploitation than they were with the exploitation of the proletariat by the bourgeoisie in the nineteenth century. In a capitalistic society, economic interest is the driving force of social life; everything else is subordinate to it. By using the themes of Christian charity and the threat of communism, Western governments have been able to obtain certain sacrifices from their taxpayers for the assistance of underdeveloped countries. But they can never prevent large capitalistic corporations from trying to obtain the raw materials from these countries at the lowest possible price; they cannot prevent these groups from having the final word. It is in the very nature of capitalism to oppose any genuine international assistance that would enable underdeveloped countries to emerge from the contradictions of their transitional stage of development.

Nevertheless, the conflict between industrialized and nonindustrialized nations can hardly lead to a direct confrontation. The new class struggle differs from the old one in one fundamental respect. In the nineteenth century, the privileged classes were literally besieged by the proletariat; their police and military forces were not enough to defend them. Pressure from the proletariat compelled the European bourgeoisie to gradually abandon some of their privileges. In today's world, protected by distance, by oceans, by deserts, and even more, by the might of their weapons of destruction, North America, Europe, and the Soviet Union run no risk of being assaulted by proletarian societies. No underdeveloped country can afford a confrontation with industrialized nations. The conflict between wealthy nations and poor nations is not a fundamental political antagonism, because the two adversaries are too unequal to be able to engage in actual conflict with one another.

Yet this conflict aggravates the antagonisms among industrial societies. The economically developed worlds—that of the East and that of the West—are relatively fixed and stabilized; each has abandoned the idea of conquering the other, and their borders are well defined. This particular antagonism has lost its violence, like the class struggle in industrial societies. But the Third World, on the other hand, is underdeveloped and unstable. By favoring one side or the other, it is in a position to give the East or West an important trump card in the rivalry. The uncontrolled and uncontrollable reactions of proletarian nations revive the struggle between the two industrial empires, a struggle that would otherwise subside. If an important part of Latin America became communist, Washington would react strongly.

Poor nations cannot afford direct confrontations with highly developed nations, but they can push them into confrontations. This heightening of international tensions arouses internal antagonisms. The fear of communism in the West today—the fear of an external danger, that is—is a fundamental cause of internal political conflicts. So long as there are poor nations, wealthy nations will not achieve total integration, assuming that this is even possible.

Conflicts Between Corporative Groups

Like territorial groups, corporative groups depend on a variety of solidarities through similarities, solidarities that unite people who share

—or shared—the same kind of activity. Professional groups are the most important class of corporative groups, but not the only ones. Like the conflicts among territorial groups, conflicts between corporative groups sometimes serve as a cover-up for other conflicts; but occasionally, they also have a real basis. In any event, they never reach the level of violence of conflicts between nations.

VARIOUS CORPORATIVE GROUPS   In the narrow sense, corporative groups unite people engaged in the same professional activity. In the broad sense, we must add groups trained and educated in a common school, those belonging to the same government agency or professional classification, as well as associations comprised of people with a common recreational interest (sporting and athletic associations, cultural associations).

The practice of a common profession produces marked resemblances and a rather strong sense of solidarity among the practitioners. The division among professional groups (which is horizontal) should not be confused with the division among classes (which is vertical). Sometimes the two combine. Within management, professional categories produce definite affinities (between big business executives and managers of small businesses, industrialists and tradesmen, and so on); the same is true of salaried workers. The bonds of professional groups weaken class loyalties if occupational distinctions and differences in the way of life between management and labor are relatively minor; this is why the class struggle is less violent in agriculture than in industry or commerce, and less violent in small businesses than in large industries. It also explains why certain conservatives prefer small economic units.

By "paraprofessional" bodies we mean groups comprised of graduates of a prestigious school or the members of an administrative category, whose professional activities, while not necessarily identical, are not very different and are largely conditioned by membership in the particular administrative corps. To have graduated, for example, from the *Ecole Polytechnique,* the *Ecole Centrale,* the *Ecole des Mines,* or the *Ecole Nationale des Arts et Métiers* is an invaluable asset in furthering the careers of those able to take advantage of these specialized institutions. They do not all practice the same profession, but their professions are not too different as a result of their common educational background. Holding a position in the Treasury Department or the Council of State, or working as a licensed teacher in public education, produces similar results. The *esprit de corps* which binds these groups together is based on a principle of mutual assistance and on the efficacy of results, as well as on a common educational background and shared experiences. These paraprofessional groups sometimes play an important role at certain levels of political competition.

It may seem strange, at first glance, to link professional or paraprofessional groups with recreational associations whose members are engaged in nonprofessional activities, such as sports or cultural pursuits. But the comparison is justified since, in both cases, we are dealing with groups based on similar activities. The fact that professional activity is motivated by the need to earn a living, whereas nonprofessional activity is voluntary and not directly tied to economic motives, is not sufficient reason for separating the two. As a person's standard of living rises and the pressure of material needs subsides, and as the hours devoted to professional work decrease, recreational activities take on added importance. They also tend to involve the individual more directly in political activities and conflicts.

ANTAGONISMS AMONG CORPORATE GROUPS   We will distinguish between genuine corporate antagonisms and the camouflage concealing corporate conflicts arising from antagonisms of a different nature.

Professional and paraprofessional groups are based not only on similar current activities or previous educational experiences but also on common material interests. Members of one profession or organization defend their corporate advantage against the members of another profession or organization. Thus, there is a natural antagonism between different professions, and at the same time, a community of interests among the members of the same profession. But, on the other hand, there is a conflict between common professional interests and common class interests. Managers and workers in the bakery business have common interests that set them in opposition to managers and workers of other professions. But managers in every profession have interests common to managers, which set them at variance with the workers in their own profession; and workers in every profession have common interests as workers, which place them in opposition even to the managers and bosses of their own profession.

Generally speaking, class interests are stronger than corporate interests—which is why class antagonisms are more important politically than corporate antagonisms. But in certain areas, in certain societies, or under certain circumstances, corporate interests prevail over class interests. This occurs rather often in agriculture, especially in conflicts between the agricultural sector of the economy and the industrial and commercial sectors. We also find it in the area of small business economies, where the common interests of employers and employees in very small enterprises create strong human bonds, and where, at the same time, competition is very keen among artisans in the same business. In highly developed societies, we see the same phenomenon reappear in a new form: the splintering of workers' demands into separate categories. Labor unions are often hard pressed to prevent the union from breaking up as differences between the various types of workers grow more serious.

Marxists consider these corporate conflicts within the same social class to be "contradictions" rather than "antagonisms," the term used to describe conflicts between classes. This means that they are not as fundamental. Contradictions can be resolved, while antagonisms cannot. Having said that, it follows that contradictions within the same social class can weaken the development of class antagonisms. But it is also possible to use the contradictions to increase the class struggle. The exploitation of capitalistic contradictions by labor unions and political parties is one of the basic principles of Marxist strategy; corporate conflicts within management can thus be helpful in achieving workers' demands. But the reverse is also true: capitalists continually exploit the contradictions within the working class.

The best example of corporate groups acting as a camouflage for other antagonisms is furnished by the "corporative" doctrines that flourished in the 1930's, when they served as the basis of certain institutions in fascist countries. The fundamental idea was to organize the nation by professions, in horizontal categories, workers and management being represented together and working together in each "corporation." In this way, fascist countries destroyed labor unions and made it impossible for workers to make their own demands. "Corporative" solidarity actually put salaried workers in each profession at the mercy of the bosses, who controlled the corporations. Accordingly, class antagonisms were hidden behind a screen of alleged common, corporate interests. In industry and commerce, these corporative tendencies have not been able to take hold outside authoritarian states. In agriculture, on the other hand, they are always very apparent.

We find other examples of camouflage, of a different nature, in the intervention of recreational and cultural associations in political conflicts. In authoritarian states, where political struggles cannot take place openly, they are often concealed behind literary or artistic conflicts; cultural groups thus play, in effect, the role of political organizations. Other recreational groups can also serve as a blind for political action; thus, in Austria-Hungary before 1914, sports clubs of Sokols served as nationalistic organizations for young Czechs. In the examples we have given, recreational associations actually became the instruments of ideological groups.

Conflicts Between Ideological Groups

We designate here as ideological groups those with a common body of ideological beliefs, in the sense we have previously defined the term "ideology" (see pp. 96–97). Churches, philosophical sects, "intellectual societies," and political parties constitute ideological groups. A doctrine becomes an ideology when a social group subscribes to it, when it ceases to be simply the intellectual construct of a thinker and becomes an expression of the aspirations, desires, and faith of a group of people (class, nation, and so on). To the extent that this group is distinct from other groups, and acquires organizations and institutions, it constitutes an ideological group.

THE VARIOUS KINDS OF IDEOLOGICAL GROUPS   There are many possible classifications of ideological groups. For our purposes, the primary distinction is between political and nonpolitical groups.

By the expression "political ideologies," we mean ideologies relating to the nature of power and its exercise. They clearly have a direct influence on the development of political antagonisms, an influence that is felt in two ways. On the one hand, ideologies tend to unify a community by inducing its members to accept the power that governs it and by developing a sense of obedience toward the government; notions of legitimacy, consensus, and national awareness take full account of this phenomenon. On the other hand, ideologies can divide a community when several of them coexist, with each depending upon the support of a fraction of the community. It is in this manner that political ideological groups are formed.

At present, parties constitute the principal ideological groups of a political nature. Alongside political parties, certain pressure groups— those related to politics without being directly concerned with the conquest of power—fall into the same category. Such, for example, are as sociations that advocate disarmament, peace movements, and various civic clubs and organizations. At other times, ideological groups have assumed different forms—leagues, secret societies, and paramilitary organizations.

Nonpolitical ideologies are those that have no direct relationship to power, for example, religious, philosophical, and artistic ideologies. Some, like artistic ideologies, are truly far removed from questions of power. Others, especially philosophical and religious ideologies, are in fact closely connected with problems of power. Actually, it is difficult to separate political from nonpolitical ideologies. Every ideology tends, by its very nature, to be a complete system for explaining man and the world, a *Weltanschauung* in which politics naturally has its place, for the various aspects of human activity are not easily separated from one another.

Like political ideologies, nonpolitical ideologies tend to serve as a basis for groups that are more or less organized: thus religions take the form of churches, philosophies become the bases for various sects, and art gives rise to schools and movements of various kinds. These nonpolitical groups often come to play a political role, like all private groups, in a "universal" society. Their ideological nature makes the antagonisms of these groups more militant, and the more fundamental the ideology, the more pronounced the militancy. This is why the involvement of churches and religious organizations in political conflicts is generally stronger and more pervasive than that of other groups.

Religious ideologies usually have great political influence. For centuries, those in power have sought religious sanctions. Political leaders regarded themselves as God's representatives, or more simply, even claimed to be gods themselves. Furthermore, religious beliefs in a future world, one in which the inequities of the present world will disappear, has prescribed resignation to the oppressed and kept them in a state of obedience to power. But on the other hand, certain religions have taken a stand against the established order by declaring it illegitimate; they have thus become instruments of opposition. Although nonpolitical in principle, religious ideologies, in practice, have played a major role in political antagonisms. The separation of religion and politics, of church and state, of God and Caesar, is a modern idea, and has only been applied in a few instances.

THE NATURE OF IDEOLOGICAL ANTAGONISMS   Marxists maintain that ideological antagonisms have no real existence, but are merely reflections of class antagonisms. This doctrine has been greatly exaggerated, for there is at least some measure of autonomy to ideological antagonisms.

In the Marxist view, ideologies are located in the "superstructures," which depend strictly upon the "base," that is, on the position of the social classes. Ideological antagonisms simply reflect the class conflicts they express. Ideologies rationalize the aspirations of struggling classes, giving them more strength.

This theory is partially true. Overall, it corresponds rather closely to the situation that prevailed when the doctrine was formulated. In the nineteenth century, the conflict of political ideologies reflected primarily the struggle among the social classes. The conflict between the conservative and liberal ideologies after the French Revolution clearly reflected the conflict between the land-owning aristocracy and the commercial and industrial bourgeoisie, which had become intellectually enlightened and powerful in banking. Then the socialist ideology appeared, expressing the needs, desires, and aspirations of a new social class that developed with industrialization—the proletariat. The character of nationalist ideologies also reflects class situations. The concept of "nation" was forged by the bourgeoisie in the eighteenth century, serving to establish a feeling of solidarity with the common people and to mobilize community feelings against the cosmopolitan aristocracy. During the French Revolution and the Napoleonic Empire, members of the nobility who had left France served in the army of Coblenz against the French nation. During the second half of the nineteenth century, the bourgeoisie continued to use the nationalist ideology, but now they directed it against the populace, which was in the process of turning to socialism, also an internationalistic ideology. The nation served to establish a sense of solidarity between privileged classes and exploited classes in order to prevent the "workers of the world" from uniting against capitalism. Then the aristocracy joined with the bourgeoisie, and the descendants of the émigrés of Coblenz became ultranationalists. The liberal nationalism of the nineteenth century, situated on the left, changed into fascist nationalism in the twentieth century and thus moved to the right. But, beginning in 1933, a portion of the bourgeoisie in France (and in other countries) joined with the Hitlerites out of fear of the communists; the latter, for their part, became patriotic (and proved it during the Resistance). Nationalism again passed to the political left and was to remain there, after World War II, with the resistance to American hegemony in Western Europe, encouraged by the bourgeoisie.

Religious ideologies also have certain characteristics that reflect class situations. We know that Marx described religion as the "opiate of the masses," which is to say, as a means of numbing the people so they will not become aware of their exploitation. It is a mistake not to examine this judgment in its original context, where it is much more subtle, and where Marx admits a certain value to religion. Here is the exact quotation from *A Contribution to the Critique of Hegel's Philosophy of Right:* "Religion is the sigh of the creature that is overwhelmed, the heart of a heartless world, as it is the spirit of an age that has no spirit. It is the opiate of the masses." We can see that Marx is actually almost grateful to religion for alleviating the sufferings of the common people, for playing the role of an anesthetic. In a less famous but more cynical observation, Napoleon I very accurately described how conservatives use religion to protect their privileges against the pressures of the oppressed: "How can there be order in a state without religion? Society cannot exist without inequality of wealth, and unequal wealth cannot exist without religion. When one man is dying of hunger while his neighbor has too much to eat, he cannot accept this difference unless there is an authority which tells him: It is the will of God; there must be poor people and rich people in the world; but later on, and throughout eternity, the distribution will be done in a different way." [4]

This strategy is precisely the one followed by the bourgeoisie in the nineteenth century, and the one it continues to follow today in its struggle against socialism. The aristocracy had used the same methods in its battle with liberalism. "The alliance between throne and altar" from 1814 to 1830 simply reapplied an earlier strategy of the monarchy when it was under attack from the eighteenth-century Encyclopedists and rationalist thinkers. Under these circumstances, we can understand the intensity of the anticlerical struggle at the beginning of the twentieth century, when the clergy, and especially the private schools, defended and disseminated conservative ideas. In Western Europe, things have changed somewhat (even though the financial support for private schools in France still has somewhat the same meaning). In less advanced countries, where religion has retained a more archaic structure, the situation remains unchanged; there was nothing more striking than the unequivocal condemnation of Fidel Castro by the Cuban clergy, compared to its silence during the atrocious tyranny of Fulgencio Batista; or the vigor of Pope Pius XII in denouncing communism, compared to his silence on the subject of Nazi concentration camps. In Moslem countries, the role of Islam is hardly any different.

The fact that ideologies, and especially political ideologies, largely reflect the class situations is not to be denied, but many other factors besides social classes contribute to the development of ideologies. Nationalistic ideologies are based upon genuine feelings of belonging to the same community, to the same cultural entity. They sometimes express needs common to all classes. The need for national independence in a community that is oppressed by another state presents certain aspects of a class struggle, but it goes far beyond such aspects; consequently, it is a gross misrepresentation to reduce the problem to a class struggle. Likewise, the need for transcendence and spiritual communion which lies at the heart of religious ideologies cannot be ascribed to the class situation. The class struggle is indeed a factor in the

---

[4] Remarks made by Napoleon to Roderer, a French statesman.

development of religions, but religions are not merely an outgrowth of the class struggle. Certain ideologies concerned with centralization and bureaucracy reflect conflicts between the leaders and the rank-and-file, between the governors and the governed, within the same class. Ideologies concerned with decentralization often correspond to the aspirations of a region or province seeking liberation from the domination of the capital. Literary, artistic, and philosophical doctrines also have a reality of their own, quite apart from conflicts between social classes which they sometimes conceal.

How much ideologies depend upon social classes varies with the period of history. We have already emphasized that the class struggle seems to have characterized the nineteenth century—the period in which Marx developed his doctrines—but that it was much less apparent both before and after that time. We may speculate, in this connection, whether the weakening of the class struggle, which seems characteristic of modern industrial societies, will not intensify genuine ideological differences unrelated to class conflicts. At first glance, the facts would appear to belie this idea, since the most advanced nations show a certain indifference to ideologies, a "disideologization," as some have described it, probably with a touch of humor (there is sometimes a confusion between "depoliticization" and "disideologization"; see pp. 300–2). But we are speaking primarily of an increasing detachment from traditional political ideologies, which is tied to the weakening of class conflicts. If the day comes when the *primum vivere* has finally been achieved, we can imagine that men will become concerned with *deinde philosophari,* which is to say that ideologies will occupy an important place in men's minds, and that they will naturally produce conflicts.

PART III

From Antagonisms to Integration

CONFLICT and integration are not simply two contradictory aspects of politics: they complement each other as well. In studying the causes of antagonisms, we discovered that many of them are somewhat ambivalent. They generate conflicts, but, in certain circumstances, they can also help to limit conflicts and promote integration. Generally speaking, integration appears in some respects to be the final result of political antagonisms, and the notion of integration plays an important role in the very development of the conflict. Every challenge to the existing social order implies a vision and a plan for a superior, more authentic social order. Every struggle contains a dream of peace and constitutes an effort to realize the dream. Many believe that conflict and integration are not opposites, but part and parcel of the same general process —that conflict naturally leads to integration, and antagonisms tend, by their very development, to self-elimination and the subsequent bringing about of social harmony.

In the classic liberal view, integration is produced by conflict, as the latter gradually develops and intensifies; the two phenomena are concomitant. Economic competition produces the greatest expansion of production and the widest distribution of manufactured goods, and continually insures the best possible economy. Political competition achieves similar results, guaranteeing that the best, the most capable, the elite, govern to the advantage of all. Political harmony—troubled only by those who are abnormal, perverse, or ill—is analogous to "economic harmonies." For Marxists, the political struggle is also the motivating drive for social evolution, a process that will inevitably bring an end to antagonisms and the establishment of a society without conflicts. This social integration will appear only in the last phase of a very long process, in the distant future. At each stage, a partial integration is achieved—a "synthesis" between a "thesis" and its opposing "antithesis"; but the synthesis soon becomes a new cause of contradiction and conflict. Political harmony is a perpetual "becoming," which develops in a rhythmical fashion until the end of history, the final phase of communism.

This justifies our studying, in close conjunction, the forms of the political struggle and the development of political integration. We will discover, in fact, that some kinds of conflict—conflicts "within" a regime, for example—already imply a certain degree of integration, and that the first stage of integration consists in restraining the use of violence, which is to say, replacing certain forms of conflict with other forms.

5

The Forms of
Political Conflict

Political antagonisms, caused by the factors we have just discussed, develop into conflicts. We shall try to give here a typology of these political conflicts, examining first the weapons used, and then the strategies in which they are employed.

THE WEAPONS OF COMBAT

Men and organizations in conflict with each other use various kinds of weapons in the political struggle. Depending upon the period of history, the type of society, the political regime, and the social groups or classes in conflict, one weapon or another predominates, but one kind of weapon is ruled out, in principle—that which involves the use of physical violence. When groups or individuals confront each other with fists, clubs, rifles, or machine guns, we are outside the domain of politics. The first objective of politics is to eliminate violence, to replace bloody conflicts with more temperate forms of civil strife, and to eliminate wars, either civil or international. Politics is conflict, but it is also a limitation on conflict, and consequently a beginning of the process of integration. However, it is not absolute. Politics tends to eliminate violence, but it never succeeds entirely. Weapons in the narrow sense of the term—military weapons—are not totally excluded from political conflicts. We must examine them first of all.

Physical Violence

"The first man to become a king was a successful soldier": this old saying suggests that military weapons are the source of power and that power is ultimately dependent upon military might.

POLITICAL STRUGGLES AND PHYSICAL VIOLENCE Broadly speaking, there are two kinds of violence used as weapons in political combat: violence by the state against the citizenry, and violence between groups of citizens or against the state.

In many human communities, authority is based on physical violence. The strongest person with fists or knife is often the leader of a street gang, a criminal band, or on a playground. The same factor also figures in the domination of adults over children, of men over women. In the state, Roman Praetorians, Turkish Janissaries, Nazi S.S. troops, special security forces, and soldiers and policemen are bulwarks of defense for rulers, whose palaces were originally fortresses designed to protect them, not against foreign enemies, but from their own people. Instead of destroying the means of violence, military arms, politics tends to concentrate them in the hands of power and remove them from the use of citizens. The state, and political power in general, is characterized by its monopoly of the means of coercion, which tends to give a formidable power to the social class, political party, or faction that controls the government. A single armed power in the midst of a disarmed people puts the latter at the mercy of the former. We will encounter this question again. Let us merely note here that this monopoly of power has the effect of limiting the use of violence—military weapons—in political struggles, since in principle only one of the adversaries has such weapons at its disposal.

Apart from their regular use by the state for maintaining its authority over the people it governs, military weapons are also used in political struggles in three principal cases. First, arms are used during an initial stage of social development, when the state is still too weak to have acquired a complete monopoly of military weapons for its own advantage. Then, the struggle for power consists of armed factions confronting each other; political organizations assume the form of militias. In the cities of antiquity, in the Italian republics of the Renaissance, and in certain underdeveloped countries at the present time, we see examples of such situations. The Middle Ages, with its feudal wars and rivalries, provides further examples. Similar situations can arise at a more advanced stage of political development if one party organizes in a paramilitary fashion, if it becomes powerful, and if the state fails to invervene; in that case, the opposing parties must necessarily adopt the same methods and arm themselves if they do not want to be destroyed. A process of this kind took place in Germany in the 1930's as the power of Hitlerism increased; in order to resist the Nazi militias, parties of the left were obliged to establish their own militias (the Banner of the Empire—socialists; the Fighters of the Red Front —communists).

Political struggles also take a military form when the opposition has no other means of action, when it is deprived of other forms of expression, or when that which it is given is altogether ineffective. In such circumstances, armed resistance to power generally occurs in two phases: a period of clandestine resistance and a period of open revolt —the first preparing the way for the second. The two phases are not absolutely distinct. The open revolt can take the form either of violent revolution, in which power rapidly falls into the hands of the former opposition, or of prolonged civil war. Civil war now tends to replace revolution, because of development of means of constraint available to the state. Formerly, when armies were relatively weak, the populace could defeat them quickly without too much difficulty. Today, the modern weapons monopolized by the state are so powerful that popular revolt can only hope to succeed through guerrilla tactics, which take much longer. Moreover, guerrilla-type warfare does not appear to be very effective in societies that are technologically advanced.

THE MILITARY AND POLITICS   Political conflicts are settled by recourse to arms in a third situation: when the military are no longer in the service of the state, no longer at the disposal of those who govern, and when they themselves join in the struggle for power. We must distinguish this possibility from that in which the army plays the role of pressure group, which is something else again.

In Rome, during the third century A.D., the Roman legions made and unmade emperors, giving the throne to one or another of their generals, often in exchange for the promise of money and various advantages; then, later, they slaughtered the Caesar they had made, replacing him with another. Today, in Latin America, in the Middle East, and elsewhere, the military often create or overturn governments. In addition, various elements within the army often become rivals in these struggles for power. In the Roman Empire, there was intense rivalry between the Praetorians and border garrisons, and between legions in the various provinces, and these factions eventually fought each other. In Latin American nations, conflicts of this sort occur frequently between the army, navy, and air force. In Algeria in 1961, we saw hostilities between regiments of the regular army and soldiers who had been drafted for service.

When an army sets itself up as an independent political organization and ceases to obey the government, there is clearly a profound disorganization of political power. By its very nature, the military always constitutes a political danger for the state. Those who possess weapons are tempted to abuse the use of them, just as those who hold positions of authority are tempted to exceed their prerogatives. Arms are the ultimate expression of authority, the most decisive in the short term, the most irresistible at the moment. Whoever holds a sword is naturally tempted to throw it in the balance. Armed military forces are a permanent danger for rulers and a disarmed citizenry. Countries try to limit their danger, first by inculcating in officers the notion that they must always, in all circumstances, obey the state, whatever its form and whoever the rulers. Obligatory military service, which produces citizen-soldiers, also diminishes the danger by establishing an army in the image of the people. But the danger is always there. Rulers and citizens alike must constantly maintain a cautious, suspicious attitude toward the military. In nations with a long history of *pronunciamientos,* like many in Latin America, only the establishment of popular militias can prevent the army from dominating the state.

The military intervenes in political struggles in two different sociological situations. In most cases, the army represents certain collective forces and plays, with respect to these forces, the same role as political parties or pressure groups, except for the means at its disposal. Generally speaking, the military is the political instrument of privileged classes and minority groups, which need rifles, machineguns, and tanks to maintain their domination over exploited classes that threaten to submerge them by sheer force of numbers. In Latin America, *pronunciamientos* generally serve the interests of the large landowners or the wealthy bourgeoisie. Occasionally, however, the army plays the role of a political force of the left. This was the case in France at the beginning of the nineteenth century, because the officers produced by the French Revolution were usually men of humble origin and liberal persuasion. It is also true today of certain countries in the process of social and economic development, in which military schools are the principal means of social advancement for gifted children from poor or lower middle-class families. The officer corps then tends to represent these social groups against a political power generally wielded by great feudal lords. Military plots and coups d'état thus tend to replace the aristocracy with the lower middle class or even elements of the proletariat. This phenomenon was quite clear in the case of Mustapha Kemal in Turkey, of Nasser in Egypt, and of several military revolts in the Middle East and Latin America.

In a more unusual situation, an army that takes power—or attempts to do so—does not represent a collective social force, a group, or a class. It acts on its own behalf. Military regimes of this type have been called "technical dictatorships." The Praetorian power in Rome assumed this character after a period of time (at first, it probably reflected the social rise of new peoples incorporated into the empire, who provided the soldiers to oppose the established citizens of Rome, who would not relinquish their political prerogatives). The attempted putsch by General Challe in Algiers, in April 1961, was just this type of action: it was supported only by regiments of the Foreign Legion, which is to say, by mercenaries who represented no one but themselves.

Wealth

The saying "money rules" is a caricature of political reality; money has never been the only "ruler." Yet in many societies, and not only capitalist societies, money is an essential political weapon.

WEALTH AND AUTHORITY The effectiveness of wealth as a political weapon is attested to by the parallel that exists between the evolution of the forms of wealth and the evolution of the forms of authority.

In agrarian societies, where exploitation of the land is the principal source of wealth, the land-owning class possesses the political power. Here we find autocratic regimes in which authority is tied both to the possession of land and to possession of the equestrian weapon (chivalry)—societies which are simultaneously feudal and military. In commercial and industrial societies, the ownership of a factory, a store, or a bank becomes the principal source of wealth. Under these conditions, political power falls into the hands of the bourgeoisie. To be sure, the transition from the one type of society into the other occurs gradually. In the commercial-industrial society, the role of wealth is more conspicuous because money occupies an important place in the bourgeois system of values. In the agrarian society, it is less overt because aristocrats emphasize military values, of a disinterested nature, and affect a contempt for money. But this contempt is directed primarily toward wealth acquired from business, commerce, and banking, not toward wealth based on land ownership. Moreover, during the period when the power of the aristocrats was greatest, the land they held was the principal source of wealth. It was the importance of their landed properties, rather than their military function, that created the political power of aristocracies.

The rise of bourgeois societies in the nineteenth century has created the impression that, thereafter, power was based on money, and that this was a new development. This impression arose because the nouveaux-riches, socially awkward and ostentatious, were replacing the previous wealthy class, which was well-bred and more discreet. It was also caused by the fact that the aristocracy had based its power on both wealth and arms, and that the first had been largely overshadowed by the second, the source of heroic and lofty values. Lastly, the impression arose because the bourgeoisie established a system of values also predicated on wealth, but it openly admitted the source of its power rather than disguising it. The aristocracy loved wealth—whether it came from its landed estates or from royal pensions—but did not talk about it, at least in public. The bourgeoisie crudely proclaimed the source of its power and gloried in it. But, actually, it was a case of one kind of wealth replacing another as a source of political power.

WEALTH AND DEMOCRACY   The development of the bourgeoisie also corresponded to the development of the doctrines of liberal political democracy. Hence a certain contradiction appeared between officially proclaimed political values and the value attached to money. If money were to be used as a political weapon, would it not interfere with the equality of citizens and the normal processes of elections and parliamentary governments? It is noteworthy that the role of money was fairly well concealed in political struggles; the financing of election campaigns and of newspapers, for example, has always been carried out in relative secrecy. This is perhaps attributable less to the conflict between political theories and economic reality than to a certain nostalgia for aristocratic values that was not completely destroyed by the rise of capitalism (this explains why the political role of money has been less concealed in the United States than in Europe; besides, the social prestige of money is greater in a country without aristocratic traditions).

But, in any event, capitalistic theories consider the influence of money to be democratic in the final analysis. And indeed, in a freely competitive society, everyone has the possibility of making money, acquiring wealth, and exercising thereby some degree of political influence. Such was the profound meaning of François Guizot's reply to those who criticized him for endorsing the monopoly of political power in the hands of the rich: *"Enrichissez-vous!"* A whole contemporary mythology developed around this theme, especially in the United States, where there was a great deal of social mobility in the nineteenth century, and where Guizot's principle could be rather extensively applied—in a new society in which the weight of established traditions and social conditions did not yet appreciably impede the development of free enterprise and competition.

This theory fails by omission, for it overlooks the phenomenon of the accumulation of capital, which produces an accumulation of power. The hereditary transmission of acquired wealth completely undermines free economic competition by depriving it of its democratic character. Gradually, the power of money is equated with the power of birth, even if it was not so originally. In the development of liberal societies, wealth comes to depend more and more on the possession of capital than on work or enterprise. Even if we do not completely accept Marxist theories regarding the absolute pauperization of the working class, we can scarcely deny the existence of a relative degree of pauperization. In the growth of national income, the actual portion received by workers tends to decrease rather than increase, in contrast to the larger portion received by the owners of the means of production. Financial power remains chiefly in the hands of the latter through the procedure of confiscating the "plus value" of labor. The subsequent alienation of the worker is not only economic but also political: by this transfer of the plus value of labor, the worker is deprived of part of his influence over political power and some of his political weapons.

Numbers and Organization

Numbers have always been considered a political weapon and a source of power in international relations. The greater a country's population, the more workers and soldiers it had, the more powerful it was—or so it was believed. But numbers, by themselves, are ineffectual. They become a genuine political weapon only when the masses of the country are organized. As a political force, numbers are inseparable from organization.

THE ADVENT OF NUMBERS   The appearance of numbers as a weapon in internal politics is a recent phenomenon, linked as it is to the industrial revolution which permitted a general rise in living standards and in the cultural level of the masses.

In the domain of internal political competition, in struggles for power within older states and cities, population size was long a secondary factor. For many centuries, the struggle for power occurred within a restricted circle, to the exclusion of the great mass of the population. Its very low living standard permitted little intellectual development, and this kept the populace from becoming aware of its strength and organizing to improve its situation; strict surveillance by those in power and by their military personnel crushed any impulses in that direction.

Occasionally, however, in exceptional times, because their degree of degradation, misery, and oppression had become too great to endure, masses of the population erupted into the political arena like large, clumsy animals, crushing and smashing everything that stood in their way; but they were incapable of rebuilding or reordering society. Slave revolts, peasant revolts, and urban riots thus broke out at various times. A ruthless repression, commensurate with the fear aroused among the privileged classes, effectively removed from the masses any desire to repeat such a venture. Thus, after the defeat of Spartacus, the first hero of popular revolts whose name has come down to us in history, 60,000 slaves were slaughtered in Lucania, and the crosses of 6,-000 who were crucified were erected along the Appian Way.

Numbers became a political force to be reckoned with once the general standard of living and culture reached the level that enabled the mass of the population to rise from the stultifying state in which it had been imprisoned—to become aware of its wretched situation and see the possibilities of escaping it—and when it also discovered ways and means of taking action. The development of the right of suffrage has proved to be the most important method of giving the masses genuine political power.

The doctrines elaborated by the bourgeoisie in their own battle against the aristocracy have greatly assisted this evolution. To combat hereditary rights to power and privilege, which were such anathema to them, the bourgeoisie proclaimed the principle of popular sovereignty and the juridical equality of all men. This position was logically followed by the notion of universal suffrage, which is to say, a method of settling issues on the basis of numbers. Nineteenth-century liberals sought to restrain the development and offset its disadvantages. By various tactics (limited suffrage, unequal suffrage), they tried to prevent the establishment of universal suffrage, or to minimize its consequences. In capitalistic regimes, they have sought to mold public opinion and render the power of the majority ineffective, especially through the influence of money on information and news media.

THE STRENGTH OF NUMBERS: ORGANIZATION   Size by itself can be powerless as a political weapon. It is inseparable from techniques for collective action and organization, the only possible way of achieving political effectiveness. Hence the need for political organizations, principally parties and pressure groups, in modern nations.

The technique of collective organization outdates the introduction of the masses into political life, an event which made numbers a factor of great importance. Organizing techniques developed first among rather limited groups, but groups that were closely bound together. Certain secret societies, certain sects and religious orders, attained a high degree of organization, which gave them a degree of political power. There is, however, a tendency to exaggerate their power—the persistent legends about the influence of the Freemasons, for instance, or of the Jesuits. Still, there is no denying the strength of Freemasonry, Jesuits, and other similar institutions at certain periods in history, and their influence depended mainly on their organizational strength.

In our contemporary mass societies, some people dream of conquering political power by mechanisms of the same nature. This tendency is noticeable first of all in conservative circles, where secret organizations and conspiracies seem to be the only way of recovering an influence that has been progressively weakened by universal suffrage and the weight of numbers. We encounter the same tendency in the technological domain, where some scientists endeavor to apply to society itself methods which have proved successful in mastering the physical universe. The famous "synarchy," founded by Jean Coutrot of the *Ecole Polytechnique,* on the eve of World War II, is a good illustration of this tendency, even though his objectives have been distorted and his role greatly exaggerated.

By and large, the political power produced by collective organization is tied to the political power of numbers. Highly developed techniques of social organization, which have made it possible to group vast numbers of people, educate them politically, mobilize their energies, and channel and direct their actions, have created extremely effective instruments for political action. The techniques of forming "mass parties" and labor unions, invented toward the close of the last century, have served as models in this respect. They are still being used. The communist parties have perfected them; part of their strength is certainly due to the superiority of their system of organization. The fascist parties also achieved highly effective organizational methods. That such techniques present certain dangers cannot be denied: there is the possibility of "manipulating" the party members and the risk of developing an entrenched bureaucracy through the power of the government apparatus in dictatorships.

Sometimes collective organization nullifies the power of numbers, instead of making it effective. This is made clear by the technique known as "parallel hierarchies," developed especially by Asiatic communist regimes.

The method is to enclose each individual in a network of social ties and obligations, according to his various activities. As a worker, he is tied to his union; as a resident of a certain house, to a neighborhood or village association; as the head of a family, to the group for family protection; as a sportsman, to a football or cycling club; as a man interested in cultural pursuits, to a literary association, movie club, or theater group; and so on. Thus each association controls a bit of his activity, requires a portion of his time, and indoctrinates and educates him on some particular aspect of his life. Through these many different groups, the citizen is then dependent on the state in one way or another. He loses his own personal autonomy and becomes merely an element in the social structure; he has virtually no means of resisting this process. In theory, to be sure, membership in these organizations is voluntary, but anyone who does not belong is suspect—and that can be serious. Furthermore, a whole series of material benefits (such as food ration coupons, clothing, theater and movie tickets, and travel permits) can be obtained only through these associations, thus making membership a practical necessity.

This system of parallel hierarchies is clearly very effective. In authoritarian societies, it completes the work of government propaganda, as well as that of the police. The former tends to inculcate official doctrine in the minds of the membership, while the latter acts to eliminate any resistance on the part of individuals. But police repression is a crude, brutal process which provokes reactions. To tie each person into a network of parallel hierarchies is far more effective, in the last analysis: this control of each by the others, in a thousand different ways, accomplishes a surveillance that no police force could achieve. However, we must not exaggerate the effectiveness of this system. The organization of the various hierarchies is often more theoretical than real; people come to the meetings because they have to, but do not participate seriously. And sometimes, certain organizations may serve as a framework for the opposition.

In the large human communities, especially in modern states, the political battle is waged between organizations which are more or less specialists in this kind of combat and which, in a way, constitute political weapons. These organizations are structured, articulated, hierarchical groups, specially trained for the struggle for power. They express the interests and objectives of various social forces—classes, local groups, ethnic groups, and communities with special interests—for whom they are the means of political action. The organized nature of these social forces is a fundamental fact of contemporary political life. To be sure, there has always been a certain amount of organization of social forces intent on political action, but during the last hundred years, the techniques of collective organization and the methods of incorporating men into coordinated action groups have become highly perfected. The truly original feature in today's political struggle is not that it takes place between organizations, but that these organizations are so tightly developed.

We can classify political organizations into two main categories—political parties and pressure groups. The primary objective of parties is to acquire power or a share in the exercise of power; they seek to win seats at elections, to name deputies and ministers, and to take control of government. We may consider them simultaneously as causes of social antagonisms, because of their ideological nature, and as weapons of political combat, because of their function as a means of expressing these antagonisms (this observation is also valid for pressure groups, some of which are "horizontal groups," in the meaning previously given this term). Pressure groups, on the other hand, do not themselves seek to win power or participate in its exercise; their aim is to influence those who hold power, to bring "pressure" to bear on them: hence, their name.

Parties and pressure groups are not the only political organizations. Further on, we will discuss the clandestine movements that develop in authoritarian regimes where political struggles cannot take place openly (p. 206). Likewise, in these regimes, nonpolitical organizations can serve as a framework for political struggles, assuming thereby more or less the character of pressure groups. Newspapers and information media are also frequently organizations for political struggles. Finally, political parties generally develop auxiliary movements—women's groups, youth groups, sports clubs, artistic or cultural associations—which are also pressure groups. Conversely, certain pressure groups play an important role vis-à-vis political parties—the trade unions vis-à-vis the British Labour party, or managerial organizations vis-à-vis conservative parties.

The Information Media

We have said that the significance of numbers as a political weapon dates from the moment when the mass of the population attained a certain level of education and access to information. The media available for disseminating this knowledge and information are themselves political weapons, capable of being wielded by the state, by capitalistic organizations, or by popular parties and movements. In this sense, their strength is tied to that of power, money, or numbers, but they also have a force of their own.

The importance of information as a political weapon has always been recognized. The invention of printing had already proved to be a decisive factor in the development of the Renaissance, the Reformation, and the liberal movement which eventually culminated in the French Revolution. The advent of the press in the last century had a great influence on the spread of democracy—a phenomenon that impressed everyone. It was the press which was first described as the "Fourth Estate," to indicate its political importance. But nowadays the spoken press (radio broadcasts) and the visual press (television and illustrated weeklies) have as much influence as newspapers and the written press. They, too, belong to the Fourth Estate. It is now customary to call these various means of disseminating news and ideas that are the result of modern technology the "mass information media."

In authoritarian regimes, the information media are usually under state control, serving to disseminate the state's propaganda—its principal source of power, along with the police and the military. This propaganda tends to secure the population's unanimous support of the government. It is not oriented toward the class struggle or the social categories that comprise the nation, but toward the country's unification, at least ostensibly. It is not an organization in the political struggle, or at least that is the claim made by the state (in reality, the state is generally in the hands of one class or one social group, and it uses propaganda to destroy the influence of the others). It constitutes a means of social integration or of pseudointegration (we will examine this more closely in the next chapter).

In democratic regimes, on the other hand, not all of the information media are controlled by the state; many have the character of pressure groups. The pluralism of the media is an element in the pluralism of the regime, together with the pluralism of political parties. Moreover, pluralism in political parties would be illusory and merely formalistic if it were not accompanied by pluralism in the information media. However, we rarely find a democratic country in which the state does not control any of the information media, as in the United States. Almost everywhere, radio broadcasting is organized as a public service, at least in part. The same is true, if somewhat less so, of television. Only the written press is entirely independent of governmental control, though not altogether free from the pressures of special interest groups.

THE CAPITALISTIC INFORMATION SYSTEM   The influence of power upon the information media is not always injurious. Free enterprise, in this domain as elsewhere, should not be confused with genuine freedom.

The principal advantage of news reporting and editorial comment in a capitalistic system is its guarantee of a diversified presentation of news and views. Anyone who wishes to know the various arguments on a given issue is able to find them; he has only to buy several newspapers or to turn the knob on his radio or television set. From the pages of *L'Humanité* to those of *L'Aurore* and the *Parisien libéré,* a French citizen can learn each morning all the arguments presented by one side or the other, and by comparing them, he can form his own opinion. Each of these newspapers, like those in authoritarian countries, attempts to impose its point of view by using the same methods of misrepresentation and oversimplification. But their very coexistence prevents them from achieving their objective. Pluralism forces them to limit the number of untruths they can publish; when no one can raise a voice to contradict you and when it is impossible to discover the truth, it is easy to lie. It is much harder to do so when other voices can be heard and rectify the facts. It is very difficult to conceal the truth in an information system based on free enterprise and competition. Nevertheless, we must not exaggerate the range of diversity resulting from such a system; it is no easier to find a newspaper in the United States that defends communism than to find one in the Soviet Union that defends capitalism.

Free enterprise is not really freedom because, first, it is based upon money. Although legally anyone may publish a newspaper, in reality, one needs about $4 million to launch a daily in Paris. It is possible to write whatever one wishes in an existing newspaper, provided that the members of the publisher's staff, the owners of the enterprise, do not object. In a pluralistic regime, information media are free vis-à-vis the state, but not free when it comes to money. The power of information is in the hands of those who have economic power. To be sure, large political parties and powerful labor unions can raise the capital needed to start a newspaper, or even to establish a radio station, but experience shows that they have a very difficult time keeping such enterprises alive.

The domination of the information media by money today is less the result of the ownership of these enterprises than of the conditions of their exploitation. The mass media are made available to the public without charge (radio and television) or are sold to the public at less than their actual cost (newspapers). Every issue of a daily newspaper costs at least twice the price it is sold for; often the difference is much greater. The gap is covered by advertising. Advertising also finances radio and television programs, which thus depend heavily on the advertising agencies that sponsor them. These capitalistic businesses, whose customers are themselves capitalistic firms, are obviously not inclined to favor ideas opposed to capitalism; rather, they tend to direct the content of advertising toward conservatism.

But this phenomenon is relatively unimportant when compared with the essential fact that the information media are, above all, the mainstays of commercial advertising. Radio broadcasts, television shows, editorials, articles, and the news published in newspapers—all serve primarily to attract a maximum number of customers for the advertising, which constitutes the foundation of information enterprises; for the basic concern of capitalistic enterprises of the press, radio, and television, like all other private enterprises, is to make money. Capitalists sell newspapers or radio and television programs like they sell shoes or cheese. In order to make money, the problem here is to secure the greatest amount of publicity. To gain the maximum amount of publicity, one must reach the maximum number of readers, listeners, or television viewers. The editorial "sugar" that surrounds the advertising "pill" must therefore be designed to suit the taste of the greatest possible number of people. This produces a whole series of consequences.

THE RESULTS OF THE SYSTEM On the one hand, these information mechanisms in a capitalistic society are democratic, since they are tailored to the public's tastes. But democracy is predicated on the principle that each individual achieves a victory over himself, over his selfish instincts, his laziness, his apathy; it is founded on civic "virtue," as was so well perceived by Montesquieu and French revolutionist Saint-Just. On the contrary, the information media in capitalistic countries lower their sights; they do not tend to lift men up and educate them, but to keep them at the level of docile consumers.

This phenomenon is especially noticeable in the area of the press. The vast funds needed to publish a daily newspaper, and the increasing differential between its cost and selling price (covered by revenue from advertising) requires an enormous circulation to make the venture economically profitable. Consequently, there is a growing tendency for the press to fall under the control of a small handful of publishers. In most capitalistic countries, the number of newspapers is continually diminishing. In recent years this phenomenon has reached considerable proportions in Great Britain and has aroused public concern. But it is a general phenomenon. In France, for instance, the local press is almost completely monopolized by one or two large newspapers.

The consequences of this situation are obviously very serious. In the first place, the famous "pluralism," characteristic of democratic societies, disappears: diversity, a fundamental factor in the freedom of the press, tends to give way to monopoly, as in dictatorial regimes. The only difference is that this monopoly is maintained by huge capitalistic enterprises, rather than by the state. This does not solve matters, because these enterprises, which mold public opinion, have formidable means of bringing pressure upon those seeking or holding governmental offices. They can destroy the popularity of one politician or entirely create the popularity of another. Among the "pressure groups" we will examine in greater detail, the enormous journalistic empires occupy a very special place. Democracy is not strengthened by this trend implied by technological advances in the area of information.

The need exists each day to attract as many people as possible to the newsstand or to radio and television sets. A sensational news story sends circulation figures soaring and increases profits. Accordingly, the problem is to find something sensational to report each day. Thus news without genuine interest is given conspicuous attention, however inconsequential its picturesque aspects may be. If need be, trivial incidents are blown up out of proportion and given the prominence of front-page headlines, causing the papers to sell. This sociological law of the system results, first of all, in exaggerating the importance of crimes of passion, notorious love affairs, and scandals of one kind or another. In politics, it leads to dramatizing problems to interest the reader. Consequently, public animosity or public enthusiasm is artificially aroused in order to sell more newspapers.

The "personalization of power," a frequent topic of conversation in recent years, is partly the result of this process. The general public is not very interested in abstract ideas or doctrines, which hardly lend themselves to huge headlines and photographs. But everything is different if these ideas are embodied in an individual to whom one can assign the attributes of a hero. The theater and film industry have demonstrated the economic advantages to be gained from publicizing "stars," created by the modern advertising media. The system is also profitable when transferred to the political domain. The press, illustrated weeklies, radio, and television can, in the same manner, create political "heroes," largely mythical and contrived inventions, who are all the more pleasing to the public if it feels it is on familiar terms with them. But these "heroes" created by the news media naturally exploit their public image in their political struggles.

The basic rule for reaching the largest possible audience is not to offend anyone. The press, radio, and television seek to avoid, insofar as is humanly possible, topics that are controversial, important, or dangerous, for if they were to take a position on such matters, they would risk alienating part of their public and driving it away. If there is no possibility of avoiding such topics because of their centrality as public issues, they are then handled with the greatest precaution in an attempt to satisfy everyone, which is to say, the mass media avoid the heart of a problem by skirting it or touching on it only indirectly, thereby diverting public attention from it. Accordingly, the citizenry is treated as if it were composed of slightly retarded children, incapable of facing and coping with difficult problems. Instead of being prepared to assume their obligations as citizens, they are steered away from them.

However, if it seems that public opinion is moving in one direction or another, if it is undergoing a crisis, then it becomes profitable to fall in line and move forcefully in the same direction. The information media in a capitalistic society tend to lull the people in normal times —just when they should keep them alert—but the same media tend to excite the people as soon as they become aroused—just when they should calm them. The anticommunist hysteria in the United States in 1953 (at the time of McCarthyism), the widespread war fever in the fall of 1961, and the rush to construct private atomic shelters are just a few of the innumerable examples of this second attitude. The capitalistic information system thus plays a role exactly the opposite of that which it should play in the general interest.

Moreover, the defense of traditional values, established systems, and existing institutions is much more profitable, since it does not disturb anybody, than a critical or reformist attitude. People are naturally conservative; they are naturally afraid of novelty or change. If the theme of progress has to be dealt with often because it is a fashionable subject, then it must be treated as a remote, abstract proposition, vague enough not to upset people whose present situation might be threatened. It will be conceded that everything must change, without specifying what is to change. Existing abuses will not be attacked if such attacks shock the average man or if they contradict the interests of the speakers. Hence the search for the ordinary man's opinion leads to conservatism.

Although the modern mass information media could provide all men with the elements of a genuine culture, the capitalistic information system results in what we might call a "cretinizing" of the public. It tends to enclose people in a childish world of a very low intellectual level. Nothing is more interesting in this connection than the development of romantic tales, designed to furnish sensational news during otherwise uneventful periods, replacing the sea serpent of the heroic age. Kings, queens, princes, princesses, and other aristocrats of a bygone era, who survive in the modern world, furnish good subject matter with their resplendent clothes and paraphernalia and the surroundings in which they live, tied to vague recollections of historical events or of legends they revive. Moreover, the public relishes love stories. These romantic tales, which loom larger than life and border on the legendary, thrill the general public like fairy stories for grown-up children. Thus Princess Margaret, Farah Dibah, Soraya, Paola, and others are condemned to a life perpetually beset by fresh trials and tribulations, all of which provide a munificent income for the press, radio, and television.

We could mention many other techniques for cretinizing the public. Films and sports offer many examples of escapism. By these various methods, the public is plunged into an unreal and artificial atmosphere, one that is childish and fantastic. Thus the public is spared any confrontation with actual social problems. Communists say that these methods are intentional, that capitalists deliberately use "affairs of the heart," the stories of Princess Margaret, the adventures of sports and movies, to make the masses forget the exploitation they endure, to nullify their desire to revolt. Objectively speaking, the mass media in liberal regimes tend to achieve this result. Subjectively speaking, this situation does not appear to be the result of any deliberate or conscious effort on the part of those who control the media, but from the mechanism itself whose overriding purpose is to find customers.

POSSIBLE REMEDIES In a sense, the picture just presented seems worse than it actually is. It describes the natural tendencies of information media in a liberal regime, but these tendencies are more or less restrained by various obstacles that can be reinforced. The actual situation is less serious and could be improved in various ways.

One remedy consists in allowing both the capitalistic and socialistic information systems to exist side by side, each correcting the other in a reciprocal manner. In practice, the press in many Western states is organized along capitalistic lines, but radio and television are in the hands of the state or a public agency. No longer slaves to advertising and the profit motive, radio and television can serve an educational function and compensate for the stultifying effects of capitalistic news media. Moreover, the pluralism resulting from the presence of a free press does not permit them to indulge in propaganda of an authoritarian type.

It is also possible to introduce, within a state-controlled radio and television system, some new methods of pluralism that will acquaint the citizen with various opposing viewpoints. For capitalistic pluralism is, to a great extent, illusory. Few people buy several newspapers; most people read just one and therefore have only a partial view of things. But institutions such as the Panel of Parliamentary Journalists, as it formerly existed at the French broadcasting network (RTF), represented a genuine pluralism in the true spirit of democracy. The same is true of the allocation of equal time on radio and television to the various political parties during election campaigns.

In general, the coexistence of the two systems gives good results. In certain countries—Great Britain and Canada, for example—radio and television have undertaken a remarkable task in educating the citizenry, an effort that greatly strengthens democratic institutions. But abuses are always possible. Governments tend to utilize radio and television for their own propaganda purposes as in authoritarian states. In France, for example, although the general level of programming of the government's network remains superior to that of privately controlled radio and television (of the American type), it has been guilty of mediocrity and partiality in the political and social domains.

Lastly, in capitalistic societies we sometimes discover a few original institutions, few though they be, that tend to provide truly independent news and opinion, in other words, that are not mouthpieces of the state or of capitalistic interests. Certain institutions tend to respect and guarantee the personal independence of journalists and commentators. Some countries have what is known as the "clause of conscience," permitting a journalist to refuse to write what is asked of him and even to resign from the newspaper, with important indemnities provided. In practice, however, it is not always easy to invoke this clause, and promotion in the profession presupposes that it will not be invoked. However, some journalists succeed in making a name for themselves and are in public demand; their situation is then such that they can say virtually anything they want to. The case of Walter Lippmann in the United States is typical. There are others, but very few of them in any country.

Much more important is the situation of certain independent newspapers like *The Times* (of London) before 1967, *Le Monde* (Paris), and *The New York Times.* There are various explanations for their independence. Sometimes it is the result of a venerable tradition and reputation (as with *The Times* of London). For *Le Monde,* it was the result of a provisional status granted in 1944. All newspapers published during the German occupation were seized and the enterprises were handed over to groups of independent journalists. One by one, the new journals succumbed for financial reasons, except for *Le Monde,* which never had a deficit. On the contrary, regular profits enabled the newspaper to compensate its former owners. The independent spirit of the news staff established in 1944, and expanded since then, has not suffered any setbacks; a tradition was created and a spirit developed, with the considerable assistance of a strong-willed, respected, and uncompromising director.

Newspapers like *The Times* and *Le Monde* now seem to have a firmly established basis for independence. The character of their readership gives them a special status vis-à-vis advertising (however, the fact that *The Times* lost its independence in 1967, falling into the hands of a newspaper chain, shows that such papers remain vulnerable). For other newspapers, an ever larger circulation is needed to keep the enterprise economically viable; hence the increasing number of mergers. The newspapers of the "elite," on the other hand, can demand higher advertising rates because of the quality of their clientele. Every influential group or individual in France, all cadres of the nation, read *Le Monde.* Accordingly, advertisers need *Le Monde.* It can live by itself. But the independence of elite newspapers does not extend to those published for the masses. Is freedom of the press thus reserved only for a limited few? And the elite papers themselves risk losing their independence, as did *The Times.*

The organization of radio and television as public agencies, autonomous with respect to the state, and operated by an administrative council consisting of representatives from the field of journalism, from the public at large, and including a panel of independent members, appears to be a very effective way of handling this problem. The English BBC is organized along such lines, and its independence is quite remarkable. The question of adopting a similar statute in France was under discussion for a long time, and certain specific proposals were advanced, but neither the government nor the parliament ever enacted them into law. The creation of the *Office Radiodiffusion-Télévision Française* was only a timid step in that direction, and it does not enjoy the independence of the BBC. We can, however, speculate whether it may not point the way to organize truly free and independent information media, including even the press. Perhaps the French statute pertaining to newspapers, established in 1944, will one day appear as the forerunner of such an arrangement.

INFORMATION IN AUTHORITARIAN REGIMES   In authoritarian regimes, the information media tend to be state monopolies that are used for government propaganda. The result is the dissemination of a generalized lie, but occasionally there is also a certain level of cultural content.

A lie becomes effective when repeated over and over again. Doubtlessly, people do not believe all the propaganda they receive from their newspapers, radio, and television, as is evidenced by the little anecdotes that circulate by word of mouth in authoritarian societies. The critical spirit of man can never be totally destroyed. Moreover, the boredom generated by the mass news media in authoritarian regimes is self-defeating. During the first four years of the Nazi regime, newspaper circulation dropped considerably. In 1934, Goebbels himself asked the newspaper publishers to try to make their papers more interesting, but the very rules imposed by the Propaganda Ministry precluded any such possibility. In the Soviet Union, there are periodic outcries against the drab content and the heavy-handed, monotonous quality of the press, but these defects are inherent in the system.

Yet, despite the persistence of a certain critical spirit among the citizenry and despite the boring effect of government propaganda, authoritarian regimes do, in some measure, achieve their objective. Deprived of any opportunity for comparison and subjected day after day to the same pronouncements, people gradually come to believe them—or at least to believe a great many of them. William L. Shirer, author of *The Rise and Fall of The Third Reich* (1960), the best work yet to appear on National Socialism, and a journalist who lived for a number of years in Nazi Germany, has given valuable testimony on this point: "No one who has not lived for years in a totalitarian land can possibly conceive how difficult it is to escape the dread consequences of a regime's calculated and incessant propaganda. Often in a German home or office or sometimes in a casual conversation with a stranger in a restaurant, a beer hall, a café, I would meet with the most outlandish assertions from seemingly educated and intelligent persons. It was obvious that they were parroting some piece of nonsense they had heard on the radio or read in the newspapers. Sometimes one was tempted to say as much, but on such occasions one was met with such a stare of incredulity, such a shock of silence, as if one had blasphemed the Almighty, that one realized how useless it was even to try to make contact with a mind which had become warped and for whom the facts of life had become what Hitler and Goebbels, with their cynical disregard for the truth, said they were." However, in time this gullibility wears off. We must not forget that Nazism lasted only twelve years in Germany, six of which were not war years. The example of the USSR and the European people's democracies shows that the critical spirit tends to recover after a period of eclipse. It is also true that in these countries, the controlled information media have developed a certain level of culture.

The information media in authoritarian regimes have, nevertheless, a few positive virtues. They have sometimes been praised for their discretion in reporting crimes, sensational news items, the amours of stage and screen stars, and so forth. This is no doubt commendable, but when they feature incidents of political violence in huge black headlines or indulge in vituperative attacks on the opposition in a sensational manner—as they so often do—then their progress is debatable. A grisly crime story or an account of the lastest flirtation of a film actress is less objectionable than the complacent reporting of the pilfering of Jewish-owned shops by a band of Nazi hoodlums. However, one cannot deny the laudable effort of certain authoritarian regimes to divert public attention from the superficial, from the cheap and tawdry, from false values, and to direct it to serious subjects, such as the family, the community, work, and art. The edifying aspect, the pious rhetoric of Soviet prose and its counterparts in the people's democracies, can be exasperating. But its human value is certainly superior to that of the sensational press or the romantic and sentimental journalism so prevalent in the mass media of liberal societies.

Moreover, communist propaganda eventually imbues the masses with the rudiments of a genuine culture by presenting all problems in terms of a general system that offers a coherent explanation of life and the world. For culture does not consist in the accumulation of countless thousands of bits and pieces of information, unrelated to each other and tossed at random into the minds of readers and viewers. A pile of rocks is not a building. People in liberal societies receive far more information than those in communist countries, and information that is far more accurate—but they are like so many rock piles. The citizens in communist states receive far less information, and information that is far less accurate, but it is coordinated, situated in a frame of reference in which each item has its place. As a result, the average Soviet citizen can retain more information than the average American, and his vision of the universe is more coherent, less disconnected.

However, this kind of cultural diffusion is not found in all authoritarian regimes. The advantage communist states have in this respect is that their basic doctrine, Marxism, is a highly developed, very comprehensive, and also modern conception of the world—in other words, it corresponds to contemporary problems. Even if it is inaccurate in many areas, it nevertheless constitutes an instrument of observation and comprehension that is carefully worked out and adapted to the world today. Fascist regimes, on the other hand, utilize a much more primitive doctrine, one that is far less complete, poorer, much less suited to the twentieth century—and, above all, a doctrine that is much more inaccurate. The culture it disseminates tends to be sketchy, superficial, and outmoded, characteristics that are even more noticeable in paternalistic dictatorships of the Spanish and Portuguese type.

POLITICAL STRATEGIES

In political battles, as in all complex battles, everyone acts according to a preconceived, more or less elaborate plan in which one anticipates not only his own attacks but also the opponent's responses and the means of coping with them. This battle plan constitutes a strategy; the different elements that go into it—actions against the opponent and responses to his reactions—constitute the tactics. The analysis of political strategies still remains rather sketchy, except in the areas of international relations and labor-union conflicts. Elsewhere, the studies have dealt chiefly with battles accompanying particular decisions. In recent years, some scholars have tried to apply mathematical methods to their analysis, using the theories of "games of strategy" and the techniques of operational calculus. Research of this kind is interesting and valuable in limited areas. We will consider here another point of view —that of strategies covering the whole of the political struggle. On this global plane, only a few general outlines can be given.

The Concentration or Dispersion of Political Weapons

Our previous analyses have shown that political weapons are sometimes concentrated and sometimes dispersed. This does not always reflect a deliberate strategic choice, but rather a situation produced by the social structures, which is imposed by practical necessity. The dispersion or concentration of arms can, therefore, result from strategies imposed by the facts.

THE TWO TYPES OF SOCIETIES   We may define two types of political societies from the standpoint of the distribution of political weapons—societies with a concentration of arms and societies with a dispersion of arms.

In societies with a concentration of arms all political weapons, or at least the principal ones, are held by a single class or social group. In societies with a dispersion of arms, the primary weapons are distributed among several classes or social categories. In feudal and monarchical societies, for example, the principal weapons of the day—military weapons and the wealth of land ownership—were concentrated in the hands of the aristocracy. In France, during the monarchy of Louis-Philippe or the Second Empire, and in the United States before 1939, the bourgeoisie held the principal means of power—money and military organization, with the latter being used mainly to put down workers' uprisings (the silk weavers of Lyons, the insurrections of June 1848, the Commune of 1871). In Stalin's Russia, the ruling group controlled all mass organizations, all collective structures, all the basic political weapons in a socialist society. These are only a few examples of monopolistic situations.

On the other hand, in certain cities of the ancient world at some point in their evolution, in the Italian and Flemish republics of the Renaissance, in Cromwell's England, and in France under the absolute monarchy, the aristocracy controlled part of the wealth, the bourgeoisie another part (sometimes the larger), and military weapons generally remained in the hands of the former, passing sometimes to the hands of the latter: these were societies with a dispersion of political weapons, examples of a pluralistic situation. Today's Western societies provide another example. On the one hand, capitalists possess the wealth, which they use for propaganda purposes, thus holding very important elements of political power in their hands. On the other hand, salaried workers have developed organizations with mass membership (popular parties and labor unions, for example), which also have the opportunity to use various kinds of propaganda, and which likewise constitute important elements of political power. Other means of propaganda and information are in the hands of intellectuals and the college and university communities. Consequently, political weapons are fairly well dispersed.

THE DISPERSION OF POLITICAL WEAPONS AND DEMOCRACY   In the West, there is a tendency to believe that the dispersion of political weapons results in a pluralism that provides one of the most effective ways of ensuring freedom for everyone and of achieving democracy.

The dispersion (or concentration) of political weapons is more or less confused with the multiplicity (or unity) of "decision-making centers"—an erroneous view. The pluralism or unity of decision-making centers is a matter that concerns the organization of the state, the structure of political power. Pluralism is achieved by the separation of powers (a concept dear to Locke, Montesquieu, and several others), by territorial or regional decentralization, by the autonomy of public services and enterprises, and by the establishment of independent bodies of governing officials. The dispersion or concentration of political weapons concerns the struggle for power, as well as the situation of the various social groups or classes involved in this struggle. Of course, the two phenomena are often closely associated: a pluralism of decision-making centers sometimes reflects a dispersion of political weapons, which results in a division of the state among the different social classes or categories. But they remain rather independent of one another. A pluralism of decision-making centers can exist, for example, in a socialist regime, notably through decentralization, quite apart from any dispersion of political weapons (for example, Yugoslavia).

Concerning the dispersion of political weapons, pluralistic theories can be accepted only with reservations. In the first place, the pluralism of liberal democracies in this matter remains very uneven. To be sure, money is no longer the only weapon nowadays. Political parties, labor unions, and other organizations with mass membership wield power, sometimes a great deal of power, but they do not counterbalance the influence of wealth. In contemporary Western societies, money remains the strongest political weapon. This means that, on the whole, basic decisions are taken under the influence of people who possess or control money. Of course, other elements of political power force some less important decisions to be made and others to be modified. At certain times, these other elements may be in a position to impose a critical decision, but this situation is very unusual. Normally, Western societies are dominated by money, and other political weapons are much weaker. However, the disparity varies according to the country: it is very large in the United States, less so in France. And to a certain extent it is tending to diminish.

Moreover, the dispersion of political weapons does not always result in the strengthening of democracy. It can also lead to dictatorship. If a hitherto dominant social class feels itself divested of a portion of its political power by another group, it may resort to violence to avoid being driven from power or being obliged to share it. The rising class may also resort to the same tactics to hasten the elimination of the declining dominant class. The great waves of dictatorships in history have generally corresponded to these situations of equilibrium, in which the political weapons are divided between rival social groups. So it was in the cities of the ancient world, in Europe during the Renaissance and the eighteenth century, and again in the nineteenth century, when the rising bourgeoisie divided power with the aristocracies which had ruled until that time. Likewise, when the domination of money appeared to be seriously threatened in the center of Western "pluralism," we witnessed the rise of fascism. The balance of power between rival social forces and the dispersion of political weapons is less important than the reduction of social antagonisms in fostering the development of democracy.

The Open Struggle and the Clandestine Struggle

The distinction between the open and the clandestine struggle is a basic one, corresponding to the two major types of political regimes. In a democracy, the political struggle occurs openly, in full view of the public; in autocratic regimes, it has to be masked or concealed. This correlation is fairly accurate, unlike the one that some have tried to establish between democracy and a dispersion of political weapons.

DEMOCRACIES AND THE OPEN STRUGGLE Political conflict in democracies has an official character that is acknowledged and recognized. It is most intense during election campaigns, but continues in the intervals between elections.

In democracies, political battles acquire a cyclical character. General elections, at regular and fixed intervals, have the effect of turning the state as a whole into a political battleground, with the fate of the state dependent upon the outcome. All the coercive measures of power, the whole apparatus for forcing compliance, are thus relinquished by the vanquished and transferred to the hands of the victor until such time as the latter, defeated in his turn, transmits them to a new victor. General elections therefore quite naturally become the decisive moment of battle. Political struggles occur according to a rhythmic pattern, passing through a phase of intense activity every four or five years, which subsides in the intervening period. Dictatorial regimes, on the other hand, never experience these systolic and diastolic movements, this regular ebb and flow of the political pulse. There is continual plotting and scheming, with various factions falling in and out of favor, but any popular waves of political fervor occur only under fortuitous circumstances.

Outside the general elections, political struggles in democracies preserve the same open and continuous character. In parliamentary debates, in the polemics of the press, in meetings and discussions, in demonstrations by parties, unions, and various organizations, the battle goes on in full view of everyone. Of course, this openness is not absolute. Even in democracies, a certain amount of politics takes place behind closed doors, in an atmosphere of secrecy or discreet privacy. For example, it is difficult, if not impossible, to learn all the facts about the financing of campaigns or the intervention of certain private interests in government and administration. The activities of certain pressure groups are discreet, if not secret, but shadowy dealings are limited. In an authoritarian regime, on the other hand, secrecy is everywhere. Debates, polemics, discussions, and 'demonstrations are generally forbidden. Officially, public opinion is unanimous in its admiration, love, and loyalty to the government. The nation is united and contains no dissident factions. To disturb this unity, or to create factions, is an offense punishable by law. In practice, however, unanimity and unity are more apparent than real. Political struggles occur, but they are concealed or camouflaged.

AUTOCRACIES AND THE HIDDEN STRUGGLE   To judge from appearances, democracies are more divided than autocracies. In reality, their divisions are more visible only because democracies allow them to be expressed, and even encourage such expression. The divisions within autocracies are perhaps deeper and more serious, not unlike repressed psychological conflicts which poison the individual personality and plunge it into neuroses. In autocracies, the political struggles are either camouflaged or clandestine.

Camouflage in political struggles assumes many different forms. Even state agencies and institutions can become the spokesmen for certain groups or classes. Every administration, organization, or corporation has a tendency to defend its point of view against the others. Hence there is a natural rivalry between ministerial departments, administrative bodies, and so forth. This technical rivalry can turn into a political struggle if a certain institution identifies itself with another social force. In authoritarian regimes, we sometimes see the labor unions (a single organization) opposing the political party (the state's only party), thereby turning these two instruments of unanimity into instruments of diversity. Universities, the army, and certain administrative agencies can also become channels of opposition.

Moreover, political conflicts are usually concealed behind nonpolitical conflicts that are tolerated in certain sectors of society. In the Soviet Union, the struggle between classicists and modernists in literature, painting, and music is now actually a struggle between Stalinists and advocates of "liberalization." Nonpolitical organizations can thus become in effect political organizations. Student associations, youth movements, even sports clubs (the Czech sokols before 1914) have played such a role in many authoritarian countries. The farther removed their official function is from political issues, the less likely they are to arouse the government's suspicion. Three types of organizations that are closer to politics are, consequently, more dangerous—churches and philosophical or ethical societies, organizations of an economic or social nature, and literary institutions (since the human conflicts analyzed in literature are inseparable from social and political conflicts).

One must not confuse these camouflaged struggles, in which political objectives are concealed behind nonpolitical objectives, with the technique of deliberate political camouflage, so widely used in the open conflicts of democracies. The latter consists of concealing one political objective behind another that is broader, less partisan, and nobler than the first, and consequently more likely to win popular support. Every class, every social group that is actually fighting for its own special interests, claims to be fighting in some measure for the common interest—for the nation, for justice, for truth. It thus strengthens its position by sowing seeds of doubt among its opponents. This kind of camouflage presupposes an open political struggle, where power is acknowledged to be the prize at stake. The other type of camouflage masks political objectives behind nonpolitical objectives because the struggle for political objectives is forbidden.

In democracies, conservative parties often succeed in giving "politics" a bad name, which results in political struggles being disguised behind nonpolitical façades. Many organizations affiliated with political parties—youth groups, women's clubs, literary, artistic, and athletic associations—thus hide under a nonpolitical guise. Many pressure groups, actually pursuing political goals, pretend to have only economic, social, or corporate objectives. Hence there is no clear-cut distinction between the two kinds of camouflage. The fact remains that, in a democracy, both kinds are possible because political struggles are openly recognized and authorized. In autocratic regimes, on the other hand, only one type of camouflage is possible—the concealment of political objectives beneath seemingly nonpolitical objectives —since open political conflict is not tolerated.

Moreover, this kind of camouflage can occur only in relatively liberal autocratic regimes. In dictatorial and totalitarian regimes, camouflaged struggles have only a superficial character. They reflect a diversity of cliques and factions within classes and ruling groups, rather than bona fide opposition to political power. Genuine political struggles can only take place in secret, through clandestine organization. The resistance of democratic Germans to Hitler's regime and especially the resistance of people in occupied European countries to his armies between 1940 and 1945 provide good examples of this situation. They may be compared with the underground nationalist movements which have triggered revolts against colonial powers in recent years, and also with the secret societies that sparked struggles for independence in Europe in the nineteenth and early twentieth centuries.

In every authoritarian regime, there is a natural tendency for such clandestine groups to arise. But they can develop effectively only if two conditions exist. First, the regime must be considered intolerable by a large portion of the population. Mass support is indispensable for clandestine action; without it, secret organizations can do nothing but commit a few acts of violence without achieving any lasting results. Second, there must be a plausible chance, a reasonable hope, of being able to overthrow the government. If the regime appears to be solidly entrenched, only a few diehards will have the courage to carry out clandestine activities. The masses will support them only if they perceive a real possibility of success. These factors explain the development of underground movements during World War II and the rise of nationalist organizations among colonial peoples after 1945. They also account for the ineffectiveness of anti-Nazi movements in Hitler's Germany before 1944, the failure of OAS terrorism in France in 1962, and the limited effect of Quebec nationalists in Canada today. In the last two cases, the clandestine struggle has occurred in a democratic regime where the opposition has other means of expression. It therefore generally represents small minorities, without much influence, who have little hope of winning representation by electoral or parliamentary methods. Such is the case unless we are dealing with outlawed groups or parties deprived of any legal means of action; if a ban is placed upon an influential organization, such a ban constitutes a restriction on the democratic process.

Clandestine movements are distinguished from all other organizations both by their methods of action and by their structures. In addition to secret meetings, the spreading of rumors by word of mouth, undercover propaganda, and the distribution of anonymously published tracts and brochures, they generally engage in acts of violence, such as secret plots, assassination attempts, terrorism, and infiltration of the government. The demands of secrecy force them into the same type of organization used by all clandestine movements: the Christian church in the catacombs, oriental secret societies, the Carbonari in nineteenth-century Italy, the Serbian Black Hand before 1914, the Croatian Ustachi of 1930, the European resistance movements of 1940–45, and the French OAS of 1961. They are always characterized by a fragmentation of the basic groups. Only the leader of each group, at each organizational level, is in contact with the higher echelon. In this way, information leaks are kept to a minimum. If one member of the organization is arrested and tortured, he can implicate only a few people; the same is true of any informers planted in the movement by the police.

Struggles Within the Regime and Struggles for Control of the Regime

Even in democracies, the open political struggle remains limited. A basic distinction in this connection must be made between struggles *within* and struggles *over* the regime. This not only defines the forms of the struggle, but its limits as well. From this standpoint, it is especially relevant to the study of social antagonisms and social integration.

THE DISTINCTION BETWEEN THE STRUGGLE WITHIN THE REGIME AND THE STRUGGLE OVER THE REGIME   In a way, it resembles the distinction between a game played according to the rules, and a contest that is waged against the rules in order to establish new rules. It is closely related to notions of legitimacy and consensus.

The best way to grasp the distinction between struggles within the regime and struggles over the regime is to look at some examples. In Great Britain, Scandinavia, and the Netherlands, all parties accept the existing political regime, based upon a liberal parliamentary democracy; no party challenges the regime itself: the political struggle takes place *within* the regime. In France and Italy, on the other hand, small fascist groups on the extreme right and a large communist party on the extreme left reject the parliamentary system and democratic pluralism: their political struggle is also directed *against* the regime. In the first instance, the political struggle consists of each party's attempt to secure power and then exercise it in the interest of the social groups and classes it represents, all the while maintaining the existing institutions and the established rules of political competition. Accordingly, these rules and institutions are almost unanimously accepted. In the second case, certain parties hold that the interest of the classes and groups they represent cannot be satisfied within the framework of these institutions; they believe that the established rules of the contest are biased, that they favor their opponents and discriminate against themselves. Consequently, they want to establish other rules and create different institutions.

The distinction between a struggle over the regime and a struggle within the regime is linked to the concept of legitimacy. Conflicts remain within the governmental framework if a majority of the citizens regard the government as legitimate, if there is a consensus on this point. The struggle becomes one over the government itself if this consensus falls apart, if only certain classes, groups, or parties regard the existing regime as legitimate, whereas the others favor another form of legitimacy. Consequently,· the struggle within the regime and the struggle over the regime are not alternate strategies one may choose between under normal circumstances. Each is dictated by the prevailing situation. If the political consensus is deeply divided, then a revolutionary situation produces a struggle over the regime. Conflicts cannot be contained within the governmental framework unless there is consensus on its legitimacy. A choice is possible only in intermediate situations—when the consensus is in danger of falling apart but has not yet been irreparably destroyed, or when it is in the process of being reestablished but is still vulnerable and under attack. Only then do the parties have a choice between accepting or challenging the rules of the governmental system.

We must distinguish between appearances and reality in our study of struggles over governmental regimes, and especially take note of the disparity between the evolution of events and of the image people form of these events. As they grow older, revolutionary parties tend to become integrated into the existing social order, particularly when it moves in their direction; instead of being opponents of the regime, they become opponents within the regime. But they try to conceal this transformation from their party militants as long as possible, since the idea of revolution generally carries more prestige than the idea of reform (especially in France). Their opponents assist in this dissimulation, since it allows them to indulge in the scare tactics so effective in winning conservative votes. The socialists, who were revolutionary in 1900, began to integrate with the system after 1920, but they did not admit it until after 1945.

The communist parties in France and Italy are moving in the same direction. Most of their members no longer seek the establishment of people's democracies. They have become part of the Western pluralistic political system and do not wish to see it abolished. Among the militant minority, the evolution is less advanced, but it has accelerated noticeably in the past few years. Many have become dedicated to civil rights, to freedom of expression and diversity of opinion—in short, to liberal democracy. They are looking for a way to establish pluralistic socialism, which would eliminate capitalism without destroying political liberalism. Although aware that a revolution is no longer possible in highly developed societies, they still refuse to admit this publicly and, in fact, do not always admit it to themselves. But the change in their outlook is no less fundamental. As always, the evolution of party rhetoric and declared principles lags behind the evolution of the facts and the attitudes of party members. They want to appear revolutionary long after they have ceased being so. In present-day France and Italy, the role of the communist parties outwardly remains one of opposition *to* the liberal democratic regime; in reality, it has become increasingly one of opposition *within* the regime.

THE FORMS OF STRUGGLE OVER THE REGIME   The struggle over a regime can assume two very different forms, depending on whether it concerns only the ends to be achieved or also the means to be used in reaching these ends.

The struggle over a regime always means that a portion of the citizenry does not accept existing institutions and is fighting to replace them with other institutions. The objectives of the struggle are necessarily revolutionary. But to accomplish the desired overthrow, one may either reject the rules of the game established by the existing regime and fight it with violence and illegal actions or, on the other hand, one may follow the established rules to secure power, and then use them to overturn the existing order and replace it with another. This second attitude more or less corresponds to the attitude of the communist parties in France and Italy in recent years. They had renounced illegality and violence in the pursuit of power and accepted the rules of liberal democracy to achieve their goals. But had they succeeded in taking power within the framework of the existing system, they would have used it to destroy the system completely.

In dictatorships, the preceding distinction has no relevance. A struggle over the regime is simply not tolerated. Political conflicts can occur only among people who do not challenge the existing institutions, for these can only be opposed by illegal methods and violence. In democracies, the situation is different. The very nature of democracy—and the source of its greatness—is that it permits its opponents to express their views. Consequently, it opens the way to a struggle over the regime itself. This brings up a fundamental question: can democracy defend itself against its enemies? In giving freedom to its enemies, is it enabling them to destroy freedom? Is democracy condemned, by its very principles, not to defend itself against those who seek its destruction? On at least one point, the answer is simple. Democracy allows its adversaries freedom of expression when they exercise this privilege within the framework of democratic processes. Respect for the other person's opinion does not mean that one must allow this opinion to impose itself by force. Democracy has the right (and the duty) to outlaw and destroy political parties or organizations that seek to overthrow it by violence.

If, on the contrary, opponents of the regime agree to play according to democratic rules, if they fight within the framework of democratic institutions, then democratic principles require that they be allowed to express themselves; under these conditions, a struggle over the regime is possible. But it is possible only up to a certain point—a point that no longer depends upon theories, but upon the existing balance of power. If a communist party, acting within the framework of legality, wins only 5 percent or 10 percent of the votes in an election, there is no problem; democracy can function smoothly despite this opposition to the regime. If it gains 20 percent to 30 percent of the electorate (and providing this is a stable rather than a temporary percentage), certain precautions must be taken: communists must be eliminated from positions of authority and only allowed to participate in government departments or agencies not considered vital to national security. In this manner, the regime can function without too much difficulty, as the French and Italian governments have demonstrated since 1948.

But if in a liberal democracy a communist party (still revolutionary in pursuit of its goals) approached 50 percent of the vote, which would confer an absolute majority and complete control of governmental power, the situation would be very different. Under these conditions, to allow the party to function within the framework of the regime would be tantamount to condemning the regime to an early death. But at the same time, outlawing the party would also destroy democracy. For if a powerful communist party is to be suppressed, it cannot be allowed to reform itself through the trade unions, through parallel organizations, through other parties of the left. In short, banning the party would necessitate an immense program of repression and intimidation against half the nation's population, which only a dictatorship could accomplish. If a revolutionary communist party acquires 50 percent of the votes in a liberal democracy, that simply means that conditions within the country are no longer conducive to liberal democracy and there is no choice left but a dictatorship of the right or one of the left.

Strategies of the Two Blocs and Centrist Strategies

The political struggle in a two-party system is different from that in a multiparty system. In the first, it assumes the form of a duel; in the second, a number of adversaries confront each other and form various coalitions. The political distinction between right and left enables us to compare the two situations and to establish a fairly accurate classification of political strategies in pluralistic democracies.

RIGHT AND LEFT, REFORMISM AND REVOLUTION Reduced to its simplest terms, to its basic element, the political struggle is made up of those who are relatively satisfied with the existing social order and wish to preserve it and those who dislike the social order and wish to change it. The former comprise the political "right" and the latter, the "left," in the broadest sense of these terms, deliberately disregarding any precise historical context. At this point, we are not considering motives, the reasons for the satisfaction of some and the dissatisfaction of others, or the forms of their expression. We simply submit that in any social group, in any human community, there are those who are satisfied and those who are not. Moreover, this premise is not an arbitrary one, but a fact of experience. The right and the left are thus defined by their objectives: to preserve the existing order of things or to replace it. But one can try to achieve either of these objectives by employing different means and methods, each of which constitutes a particular type of strategy.

The distinction between revolutionaries and reformists of the left has long been recognized in the parties of the left. The overthrow of the existing order brutally, completely, in a single operation, and the substitution of the new social order, all at once, also brutally—this is the revolutionary method. The destruction of the existing order progressively, piece by piece, replacing each item, as eliminated, with an element of the new order—this is reformism. At the beginning of this century, many violent arguments took place in the socialist parties between reformists and revolutionaries. On the other hand, when the communist parties were all revolutionary, the problem never arose. It is now beginning to appear in Western communism in societies where revolution seems neither possible nor desirable. The question will probably acquire greater importance in the years ahead.

The debate between reformists and revolutionaries is usually distorted by strong feelings and passions. Since revolution was generally the old dream of French socialists and communists, reformism seems like a form of treason to them. On the national level, the proponents of revolution declare that reformism is an illusion, because it will never be possible to destroy the old order piecemeal. By this method, they argue, one can only modify matters of secondary importance; as soon as the essential is threatened, the defenders of the existing order will react with violence, and since they hold the positions of strength within the system, they will inevitably triumph. We are not taking any position in this debate. Suffice it to say that the two strategies—that of reformism and that of revolution—can be employed, at least in theory, to change the existing social order, and that certain parties have subscribed to the former, while others prefer the latter.

Two parallel attitudes on the right—moderate and ultraconservatism—reformism and revolution on the left. The distinction is less well known, has seldom been clearly formulated, and has engendered fewer debates. But it is equally important from a practical point of view, perhaps even more important, because it has definitely inspired the actions of many conservative parties. In maintaining the existing social order, one may defend it in its entirety by refusing to change anything, by opposing all reforms, even the slightest modifications. On the other hand, considering that certain changes cannot be prevented, one can yield on certain minor points in order to preserve the essential—to prevent the fire from spreading, as it were. The first attitude corresponds on the right to the revolutionary strategy on the left: it is the position of the ultraconservatives and fascists. The second attitude corresponds to the reformist strategy on the left. It is characteristic of moderate conservatives. The best example of it is the politics of Disraeli in nineteenth-century England.

THE TWO FORMS OF "CENTRISM"   The foregoing analysis leads us to separate the dualistic opposition of the right and the left into four basic types of political strategy, defined both by their ends and by their means—the extreme right, the moderate right, the reformist left, and the revolutionary left. The confrontations and alliances among these basic tendencies do not occur in the same way in all countries and periods of history. Two basic situations are discernible—the English type and the French type.

In Great Britain, the moderates and extremists of each tendency have generally united within a common organization, one on the right, the other on the left: the Conservative party and the Liberal party in the nineteenth century; the Conservative party and the Labour party in the twentieth century. The political struggle has thus been dominated by the strategy of "the right against the left," or what is known in France as the struggle between two blocs. Contrary to what one might expect, political antagonisms have been weakened, not intensified. Actually, the strategy of the two blocs is a form of centrism, since each of the blocs is forced to orient its politics toward the center.

Within each tendency, the extremists have had to accept the domination of the moderates, whether they wanted to or not. In a contest between two political parties, electoral victory normally goes to the party that attracts the marginal voters of the center, whose votes can tip the scales one way or the other. In order to win, each party must appear moderate, the reformists prevailing over the revolutionaries on the left, and the "evolutionists" over the ultraconservatives on the right. The permanent, regular, organic tie linking the extremists and moderates in each camp prompts the former to soften their extremism, so to speak, through contact with the moderates, whereas isolation would lead them to harden their position. Also, the fact that they are associated with governmental and parliamentary responsibilities, at least indirectly, within the framework of a great party moves them in the same direction. Hence the coalescence of political tendencies into two opposing blocs—one on the right, the other on the left—results in pushing them both toward the center.

In France, the political tradition is quite different, whatever one may say of it. The rather widespread notion that French political life has been dominated since 1789 by a struggle between the right and the left does not correspond exactly to the facts. The right, strictly speaking—extremists and moderates united—has rarely governed (from 1814 to 1830, with interruptions; in 1871; in 1919; and in 1940). The left, defined in the same manner, has held power even less often (from 1793 to 1794, from February to May in 1848, from 1936 to 1937, and from 1944 to 1947). Most of the time, the government has been in the hands of centrist coalitions, uniting the reform-minded leftists and the moderate rightists against the extremes—the ultraconservatives and the revolutionary left—who are forced into a defensive position or reduced periodically to a supporting role. The real battle is waged between the two centers for domination within the coalition. The pendulum does not really swing from right to left, but only from right center to left center. Accordingly, the political struggle is controlled by a centrist strategy.

The coalition of moderate conservatives and reformists of the left has a natural basis. They have a common ground for understanding; both are willing to accept reforms. For conservatives, it is a regrettable but necessary stance to stave off disaster, and reforms must be limited. For the moderates on the left, reforms are seen as desirable and must be extended. Final objectives and ulterior motives are different, but on the plane of practical politics, there is room for a certain amount of collaboration. They can "travel a while together." Having said that, each one within the centrist alliance tries to secure the strongest possible position, which leads to some degree of dependency upon the extreme wing of the party corresponding to one's political tendency. The ties between the reformist left and the revolutionary left are never completely severed, because the former seeks the support of the latter in order to dominate the centrist coalition; the leftist bloc before 1914 roughly corresponded to this situation. Likewise, the moderate right always retains contact with the far right for the same reason; this was reflected in the National Union or the "enlarged coalition" of the Third Republic in France.

Reduced to an occasional supporting role, deprived of any real influence over the government, and isolated within separate organizations, extremist parties in France are naturally inclined to intensify their extremism. Their members also have a sense of alienation that neither the left wing of the Labour party nor the ultraconservatives experience in Great Britain. In addition, the daily, down-to-earth, pragmatic side of centrist politics, which is unrelated to any fixed principles—because the principles of the two halves of the center are different—inspires feelings of disdain and dismay among extremists. They thus tend to draw a sharp line between a political ideology, pure and unapplied, and real politics, which consists less in making political compromises than in compromising one's own principles. To oppose this state of affairs, the two extremes have only one means at their disposal—the formation of a coalition against the centrist alliance. Besides, the support they are asked to give to incline the centrist alliance one way or the other compromises their principles without giving them any real influence over the political structure. But this coalition between the revolutionary left and the ultraconservative right can only be negative. It can prevent the center from governing, but cannot replace it. If the extremes, by themselves, become stronger than the centrists, and if they unite, then government of any kind becomes impossible. This was the case during the last years of the Weimar Republic, and, to a lesser degree, during the Fourth Republic of France in 1958.

Camouflage

Reformism and revolution, centrism and extremism—these strategies are applicable only in pluralistic democracies. On the other hand, one strategic device is utilized in every kind of political regime, even in unitarian and authoritarian states. As previously mentioned, it consists in concealing the true aims and motives of political action behind pseudoaims and pseudomotives that are more popular and, therefore, benefit from greater public support. We will call it "camouflage." It is a natural development in democracies where public opinion plays a significant role, but it also exists in authoritarian societies, which cannot afford to be completely indifferent to popular support. It is used by individuals, parties, and pressure groups in their struggles to win or influence power. It is also used by the government to obtain the obedience of the citizenry and to develop an apparent social and political integration.

THE FORMS OF CAMOUFLAGE Camouflage takes numerous forms. We will consider a few, by way of illustration, but our description is by no means exhaustive.

The most common technique of camouflage is to mask a less reputable objective behind one that is more respectable in terms of the value system of the particular society. In the West, this technique is used on a large scale for the defense of capitalistic interests. Instead of saying that private ownership of the means of production guarantees them substantial profits, owners and managers declare that the system is necessary to insure individual freedom for everyone. Moreover, there is less talk of private enterprise than of free enterprise, less talk of property than of freedom (meaning economic freedom). Nowadays, "liberal" parties play on the double meaning of the word "freedom." They exploit its political prestige in an attempt to conceal its economic aspects. Whenever the state imposes price controls on businessmen, they will not admit that their resistance to such measures is dictated by a desire to retain large profit margins. They protest against government interference which threatens the principle of freedom. They accuse the state of "meddling" with the economy, of "socialistic planning"— language certain to find a sympathetic audience among the general public.

This kind of camouflage is based on an appeal to social values. We have already indicated the political importance of a society's concepts of good and evil, of right and wrong, in a word, value system. It is one of the most significant aspects of social life. Values are established simultaneously within the framework of universal society, through a system of values common to all members—national values in the state—and within the framework of each class or group contending against the others, through value systems that are peculiar to each one and expressed in various ideologies. Values serve as camouflage in different ways. In the first place, every social class and every political party tries to conceal its own private interests and to identify with the national system of values, by masking its objectives behind values common to all society. Each group accuses the other of being partisan, while proclaiming itself to be national. It is not too much of an exaggeration to say that each group feels it is "the nation," while the other groups are "parties."

Each partisan system of values, each particular ideology, also serves as a camouflage, both internally and externally. There is always a disparity between the values we proclaim and those we really believe. The image that a party, class, or group projects of itself is an idealized image, like that of a product praised by advertising: idealization is a means of attracting customers or supporters, of fighting a competitor or opponent, who, in turn, practices idealization in the same way. Within a group or party, there are various degrees of adherence to the system of values. The image of leaders who exploit great ideas to attract the masses is only partially true, reflecting the strategies of only certain politicians. On the other hand, in parties with strong ideology, adherence is usually greater at the top than at the bottom. Religions have little influence if the clergy is less devout than the faithful followers. Broadly speaking, value systems are a means of self-justification, corresponding to self-deception: every ideology tends to give its followers a rather glorified image of themselves, one they can contemplate with satisfaction. Frequently, there is only a partial awareness of the deception.

Another technique in camouflage is to persuade a large part of the population that its interests are being threatened, whereas the issue concerns only the private interests of a small minority (which may indeed be very valid). Thus, French colonists, who would have been ruined by Algerian independence (as indeed many of them were), justified a continuation of the war by arguing that Algeria was an important customer of France and that her loss would compromise the entire French economy.

Very often camouflage based on an "enemy" takes the form of a scare tactic. A nonexistent enemy is invented or the importance of an actual enemy is greatly exaggerated to justify certain measures that are ostensibly to defend the homeland against the "enemy," but actually serve the personal interests of those in power. By shouting "Wolf!" one can distract the attention of a traveler and steal his baggage while he is concerned only with saving himself from the ferocious animal.

The communist specter plays a very important role in this respect in most Western countries. The danger of Sovietization in these countries is really very slight, but public opinion is unaware of this fact, recalling only the establishment of people's democracies in Eastern Europe between 1945 and 1948. The "red peril" is always present in many peoples' minds—which makes it possible to use this fear to divert public attention from other phenomena, such as economic exploitation or attempts to establish political dictatorships. Conjuring up the specter of a foreign enemy in order to weaken the opposition and compel it to rally to the government in power is a strategy that has been practiced by every government for hundreds of years. Carried to its extreme, it plunges a nation into war in order to weaken internal conflicts that threaten to get out of hand.

CAMOUFLAGE AND THE LEVEL OF ECONOMIC DEVELOPMENT Is the use of camouflage dependent on a society's level of technological development? The hypothesis has been advanced that camouflage reaches its peak in an intermediate stage between underdevelopment and overdevelopment.

The idea that camouflage corresponds to an intermediate level of development is based on a certain number of observations. In primitive societies, the mass of the population—undernourished, illiterate, and oppressed—is virtually excluded from the political struggle. That takes place exclusively within a narrow circle, among experienced people, among "princes." In such circumstances, camouflage is futile since it would be quickly discovered by everyone. As the old proverb goes: "You can't teach an old dog new tricks." All the participants in the political struggle are "old dogs" in this instance. We might compare them with the ancient soothsayers of whom it was said that they could not look each other in the face without laughing, for each knew the other's bag of tricks. In a very highly developed society, where most of the population is well educated and where the development of the social sciences has made people aware of the techniques of camouflage, such deceptions will prove equally ineffectual. In this case, the general population will be as well informed as the political elite in primitive societies. Moreover, each party or group spends its time unmasking its opponent. Therefore, camouflage is characteristic of the "intermediate phase" that began in Western societies with the French Revolution and is now gradually disappearing. In this intermediate phase, the masses participate in the political process; they cannot be excluded from it. But they are not sufficiently informed about the country's problems, a fact that enables others to conceal the disturbing aspects of these problems by means of camouflage.

The foregoing propositions can be accepted only with strong reservations. In primitive societies, the small, knowledgeable minority is not too advanced to make camouflage entirely useless. In highly developed societies, human gullibility probably remains great enough so that dissimulation can still be quite effective. This is all the more likely because people do not know enough about their opponent's point of view—which would enlighten them—and also because the news media tend to use other forms of camouflage, the kind that is soothing and insipid. Moreover, camouflage is not only a process of conscious deception, but also, in part, a means of avoiding a truth one would rather not face up to. In politics, many people wear blinders and do not wish to have their eyes opened. Nevertheless, camouflage will probably decrease and become less obvious in time; it is less likely that it will ever lose its importance in the political process.

6

The Development of

Integration

The two faces of Janus—struggle and integration—are inseparable. In the first place, they are not always easy to distinguish. Political regimes, for example, are concerned with both phenomena. By establishing the rules of combat and defining its scope, the regime organizes the means for expressing antagonisms and tends to lessen their intensity at the same time. Struggles within a regime are simultaneously a form of combat and a form of integration, since they reflect agreement on the basic principles of society and the institutions which apply them. When a regime's legitimacy is challenged, it becomes a weapon in the ensuing struggle; when it is accepted by a consensus, it is a means of integration. Many of the ideas we have examined thus far within the framework of conflict can also be studied within the framework of integration.

Moreover, almost every political ideology maintains that struggle leads to integration, that the development of antagonisms tends toward their elimination and the establishment of a genuine social order. When in the role of opposition, each party regards politics as a struggle; when in power, it regards politics as integration. In the West, there is a tendency to believe that integration is already an accomplished fact, or close to it. This attitude merely reflects public relations techniques or psychoanalytical treatment; soon only a few sick, abnormal, or antisocial individuals will dissent. In the East, it is thought that a long transitional period is still necessary, even after the seizure of power by the proletariat, before a just society will finally be established. Opposition affects only the speed and rate of its evolution, not the evolution itself.

The latter appears indisputable. But the optimism on the subject, in the East as in the West, is far more questionable. The end of conflicts, which is supposed to follow from the "society of abundance" of the "final phase of communism," will probably occur in Utopia. Some conflicts are in the process of disappearing, or rather, diminishing. Others persist and even grow sharper—especially the conflict between citizens and governmental power, which technological progress has made more dangerous than before. New conflicts arise which relegate the old ones to other levels.

THE NOTION OF INTEGRATION

The *vocabulaire philosophique* of Lalande defines integration as "the establishment of a closer interdependence between the parts of a living organism or between the members of a society." Integration is therefore the process of unifying a society, which tends to make it a harmonious city, based upon an order its members regard as equitably harmonious. By political integration we refer to the role played in this process by organized power (that is, the state, in a national society). Integration involves two aspects—one that is negative, another that is positive. To unify a society means, first of all, to eliminate the antagonisms dividing it, to put an end to struggles which threaten to tear it apart. But a society without conflict is not really integrated if the individuals who comprise it merely remain juxtaposed, side by side, like a crowd in which each person is isolated from his neighbors and has no realties with them. Integration assumes not only the elimination of conflicts, but also the development of solidarities. In practice, these two aspects are sometimes confused.

Limiting the Conflict

By their very nature, political antagonisms tend to be expressed violently, because they concern fundamental human questions. When certain men struggle to escape from wretched conditions, from a world of privation and alienation, and when others fight to avoid falling into a similar predicament, it is natural for each man to use every means at his disposal, including violence, to defend his privileges against the assault of the oppressed and exploited and assure victory. Riots, insurrections, revolutions, civil wars, acts of terrorism, repression, executions, reprisals: politics is strewn with corpses. Conflicts are constantly being settled by bloodshed.

THE ELIMINATION OF VIOLENCE However, we can also give politics another definition: a continual effort to eliminate physical violence and give social and individual antagonisms other less crude, less brutal, and less bloody means of expression. Politics is a civil war carried on in other ways; in other words, it is the negation of civil war, for war (whether civil or international) is defined precisely by the means it employs. There is no such thing as "cold" war. War means the use of physical violence to resolve conflicts. Politics is the use of nonviolent or, more precisely, less violent means. When class struggles, racial disputes, regional rivalries, and arguments between individuals are settled with lethal weapons and bloodshed, we are really outside the domain of politics. Politics tends to replace fists, knives, clubs, and rifles with other types of weapons. It is not always successful in doing so.

We can discern three stages in the process of eliminating weapons of violence. In its first stage, established power is not strong enough to prevent determined adversaries from confronting each other with physical force. It can only restrict the use of the latter, limit it, and regulate it. This situation corresponds to the legalized systems of private revenge, dueling, and the mutual observance of periods of truce. Fist or sword fights are not outlawed, but only governed by rules that reduce their harmful consequences. In the second stage, these brutal and barbarous forms are replaced by more civilized forms of violence: pillage and slaughter are replaced by strikes; forced labor and imprisonment are replaced by the lock-out. Finally, in the third stage, politics completely eliminates physical violence, replacing it with other types of combat, such as election battles, parliamentary debates, and committee discussions.

Democratic processes are thus more moderate, less brutal means of expressing political struggles than physical violence. To criticize democracies for publicly displaying their conflicts, controversies, and disagreements is to fail to recognize one of their fundamental objectives. Democracies tend to substitute discussion for armed conflict, dialogue for guns, argument for fistfights, and the ballot box for muscles and weaponry. The law of the majority is a more civilized, less brutal form of "might makes right." We may question whether numbers alone are capable of solving important social problems. The idea is not altogether satisfactory, although the principle is based on the idea that all men are equal as human beings, and that in itself is an indication of a very advanced civilization. In concrete terms, we have a choice between law based on numbers and law based on force and machine guns. To substitute the first for the second is a great step forward.

Limitating combat by the exclusion of violence is not, properly speaking, integration. Limiting the means of settling a conflict, having the opponents confront each other in the polemics in the press, in election campaigns, and in parliamentary debates—instead of having them fight a civil war—is not the same as eliminating conflict. We are still in the domain of political struggle, but we are now moving toward the area of integration. Changing the means of battle also means changing its character. Violence produces a relentless, uncompromising struggle; it develops a spirit of hatred and revenge which only intensifies the initial antagonism. Original motives tend to disappear and give way to another—the desire for revenge. So it is with groups who over the years have lost their motives for fighting one another, but who find reason to do so in the memory of their previous violent encounters. They want to return the blows received, even if they have no other reason for doing it. Moreover, and above all, excluding violence from conflicts assumes that all the adversaries accept the limitation. Agreement is required on the rules of nonviolent competition: without it, there will be a return to violence as the last resort. Limiting the conflict is a first compromise, a first act of cooperation, an initial step toward integration.

LIMITS TO THE SUPPRESSION OF VIOLENCE   Violence is never totally eliminated. Although politics is an effort to suppress the use of violence, it is never completely successful. Violence is always present, even in the most civilized, best organized, and most democratic societies.

In the first place, there is a residual amount of violence; a few isolated individuals, certain small minority groups, and some fanatical elements will resort to the use of fists, clubs, even bombs and revolvers. And there is always a certain amount of latent violence in society generally: classes, groups, and individuals use normal, nonviolent procedures as long as these allow them to express their true feelings; otherwise, there is an explosion.

Above all, power (the state itself) rests on violence: the army, the police, executioners, and prisons constitute its ultimate foundation. Of course, to the extent that these means of physical coercion are used in the public interest and for the common good, their significance changes. Power employs violence to prevent greater violence; legal violence is a way of restraining violence. But its practice does not always conform to its theory. In describing the state, and power in general, as the collective means of constraint employed by the dominant class to insure its exploitation of the subordinate classes, Marxists express at least part of the truth. In this sense, politics is not the suppression of violence, but its centralization, monopolization, and organization; wrested from various groups and individuals, the means of violence are placed exclusively in the hands of those in power.

However, this centralization, monopolization, and organization produce a decrease in the use of violence. Lenin recognized this fact when he wrote, in *The State and Revolution:* "The state is an organism for the domination of classes, an organism for the oppression of one class by another; it is the creation of an 'order' that legalizes and reinforces this oppression *by restraining* the class conflict." Moreover, the same expression, "restraining the conflict," is borrowed from Friedrich Engels, who formulated it in *The Origin of the Family, Private Property, and the State.* For Marxists, the appearance of the state and of organized power reinforces the oppression of one social class by another, by institutionalizing it, regularizing it, and making it official. The power of the ruling class is strengthened by the possession of this apparatus of coercion, which is the state. But its domination takes less brutal, less violent, and more moderate forms. Therefore, we are describing a general characteristic when we define politics in terms of limitations on the means of combat, in terms of its tendency to eliminate physical violence. But rather than an elimination of violence, there is a transposition of violence: physical, elementary violence is replaced by legal, juridical violence—a violence in the hands of those authorized to wield it.

The Establishment of Compromises

The elimination of violence presumes an initial compromise on the rules of combat. With the idea of a compromise on content, not just on form, we begin to make genuine progress in the process of integration.

THE NOTION OF COMPROMISE   We are no longer concerned with regulating the political struggle, but with putting an end to it by an adjustment of the issues at stake. Reaching compromises is one of the main functions of politics. In a democratic society, its institutions are specifically adapted to this objective. Democratic processes not only serve to express political struggles by nonviolent means; they are also designed to resolve these conflicts by compromise. The mechanisms of discussions, debates, and committee hearings allow each party to present his arguments; in addition, they assure an awareness of all aspects of the problem, so that everyone recognizes the diversity and complexity of the interests involved. Each contender can make his weight felt by his interventions and his votes, but agreements and coalitions are often necessary and require mutual adjustments and concessions.

We must distinguish between two important techniques of compromise—negotiation and arbitration. The contending parties can try to adjust their differences by themselves through discussion and dialogue, the normal democratic process. Representatives of the opposing parties meet around a bargaining table and attempt to work out the terms of a settlement, taking into account their respective interests, and each must make mutual concessions. But the adversaries can also appeal to a disinterested third party, whom they commission to settle their dispute. Such recourse to arbitration is a fairly common practice in international relations and in social conflicts. It has sometimes taken very interesting forms in politics. In the seventh century B.C., during a period of great social strife, many Greek cities were in danger of being torn apart or plunged into tyranny. Some of them appealed to oracles for new constitutions and new codes of law, and these were based on compromises that allowed the citizens to continue living together. Often a foreigner was called upon to lead the cities for a while, because he appeared to be more neutral and more impartial.

In general, democracy corresponds to the first type of compromise: its processes provide for the permanent confrontation of contending groups and parties. Some people claim that autocracy corresponds to the second type of compromise. Independent of parties and placed above classes, factions, and individuals, the state is in the position of an arbiter. It reaches compromises through an objective and impartial analysis of the facts, rather than through negotiation between the adversaries (in the manner of Solon and other lawgivers of his time). To be sure, the state is also regarded as an arbiter in Western democratic doctrines, but the theoreticians of autocracy criticize this concept. In their view, the democratic state is in the hands of a faction, a party, or a class, which uses the state in its own interests and to the detriment of other factions, parties, or classes. Only the autocratic state can be a true arbiter because of its independence with respect to all social groups or classes. Now this theory confuses appearances with reality. Although the autocratic state claims to be above parties and classes, this is never really true. Like the democratic state, it is always more or less in the hands of one class or party, and generally more completely than in a democracy because the opposition is unable to reverse the situation. No form of government is entirely above the fray, but the autocratic state is less so than the others.

It is often said that publicizing initial positions makes compromises more difficult in a democratic society. In international relations, it is traditional to extol the desirability of private negotiations over "diplomacy in the public forum." Autocracies, which keep political struggles behind the scenes, supposedly have an advantage in this respect, although their institutions are less formally organized for reaching compromises. There is some truth in these observations, but they are exaggerated. In modern states where the general population has reached a high level of political understanding, and where the news media have informed the public of the essential aspects of the issues, the need for compromises is widely recognized. The advantage of secrecy, enjoyed by autocratic institutions, is relatively unimportant compared with the fact that their entire structure tends toward unilateral solutions, imposed from above—and this is the very opposite of compromise.

THE LIMITS OF COMPROMISE   Political compromises are limited by their very nature. The principle of compromise is "cut the pie in two" and give one half to each. The ideal compromise, the perfect compromise, would balance out the advantages and sacrifices of each of the contending parties. It would be based on justice in its fundamental form of equity, symbolized by the scales. Each individual, each group, each class, would thus be satisfied, and their reasons for conflict would disappear. The fairer the terms seem to be, the easier it is to reach a compromise. Thus the notion of justice plays an important role in the process of integration.

The definition of justice depends on the ideologies and value systems of a particular society. It is almost always related to the distribution of goods and social advantages, and these goods and advantages are less abundant than the demand for them. When aristocratic societies evolved into bourgeois societies, the principle "to each according to his birth" was replaced by the principle "to each according to his ability." Socialism seeks to replace "to each according to his ability" with "to each according to his work," a principle that erases more completely the inequities of birth. But it has not been wholly successful. For Marxists, the transition from socialism to communism will be reflected in the replacement of "to each according to his work" with "to each according to his needs." This presumes that poverty will end and a genuine society of abundance will be established—one in which goods will be sufficiently plentiful to satisfy everyone's needs.

There is a wide gulf separating theory from practice. In reality, compromises reflect power relationships as much or more than they express justice. If two opponents carried exactly the same weight, and if they both negotiated with the same skill, the compromise they arrived at would be perfectly equitable. But this kind of evenly balanced situation is rarely encountered in real life. Of course, if the imbalance is too great, if one of the adversaries is in a position to crush the other, there is no compromise. Compromise is possible only if the disproportion in their relative strengths is not too great, and if a continuation of their conflict entails more liabilities than advantages for both sides. An imbalance generally remains, which gives an inequitable character to the compromise. The notion of justice can do no more than temper the demands of the stronger adversary—and never very much. Compromise therefore reflects the balance of power prevailing when the contending forces have resigned themselves to mutual accommodation.

Lastly, the contrast between conflict and compromise is not absolute. Compromise is not the end of the struggle, but only a truce, an armistice, which a change in the balance of power will replace with another. The political life of a democracy illustrates this process very well. It is not as noticeable in autocratic regimes where compromises are less open. Nonetheless, the process goes on as long as the imbalance of forces is not too great or the antagonisms too serious. But since changes in the balance of power are often slow to develop, many compromises last quite a long time. Custom, habit, and social inertia in general help to prolong their existence.

In order to eliminate, not just suspend, political struggles, their causes must be eradicated—that is to say, the antagonisms between individuals and groups comprising human society. We may doubt that it is possible to totally eliminate all the causes of antagonisms (this question will be pursued further). But certain factors can be diminished, and the natural evolution of society appears to be moving in this direction. If the range of conflict is thus reduced, then compromise is naturally easier to achieve and more durable, and an armistice tends to turn into peace. The line between the two is not clear. A long armistice strongly resembles peace, and, in any case, nothing can guarantee a permanent peace.

The Development of Solidarities

Even if it could exist, a society without struggles, without conflicts, without antagonisms, would still not be fully integrated if its members remained isolated from one another, without personal ties or relationships. They would be like Sunday-night motorists on an American highway, each enclosed in his car, mechanically obeying traffic lights and signals, showing disciplined respect for all rules and regulations, lacking any competitive spirit or aggressive impulses, so close that they bump into one another from time to time like a line of enormous beetles—and yet they are so distant from each other, so solitary despite appearances to the contrary. No social integration is possible without a development of social solidarities.

MECHANICAL SOLIDARITIES Solidarity results, first of all, from the very structure of community life, where each individual needs others in a network of interlocking relationships.

Durkheim saw in the division of labor the origin of an early type of solidarity. Only slightly developed within closed, primitive economies, solidarities of this kind grow as human activities become more specialized and contacts and exchanges increase. The simple little poem which used to adorn old civics textbooks expresses this idea in its most rudimentary form: "Without the baker, would you have any bread?" This type of solidarity is constantly developing. In this sense, we may say that the world is becoming "socialized," as Pope John XXIII emphasized in his encyclical *Pacem in Terris.* But in a capitalistic economy, this solidarity remains purely materialistic. It is not felt in a psychological sense because each individual's activity is dictated solely by his selfish personal interests.

Objectively speaking, by making bread, the baker renders a service to his neighbors. But subjectively speaking, he is only trying to earn money, and his fellow citizens know this. The publicity business firms give to the "services" they render is merely designed to attract consumers for their products. They are not in business to give "service" but to make money.

Socialist theoreticians strongly believe that the relationships of exchange should be radically altered and move in the direction of genuine solidarity. For socialists, the notion of social service must truly replace that of personal interest. In practice, it has been noted that this type of social progress is difficult to achieve. In the Soviet economy, it was found necessary to introduce private incentives to obtain higher productivity. However, personal interest is merely one of a number of factors in an individual's activities, and it is not the fundamental factor. Its importance derives from the persistence of capitalistic mentalities. Social evolution tends to reduce it gradually. To eliminate selfish personal motives and replace them with altruistic motives remains the overriding goal of socialism, even if this goal seems less easily attained than was first believed. Egoism is also a form of alienation.

PSYCHOLOGICAL SOLIDARITIES   The problem of substituting social service for personal interest is that of moving from mechanical solidarities to psychological solidarities—solidarities that are truly felt, shared, and experienced by all members of a society.

Durkheim thought that similarity constituted the second source of solidarity. Every society rests, in the first instance, on resemblance: the community of language, religion, customs, myths, and value systems—and, in a more general sense, of culture—are fundamental to it. Important, too, are physical contact, proximity, the fact of finding oneself in the company of others. Also important is the location of the community with respect to other communities. By tracing clearly defined boundaries and giving them a natural character, isolation strengthens the sense of a collective community relationship. Similarities are more readily perceived in comparison with members of other groups: the image of the foreigner has played an important role in the development of solidarities. The existence of an external danger or the threat from an enemy are also important, whether the danger and the enemy are real or imaginary. Arnold Toynbee has stressed the influence of adversity, of a "challenge," of a struggle against obstacles, in the development and strengthening of communal ties.

A sense of solidarity is based less upon the resemblance or physical proximity of the members of a community than upon the images they form of this resemblance and of this proximity. Three kinds of collective images are especially important in this connection: the image the members of a community have formed of their past, the image they have of themselves at the present time, and the image they project for their collective future. We have mentioned the essential role of history, whether authentic or legendary, in the development of nations; the role is similar in other types of human communities. Not to be overlooked is the role of national stereotypes, simplified images of a country's citizenry—in France, Jacques Bonhomme; in Germany, Michael; in the United States, Uncle Sam. The image of a great collective goal to be accomplished together is probably even more powerful in social integration. To quote the Bible: "Where there is no vision, the people perish." Every society needs a Promised Land.

Lastly, the development of solidarities is probably based on one of man's deepest instincts. In explaining certain animal societies, a biologist has spoken of the "interattraction" that drives the members to live together, a phenomenon that also exists in human societies. Describing the anguish of solitude, psychologists cite Genesis: "It is not good that man should be alone." The desire for communion within the group, where each individual finds total fulfillment of his being, probably constitutes the mainspring of collective life. Beyond the present city—imperfect, unjust, and superficial—looms the dream of a harmonious city, whose members are finally liberated from their egocentricity, from their self-imposed isolation, from their fragmented existences. In this city, each member will be tied to the others, not by legal contracts, the mechanisms of the exchange and division of labor, or the chains of debits and credits, but through mutual understanding, altruism, and love. Though taking different avenues of approach, both Karl Marx and Pierre Teilhard de Chardin believed that this is not simply a visionary dream, but that mankind is evolving in this direction.

TIES WITH OTHER GENERATIONS   The solidarities mentioned above unite men who are living in a society at a given moment in its history, which is to say, people of several generations who coexist at the same time. Another type of bond uniting succeeding generations constitutes a very important aspect of integration.

The characteristics a man acquires during his lifetime are not biologically transmitted to his descendants; this fundamental law of Mendelian genetics is almost universally accepted nowadays (the opposing theories of the Soviet scientist Lysenko, of the Stalin era, have hardly received serious consideration outside communist countries, and even there they have now been abandoned). This means that the whole heritage of civilization, since its earliest beginnings, devolves entirely upon society. Biologically speaking, contemporary man is identical to Neolithic man, apart from some genetic mutations that have occurred in the meanwhile. It is through society that man inherits all the progress achieved by those who have preceded him.

Society thus serves as a repository for civilization. It also guarantees the transmission of what has been preserved through education. This bond between present and past generations is of fundamental importance. Should the chain be broken, all civilization would crumble.

This solidarity through time is not a one-way street; it not only moves in the direction of the past, but also toward the future. Just as society has preserved and transmitted past civilization down to the present generation, the present generation will continue the cycle for future generations. The problems that arise in protecting works of art and monuments of the past illustrate this aspect of solidarity achieved through time.

The problems are not always simple. No generation is content to retransmit the heritage it received from the past: it makes its own contributions. In some cases—for example, on the question of urban development—new ideas can be developed only by destroying and replacing the work of the past. If every generation were to preserve everything, humanity could not develop. A certain balance must be achieved. We cannot pursue this question further here; we merely call attention to it, noting that it is especially important in periods of great expansion. At the present time in Western societies, land and real estate speculation can produce as much destruction as was wrought by the barbarian invasions that marked the dissolution of the Roman Empire. The forms of vandalism are different, but the results are comparable. Hence the necessity for intervention by political power, which is one way it achieves social integration.

POWER AND INTEGRATION

Many of the factors contributing to social integration are independent of political power. "Interattraction" is a natural phenomenon; similarity and proximity are not created by the state or by power in general. Diversification of the economy, the division of labor, and a multiplicity of exchanges develop, at least in part, by themselves. If integration is the primary aim of politics, the means of achieving it are not all political. All the same, the state—and political power in general—play a major role in social integration. The classic concepts of power as the arbiter, the embodiment of justice, the protector of the commonweal, and the guardian of the public interest underscore its importance. To some extent they exaggerate it, because integration through the use of power is sometimes deceptive, and it contains an element of camouflage.

Political Means of Integration

Generally speaking, power and the state intervene in the integration process in four major ways: (1) by defining rules and procedures; (2) by organizing collective services and the general pattern of social activities; (3) by providing education for the citizenry; and (4) by using force in dealing with those who break the laws.

THE ESTABLISHMENT OF RULES AND PROCEDURES   The state within the nation and organized power within any collectivity play their role in social integration by participating, first of all, in the establishment and enforcement of rules and procedures. The latter, taken together, constitute the laws of the society. To be sure, there is a law based on tradition (commercial and rural customs) and another based on agreements (contracts made by private individuals). Customary law, essential in primitive societies, plays a minor role in modern societies, whereas contractual law remains prominent, even though state regulations are continually reducing its influence. In any event, neither type can be effectively applied except when recognized and sanctioned by the power of the state. It is not possible to invoke tradition in a courtroom or before an administrative agency unless the law, which is established by power, has agreed that one may do so. Likewise, contracts only have as much effect as the legislature decrees. Finally, law is defined by power; it is made up of the body of rules and procedures established or recognized by political power—which is to say, by the state in a national society—and sanctioned by it.

Rules and procedures serve first to limit the expression of antagonisms by excluding the use of violence. In struggles between private individuals, controlling personal acts of revenge is the first and simplest form of law. At this stage, violence is merely contained or restrained. In the second stage, all forms of private revenge are abolished; reparation is assured by the government. At the same time, it punishes those who injure persons or property, and who thus transgress the laws established by power. In conflicts between groups or classes and in collective political struggles, law defines nonviolent means of combat—elections, parliamentary debates, committee meetings, and so forth.

Rules and procedures also tend to eliminate conflicts by facilitating compromise. In its first stage, the state limits itself to ratifying compromises reached between private individuals, by giving them executive force, by lending them its secular authority to ensure their application. This system is used extensively in modern societies where it corresponds more or less to "contractual law." Contracts between individuals, understandings between groups, agreements between local communities or public services: all these mechanisms insure the regulation of a great many struggles and conflicts. Moreover, the state intervenes in the compromise itself by excluding certain clauses or by insisting that certain other clauses be included: clauses characterized as "in the interest of public order" thus tend to multiply in comparison with those left to the private negotiation of the interested parties. Generally speaking, governmental power intervenes either to protect the weaker party from domination by the stronger one or to prevent private agreements that would be contrary to the general interest of society.

In a second stage of development, the state makes it easier to work out difficult compromises. A typical example is that of government mediation to achieve conciliation or binding arbitration. In the field of international relations, these methods correspond to the embryonic situation of supranational communities, whose power is not sufficiently organized to be able to settle conflicts and establish compromises. However, the pressure they apply on nation-states constitutes the greatest intervention by political power in matters affecting international society. It represents some progress in integrating the international community. On the other hand, in labor conflicts within nations, these same methods reflect a regression in the integration process produced by the intensity of class struggles during the nineteenth and twentieth centuries. Incapable of imposing authoritarian solutions in this area, as it could in others, the state has had to make an accommodation with violence, replacing bloody conflicts with less brutal forms of violence (strikes, lockouts) and trying to limit the use of these tactics by requiring preliminary attempts at bargaining and arbitration.

Dictated compromises are the final stage of development. In such cases, the state uses its power to adjudicate the interests involved by defining the terms of the compromise and enforcing its implementation. There is no sharp dividing line between state-imposed and negotiated compromises. Democratic processes, in establishing laws and reaching governmental decisions, attach great importance to direct or indirect negotiations between the contending parties. Parliamentary debates, for example, permit each party to express its point of view, to assess its strength, and to discuss possible arrangements with the other parties. The mechanisms provided by commissions, expert opinions, consultations, and "round table" discussions serve the same purpose. In modern societies, public debate in the press, and on radio and television, is itself a procedure for compromise prior to governmental arbitration.

Rules and procedures are inseparable from a certain amount of formalism, which plays an important role in the process of social integration. Originally, legal formalities had a religious and magical basis. Because certain gestures were made and certain words pronounced, the commitment became sacred in everyone's eyes. Today, the juridical power of an oath, the importance attached to the written word (apart from its value as evidence), and ceremonies of investiture still retain this quality. But the real basis of formalism has become more empirical. No social life is possible without rules of the game, and all the rules entail a certain formality. Eventually, the process of debate and discussion must end; after a point, we can no longer challenge the decisions and must acknowledge the authority of the thing that was judged, even if it was misjudged. The decision of a referee must be respected, even if it is questionable: otherwise, no game at all is possible. In Great Britain, because of the inequitable distribution of election districts, the Labour party can have more votes in the country than the Conservative party, yet win fewer seats in Parliament and so be kept in the role of the opposition (which happened in 1951). This is contrary to the principle of democracy, but it conforms to the rules of the game; it is legal. England must accept the situation or risk destroying the foundations of its political regime.

Moreover, formalism in itself is a factor in integration. Politeness is not simply an absence of brutality; it is also a means of preventing a resurgence of brutal behavior. Its observance accustoms people to repressing individual violence. The observance of legal formalities helps to contain social violence. Law is rarely what it ought to be: in other words, it expresses balances of power rather than equity and leads to the concealment of violence rather than its elimination. But in proclaiming what it is not, it progresses a bit beyond what it actually is. Politeness and formalism are also systems of signs and symbols by which the members of a given society recognize one another and become more clearly aware of their shared membership. Social solidarity is thereby strengthened in fact, not simply in appearance.

THE DEVELOPMENT OF COLLECTIVE ORGANIZATION   Classic liberalism limits the integrating role of the state and governmental power to this legal activity of formulating rules and procedures. Actually, the state and governmental power play a much greater role. They not only place limits on the activities of the citizenry, but they also engage in certain activities themselves.

Liberal doctrine admits the need for services of a collective nature, such as highways, postal service, information media, schools and colleges, organizations for health and medical attention, and the printing and coinage of money. But it believes that private initiative and free enterprise will guarantee that these services will work most efficiently (with the exception of areas like justice, the police, the military, and diplomacy). Only in this modest and limited domain does the liberal position see a need for social organization maintained by political power. This doctrine reflects the situation of societies that are still technologically underdeveloped, societies divided into basic groups that are more or less self-contained, societies where production occurs within the framework of small units, and where central authority plays a fairly weak role. In closed, agrarian economies, where each peasant tends to live entirely off the land, community services are nonexistent. In the first phase of capitalism, the economy opens up and commerce and exchange are developed. Community services multiply, but they are generally maintained by private initiative and remain rather unimportant in the life of the community. Individualism and distrust of the state characterize this type of social structure. We observe these attitudes today in the mentality of artisans, small businessmen, and traditional peasants, who look inward upon themselves and their personal relationships. The progressive elimination of this archaic kind of capitalism through the development of a modern form provokes among these social groups aggressive reactions, like those of the Poujadists.

The structure of contemporary industrial societies is altogether different. They have many important collective services—planning the use of land, public works, engineering projects, highways, communications networks, technological research in fundamental problems, overall social planning; the economy needs them. Social services like education, protection against risks, public assistance, and public health must be expanded. A country's defense establishment against external threats becomes very complex, very vast, and very costly. Modern armies constitute one of the world's largest human organizations and have the most expensive equipment. Some of these services can be provided through the interplay of private endeavor and competition, but the proportion supplied by private services is continually diminishing. No one denies this fact nowadays. American economists have themselves demonstrated that the public sector tends to remain underdeveloped in a purely capitalistic economy, and that this underdevelopment retards overall expansion. Because the state alone can feasibly provide these economic services, its function in social organization has become extremely important.

The influence of power over collective organization tends to go beyond this domain of common services, which concerns only the private sectors of social life. Technological evolution converts power into the general organizer of the community, the coordinator of activities in all the private sectors within the framework of universal social planning. Economic planning is only one aspect of the function of social organization in modern nations. Or more precisely, the economy is only one part of universal planning. Selecting plans for investments, development priorities, and the like involves all aspects of national life. Education, culture, art, scientific progress, land development, urban planning, life style—as well as military power and technical assistance for underdeveloped nations, in other words, the bases of diplomacy —are largely determined by the orientation of the planning. The organization of society through political power encompasses all collective activities. It consists not only in coordinating a society's present activities but is also directed toward the society's future. To this end, it tries to anticipate future possibilities and to direct collective evolution the way it deems best: it is "forward-looking."

This extension of the organizing role of political power affects the very structure of the state. The development of what was formerly called the executive branch, by comparison with the legislative, is directly involved. The preeminence of the legislature corresponds to societies still loosely integrated, where the important collective activities are carried out by private enterprise and the principal role of political power is to restrict conflicts between groups and individuals, to assist in reaching compromises that will end such conflicts, to define the general terms of compromise, and to supervise collective services of an administrative nature (police, army, monetary matters). In a planned society, in which the state coordinates the various collective activities, the function of organization cannot be performed by legislative machinery, but only by the government, which becomes the center of initiative and of political decisions. The weakening of parliaments and the strengthening of executives—tendencies common to all democracies today—are the political results of changes in the socioeconomic structures, which in turn are the product of technological advances.

EDUCATION AND PROPAGANDA Social integration is based simultaneously on material factors (justice in the distribution of goods, economic abundance, the development of interdependency) and on collective ideas and beliefs. Even material factors are unimportant unless they are seen as objects of opinions, beliefs, and feelings. The notion one has of a thing is more important socially than the thing itself. A society in which there is a just distribution of goods and property, but which the citizens believe to be unjust, is not as well integrated as a society in which the distribution is unjust, but which the citizens consider to be just. The influence of collective beliefs and images is a powerful factor in the integrating process and can be conditioned in two ways. One may take direct action by developing community feelings and by restraining individualistic tendencies; for example, by denouncing selfishness and individualism and by extolling altruism, dedication, civic virtues, and national pride. One may also act indirectly through the presentation of facts, emphasizing those that are conducive to integration and concealing or disguising the others. The state and its political power play an important and increasing role in this dual psychological process.

The psychological influence of the state begins first with children in the form of education. The primary goal of education is to incorporate new generations into society. Political power never takes this task over completely. Even in the most totalitarian regimes, the family exercises considerable influence over a child's first years. Thereafter, the social environment and close personal relationships with friends and comrades provide a very important education through a process of osmosis. But political power always participates to some degree in the educational process, and its participation is oriented above all toward integration. Integration through education assumes several forms in modern nations.

The principal objective of education is to transmit to new generations all the experience of civilization developed by previous generations, since, as we noted earlier, this kind of learning is not transmitted biologically. The elements in a civilization are so numerous and so complex that choices have to be made to render them capable of assimilation through education. These choices, which depend to a great extent on political power, are extremely important. First of all, they condition the technical development of society; if the educational system is bad, if it does not transmit the basic elements of civilization, there is a risk of stagnation or regression. But these choices also have a great influence on political behavior. An education strongly oriented toward material techniques and an immediate professional education, one that does not attach much importance to general education, discourages the development of critical thinking and favors conservatism. But, on the other hand, an education, which—without neglecting technical and professional skills—emphasizes general culture will result in producing less conformity and more originality.

The state and political power, moreover, ensure a civic education, consisting of first-hand instruction in the social ties that bind the individual to the community and the resulting duties. Education in civics consists of more than teaching about the human solidarities and the duties of citizenship; it goes far beyond the courses and textbooks officially prescribed for "civic education" as a subject matter in the curriculum. Civic education is the product of many other areas of learning —literature, ethics, philosophy, geography, and especially history. It always implies taking a position on fundamental systems of value. In a society in which there is a consensus on the subject of legitimacy, no problem occurs. But if, on the contrary, there is disagreement about legitimacy, difficulties inevitably arise. Civic education then becomes partisan rather than national because it presents a picture of society that is not shared by all of its members. It then becomes more divisive than unifying.

The same must be said of the role of the state in presenting government propaganda, its education for adults. Everywhere and at all times, political power has sought to develop a sense of cohesion and community feeling among the citizenry. The modern propaganda of authoritarian states is merely an excessive development of a function that all governments perform. The means are different, but the end is the same. In ancient societies, in which the visible world was not separated from the invisible universe of magic and religion, in which each individual was conscious of belonging to a mystical body as well as to a community of men, government propaganda tended to sanctify this view by merging it with both the secular city and the realm of divinity. It was reflected above all by myths reinforced by rituals, ceremonies, and worship. It was expressed particularly through incantations, although it did not disdain persuasion through the works of writers and authorized speakers.

Traces of the primitive mentality still persist in contemporary societies. Sometimes the sovereign, always the city, receives a quasireligious veneration, and treason remains a sacrilege. The Lincoln monument and Lenin's tomb are shrines, but propaganda employs especially modern techniques. Of course, the adaptation of these advertising methods differs according to the political regime. Fascist methods—based on brutal affirmation, repetition, and slogans—are closer to primitive propaganda, although they use highly perfected techniques. Communist propaganda, rational and ideological, is very different, although it is also monopolized by political power.

In democracies, on the other hand, propaganda is employed by individuals and groups (political parties, newspapers, private firms, pressure groups) in competition with the state. Thus it is used both as a weapon for combat and as an instrument for integration. Its first function obviously limits the development of its second function. Government propaganda is less effective if the government does not have a monopoly on the information media, if its voice is not the only one to be heard by the citizenry. Nevertheless, it is more audible than the others. Solemn pronouncements by governments always make newspaper headlines, because they are important news. In a liberal democracy, with privately owned television, a de Gaulle or a Kosygin could appear on the television screen whenever they wished to because they attracted the public. In a "star system," government leaders are stars.

Moreover, we must distinguish between propaganda for power and propaganda for the nation. Democracies limit the first more than the second, which is specifically oriented toward social integration. The role of the state in this area is much more restrained than in authoritarian regimes, but it is still significant.

RECOURSE TO SOCIAL CONSTRAINT   To resort to the police, the military, prisons, and executioners is the last means available to governmental power in integrating society.

Social constraint, that is, violence used by the state, works to bring about integration in two ways. Whether monopolizing violence to its own advantage or denying the possession of military weapons to individuals and factions, the state is initiating a form of integration, as we have mentioned, by preventing groups and individuals from using violent means to settle their political conflicts themselves. To threaten the use of force when contending parties refuse to accept a compromise is an effective method of encouraging agreements; for each adversary no longer considers only what he will gain or lose with respect to his opponent, but also what he could lose if the wrath of the government fell upon him. Even if the litigants are dissatisfied with their judge, the case is terminated through the intervention of *manu militari*. General compromises, such as those resulting from codes and regulations, would be difficult to apply—regardless of their equity—if citizens could reject them; but "force resides with the law" because law is supported by force. Beneath its negative aspect of limiting and eliminating conflicts, social integration owes a great deal to coercion by governmental power. Coercion is more frequently used when antagonisms are unusually deep and bitter, when the struggle between classes, groups, and individuals is very intense, hence when there is little integration.

Some believe that force also achieves positive integration, that is, the development of social solidarities. This seems strange at first glance. If violence has to be used against individuals to keep them within the community, one would assume that these people must lack strong community feeling. Yet certain moralists believe that violence has the effect of wresting human beings from undesirable passions, liberating them from evil, making them aware of their true interests, and turning them into more sociable members of society. When philosopher and statesman Joseph de Maistre (1753–1821) made the executioner the cornerstone of society, he meant that only the use of terror can deter individuals from yielding to their baser impulses, which prevent them from living sociable lives. These old theories, more or less inspired by the pseudo-Christianity of the Inquisition, are being revived today by the fascists who think, like French writer Henri de Montherlant, that "it is by administering kicks in the rear that society forges a people's morality" (*"c'est à coups de pied dans le derrière qu'on forge la moralité des peuples"*). Many conservatives who appear to be moderates hold the same view, but are reluctant to say so publicly. The political right is not alone in demanding that power use violence to develop sociability. The Jacobin doctrine of the Reign of Terror, which regarded violence as a necessary instrument to insure the reign of "virtue"—that is, a sense of civic responsibility—reached the same conclusion, but the reasoning was different.

From a rightist viewpoint, man is born evil. His nature is unsociable ("Man is a wolf to his fellow man") and is opposed to the development of any authentic community life. Power uses force in dealing with citizens as an animal trainer uses it in dealing with animals: to train and discipline them, to substitute for their inherent nature, which is bad, another nature, which is good. Thus in old-fashioned education, the schoolmaster used the rod to force his pupils to behave properly. For the Jacobins, on the other hand, disciples of Rousseau, "man is born good, but society corrupts him." Violence does not have a psychological aim—to change human nature—but a sociological aim—to destroy the institutions and habits that have corrupted man, in other words, to liberate him.

A Marxist would say it should "disalienate" him. The theory of the dictatorship of the proletariat is continuation of the Jacobin doctrine of the Terror. Man is born good, but capitalism corrupts him. To put an end to the system of oppression, exploitation, and alienation that has developed, violence is necessary. Violence, directed first of all against the state, as long as it is in the hands of exploiters: this is the revolution. Afterward, when the working class has seized power, through revolutionary violence, it will turn the power of the state against the exploiters, using it to destroy the last vestiges of exploitation: this constitutes the dictatorship of the proletariat. Dictatorship implies a harsh, pitiless, violent power because the former exploiters are still powerful, because the institutions and habits of capitalism are deeply ingrained in society, and because they cannot be rooted out gently. When this cleansing process is completed, when all vestiges of exploitation have been eliminated, then men can live in a brotherly, interdependent society, consonant with their true nature, which capitalism had alienated. In this society, violence will cease and coercion will be useless; power itself will tend to disappear.

Another major difference separates the right from the left with respect to the use of violence to develop sociability. For conservatives, it is a question of permanent usage. Men will always remain evil. However rigorous and thorough their training may be, it is never final or absolute. Like the lion who continually threatens to devour his trainer, to whom he owes everything, human beings continually risk falling back into their evil ways. Culture, politeness, and civilization are fragile structures, which only constant vigilance can maintain. Power must always keep its sword in hand, ready to strike when necessary. It must strike, and strike hard, at the first suspicious movement, in order to forestall the mad rush of the populace reverting to savagery, blindly destroying the foundations of a social order from which it, too, has profited. As Charles Maurras expressed it, "Whatever one removes from the rod of punishment has not been taken from the rod or from the authority wielding it, but from the whole populace; the nation and all mankind are the first victims."

For Jacobins and Marxists, on the contrary, the use of violence by the state to develop solidarity is simply temporary. The selfishness and wickedness of men stem from the social structures, which establish inequities and exploitation and give certain men the power to dominate others and to "alienate" them. When these social structures have been completely destroyed, men will recover their natural sociability, and violence will finally disappear. The state will wither away as an instrument of coercion. All that will remain will be technical apparatus insuring the planning and organization of society, somewhat like automatic traffic signals that facilitate the movement of cars and vehicles in congested cities. But there will no longer be policemen, military personnel, prisons, or executioners. Social integration will be maintained and developed naturally, without force, through the interplay of human nature, finally restored to its true nature. Power will resort to violence only to cut the Gordian knot: liberated from their shackles, men will then live without violence.

Contemporary neoliberals take an intermediate position. Like Jacobins and Marxists, they do not believe that states are founded on perpetual recourse to violence; they believe that men are naturally good and sociable, that the use of force, generally speaking, is futile and even harmful as a means of integrating them into the community. Like fascists and conservatives, however, they do not think that political power can ever entirely abandon coercive methods; sometimes force must be used to insure social harmony. But this recourse to violence is secondary, marginal, and in a way residual. It is used against only a few individuals who are incapable of integrating into the community: these antisocial individuals are also abnormal, that is, sick. They are more in need of urgent medical attention than of police violence, more in need of a clinic than a prison. These theories, which are widespread among certain Western sociologists, are extremely dangerous. To define the abnormal, the sick, in terms of antisocial characteristics, which is to say, atypical behavior, amounts to condemning all eccentrics, all people who constitute small minorities. The proposal to use preventive violence against them, violence in a white blouse, instead of policemen and hangmen, is not particularly reassuring.

In addition to the foregoing theories, we may ask whether technological progress does not have the effect of transforming social constraint in the same way. The substitution of nurses for jailers seems to be along this line. The development of collective organization leads us to imagine another form of coercion, a bureaucratic kind, resulting from a mechanical solidarity similar to that of the parts of a transmission. Each revolution of the engine forcibly affects the entire mechanism; no part of it can escape. To replace a police officer with traffic signals is not an elimination, but a transposition, of social constraint. The relation of the citizens to the modern state increasingly resembles the novels of Kafka. To be sure, the detractors of technological progress exaggerate a great deal, but their observations cannot be entirely disregarded.

Genuine Integration or Pseudointegration?

In describing the various processes of integration used by political power, we have not inquired whether we were dealing with an authentic integration or a pseudointegration, which disguises the government's participation in the political struggles in the service of one of the combatants. Rules and procedures, social organization, education and propaganda, police, and prisons: are all these means utilized by the state to develop order, social harmony, and justice? Or do these officially announced objectives conceal others that are altogether different and less acceptable? In other words, are they means of integration or of camouflage?

MARXIST THEORIES AND INTEGRATION-CAMOUFLAGE   Marxists were the first to denounce in a systematic fashion the deceptive character of political integration. However, they themselves concede there are limits to camouflage. Normally, the state is an instrument of the class struggle, but it can also become a means of integration.

The state, an instrument of the dominant class, is a product of the class struggle and develops at a certain moment in the evolution of this struggle. Political power corresponds to a change in the methods of oppression by the dominant class. A violent, brutal, and crude sort of domination is replaced by one that is more moderate in appearance, more organized, more juridical, but fundamentally more effective. The means of state action, which we have examined—rules and procedures, organization, education and propaganda, social constraints—do not serve to create a true order, to develop genuine integration, but only to consolidate the domination of one class over the others, beneath an appearance of order and integration. The only real objective of the legal, administrative, and law-enforcement apparatus of the state is to preserve the privileges of the dominant class and the exploitation of the other classes. Thus the state is in the hands of the ruling class: in other words, it was first in the hands of property owners, who used it to dominate the slaves and then the serfs; next it fell into the hands of the bourgeoisie, who owned the industrial and commercial enterprises, and who used the power of the state to dominate the working class.

Nevertheless, Marxism admits that the state may not be in the exclusive service of a single class, for instance, in those special and transitional circumstances when a certain balance of forces exists between several classes. Such is the case when a declining class (previously dominant) still has enough power not to be ignored and when a rising class (previously dominated) does not yet have enough power to oust its rival. For a brief period of time, the state maintains a balance between the two. Thus it was in France during the absolute monarchy of the seventeenth and eighteenth centuries, and during the Bonaparte regimes of the First and Second Empires, and in Germany during the time of Bismarck, and in Russia under Kerensky in 1917. In such situations, the state's position is like that of a referee, standing a bit above the battle. It does not act in the exclusive interest of one class, but tries to effect compromises between the evenly balanced classes. Thus it moves in the direction of integration. But this integration remains partial: the state does not consider the interests of all classes, but only those of the classes that are equally balanced. In France, both the absolute monarchy of the seventeenth and eighteenth centuries and the First Empire took into account the interests of the aristocracy and the bourgeoisie, but disregarded those of the peasantry and the working class.

Marxists, however, do not entirely reject the idea that the state acts for the common good, the interest of all, and for genuine social integration. In the framework of a capitalistic regime, the state is an instrument serving the bourgeoisie, protecting its private interests and maintaining its domination and exploitation. For the proletariat, revolution consists in seizing the apparatus of government, removing it from the bourgeoisie and turning it against them, and making it serve the establishment of socialism. In this second phase, the state remains an instrument of coercion in the hands of the dominant class, now the working class. The latter uses it in its own interest, namely, to destroy the vestiges of the bourgeois social order and the remnants of its own exploitation. But, by doing this, the proletariat acts in the general interests of all men, for it abolishes every kind of exploitation, domination, and oppression. In a single operation, it destroys the bases of antagonisms that produce class struggles, opening the way for the construction of a fully integrated society, one in which the state will fade away and there will be no further need for political power or the use of force. In following its class interest, the proletariat acts in behalf of all humanity. Accordingly, when it controls the state, in the post-revolutionary stage when socialism is achieved, it accomplishes a work of integration of the most authentic kind; thanks to the state and to the dictatorship which the proletariat exercises through the state, a human community founded on justice, harmony, and cooperation—which is to say, a fully integrated society—can be built.

THE MEANS OF CAMOUFLAGE   Political power has several ways of appearing to serve the public interest when, in reality, it is acting in the private interests of those who control power. There will, of course, be much reliance upon nationalistic feelings and patriotic pride, and on the use of legitimacy and legality.

All men feel a natural attraction for a state of peace and order and repulsion for a state of disorder that threatens their existence and creates a sense of insecurity. Thus they tend to confuse what Emmanuel Mounier called "established disorder" with genuine order. The state always maintains a certain kind of "order"—order in the streets, an absence of civil war or armed conflict. It fosters the idea that this material order is an authentic social order, and the resulting confusion serves its purpose. The dream of order, justice, harmony, and solidarity that all men share, the great yearning to escape from loneliness and find fulfillment in a genuine community, in a truly integrated society, serves the aims of the governing power. We always see things somewhat as we want them to be.

The natural attachment each man feels for the universal society, each citizen feels for the nation, also assists the state in its camouflage efforts. Earlier, we indicated the ambivalence of national values: on the one hand, they express community feelings and genuine social interests; on the other hand, they conceal, to a greater or lesser degree, antagonisms within the group to the benefit of the established order. To place national sentiments in opposition to "party differences" is tantamount to disguising the oppression of certain classes by others behind a façade of the elements common to all; one aspect is magnified, while the other is minimized. Utilizing an "enemy" is a very effective device in the process of camouflage. In the face of a threat, a danger, a possible aggression, every social group tends to draw together and overlook internal differences. Emphasizing the danger from a real enemy, making it appear more menacing than it actually is, and fabricating incidents—these are traditional techniques employed by every state. Sometimes it is the "enemy within our midst": Christians, Jews, Reds, capitalists, communists, and so forth. Other times, it is the "foreign enemy": England for France before the Entente Cordiale; Germany for France from 1871–1949; and the Soviet Union for Western nations.

In ancient societies, rulers were the interpreters of supernatural forces or gods who presided over the world and mankind; social order depended solely on obedience to their superior commands. Power was obeyed because it expressed the will of the gods or the power of mysterious forces. It expressed these supernatural agencies insofar as it followed certain rites and ceremonies, like a priest administering a sacrament. It was unimportant whether the priest, as a person, was good or bad: since he pronounced the sacramental formulas, divine forces acted upon their invocation. Authority among rulers of ancient societies was of the same nature, and authority among modern rulers is not much different. Notions of legitimacy, and especially of legality, result in recognizing the decisions of political power as valid because of their form, not their content, because of the power held by government leaders, not their ability or sense of justice. It is enough to be arrayed in purple and to receive a sceptre, to be crowned and annointed at Rheims, or to have received a popular endorsement in order that one's commands become law, justice, and social order.

Jurists further this mystification, usually unconsciously, by considering things from a theoretical rather than a practical point of view. They declare that the law is the expression of the general will, when in fact it is the expression of an assembly elected under conditions of one sort of another, which may or may not reflect public opinion. They declare that judges render justice, whereas judges express their conception of justice, which reflects their social status, their education, and their personal likes and dislikes. The law is one of the great means of camouflaging power. Even idealistic jurists, who distinguish between power and justice, who contrast positive law established by power with natural law founded on true equity, contribute to this enterprise. For positive law borrows some of its prestige from natural law, under the same name of Law, with a capital "L."

THE NATURE OF RULERS AND DEGREES OF INTEGRATION Every party tends to believe that when it is in power, government operates in the general interest, and when its opponents are in control that special interests are served. But this relativity of viewpoints does not obviate the fact that certain parties are closer to reality than others.

A certain theory about ends and means has contributed to spreading a state of confusion that benefits the privileged classes and "established disorder." It is true that some means (like torture) are unjustifiable, no matter what ends they are supposed to advance. But this is not to say that all ends have the same value; means being equal, power is judged by its objectives. Every dictatorship is bad per se, but a dictatorship that seeks to establish equality among men, to destroy the domination of privileged groups, and to liberate the people from exploitation and contempt is less bad than a dictatorship that maintains the oppression of an oligarchy of property owners and capitalists over a population kept in poverty and subjection. Castro is better than Battista, not only because he uses less brutal methods, but also because he is motivated by a different goal. Communism and fascism cannot be placed in the same basket. The confusion about ends and ethical principles, when applied only to means, serves the interest of the established disorder and acts as a camouflage.

The authentic role of the state in the question of integration is inseparable from the groups and individuals who effectively control the state. Any formal analysis that confuses the container with the contents, the sword with the swordsman, cannot grasp the reality of the problem. Political integration is always a camouflage to some extent. Political power is never used in the exclusive service of the social order and the general interest. Conversely, there is always some measure of integration even in the worst regimes: they build highways, regulate traffic, provide for sanitation and garbage removal, and maintain fire departments. Between these two extremes, the proportion of camouflage of and genuine integration fluctuates considerably. It depends, first of all, upon those who exercise power. When the state is in the hands of the privileged classes, they use it primarily in their own interest, and secondarily in the public interest; the proportion of camouflage increases, that of integration decreases. When the state falls into the hands of previously dominated and exploited classes, the latter act in the general interest by acting in their own interest—trying to eliminate domination and exploitation. The amount of camouflage decreases, and the amount of integration increases, at least until those who were formerly exploited become exploiters in their turn. However, by destroying their own exploitation, they succeed in definitely eliminating certain forms of camouflage.

By this process, Marxists maintain that total integration, without camouflage, will one day be achieved, since the working class cannot put an end to its own exploitation without destroying forever all forms of exploitation. Westerners question the mechanism of this process, but they offer another that would move in the same direction. They believe that by eliminating poverty and creating abundance, technological and economic development will put an end to social antagonisms, inequalities, and the exploitation of certain classes by others, and that one day political power will then fully exercise its role of achieving integration, also without camouflage.

THE DEVELOPMENT OF INTEGRATION

Although Western theorists and Marxists disagree on the road to be followed in the development of modern societies, they do agree on the destination of these different roads, and on the mechanism that will bring about the evolution. They believe that the natural movement of history tends to reduce antagonisms and develop social integration, and that this movement is advanced by technological progress.

To some extent, observable facts confirm such optimism. That technological progress promotes social integration can scarcely be denied. But integration depends on other factors besides the economic abundance resulting from technology; and technology also generates factors that cause disintegration. Certain Western observers share the Marxist vision of a fully integrated future society, one in which all conflicts have disappeared and perfect harmony reigns. The possibility of such a perfect society is more than dubious.

Social Integration

The notion that social integration develops concurrently with technological and economic progress is commonplace nowadays. We have already had occasion to touch upon it, but now must examine it more fully.

THE MEANS OF DEVELOPING SOCIAL INTEGRATION   Technological progress increases social integration in several ways: it reduces the tensions caused by poverty, it gives all men the opportunity to better understand one another and even the society in which they live, and it develops a sense of solidarity among all members of the community.

We have already indicated how technological progress tends to reduce social antagonisms (pp. 56–60), but let us review the process of this evolution. The disproportion between human needs and the goods available to satisfy those needs has always been considered an essential factor in political and social conflicts. Too many men fight over too few goods: this melodramatic picture depicts the human situation from its origins down to the twentieth century. There is no doubt that one could alleviate social antagonisms by establishing a rigorously just system of distributing goods and property. This indeed has been the ideal described by virtually every social theoretician, but in practice, it has rarely been applied.

With technological progress, we see the possibility of societies of abundance in which the level of production will not only be able to satisfy everyone's basic needs (food, housing, and clothing) but also their secondary needs (comfort, leisure, and culture). To be sure, no country has yet reached this stage of development, but some are approaching it. Of course, human needs expand and are no sooner satisfied than others arise; but as men's fundamental needs are replaced by secondary needs, dissatisfaction is less acute, and the resulting conflicts less intense. This process tends to reduce antagonisms in two ways. In the first place, it makes social inequality more tolerable. If the pie is too small, all eyes are fixed on the way it is sliced, and the argument is violent if the pieces are unequal. In the presence of a huge pie, capable of satisfying everyone's appetite, the respective size of each slice is less important. Three hundred years ago, the beleaguered silk workers of Lyons inscribed on their banners "Bread or Death": the political struggle was really a struggle for life itself. Today, in Western Europe and North America, it has become a struggle for comforts, leisure, and culture, and so the struggle has become less bitter, less desperate.

In addition, technological progress eliminates the more brutal forms of man's oppression of man. Today we measure the level of a country's development by the number of "mechanical slaves" available to each inhabitant—the mechanical slave being defined as the quantity of energy produced by technological means equivalent to the energy a man could furnish by physical labor. Mechanical slaves are replacing human slaves, which, for a long time, were a kind of necessity. Some say that the invention of the harness in the tenth century was in itself sufficient to eliminate slavery and serfdom. As long as mechanical slaves did not exist, the privileged minority could maintain its comfortable way of life only with human slaves. Today machines suffice. Inequality is based on less blood, sweat, and tears. And finally, inequality itself is diminishing because technological progress tends to reduce the gulf between rich and poor, a fact that clearly contributes to making conflicts less violent.

Technological progress does not merely bring about negative integration by decreasing social antagonisms; it also increases positive integration by developing contacts, understanding, and solidarity among men. By multiplying the means of communication and exchange of information, it ends isolation and makes all members conscious of their community. By raising the level of knowledge and information, it enables each man to gain a better understanding of the others and of society as a whole. By pushing the division of labor as far as possible, it increases human interdependency. However, these results are less conclusive than the negative results mentioned above. Human solidarity, contacts, and understanding were perhaps deeper and more genuine within the framework of small traditional communities than within large modern societies, where personal relationships often remain superficial and even spurious. But these small groups were self-contained and were violently hostile to outsiders or foreigners: their internal solidarity was merely a kind of enlarged egotism. Nationalism, racism, and intolerance are spawned by just such conditions. Technological progress, on the other hand, tends toward a broader, truer kind of solidarity, one that is open to mankind as a whole.

THE HISTORICAL PARALLEL BETWEEN TECHNOLOGICAL DEVELOPMENT AND THE DEVELOPMENT OF INTEGRATION   Observation confirms the fact that, throughout history, integration has advanced as technology progressed.

In primitive societies with closed economies, political power, whether it resided in a remote state or with a nearby feudal lord, rendered few services to the community. Those it did provide included security against invasion from neighboring lords and from foreign armies or bands of marauders; arbitration and legal justice; punishment for crimes against persons or property; use of the community mill and the community oven; and the minting and control of money. But these services cost a great deal, and power eventually took far more than it gave. Those who held power lived off the land, enjoying luxury and opulence in the midst of an impoverished population. Power served them more than it served the community; it safeguarded their privileges and perpetuated social inequality. Furthermore, it had to rely heavily on the use of violence and the force of arms. Although castles protected the inhabitants of a region against foreign invaders, their primary function was to protect the residents of the castle against the surrounding population. Royal castles were, first of all, well-armed and well-defended fortresses that sheltered the monarch from the hostility of the people. This situation still persists in certain parts of the world, in certain regions of Africa, Asia, and Latin America.

In other parts of Africa, Asia, and Latin America, the situation is slightly different. Most of the population still lives in a semiclosed economy and receives few benefits from the state. It also endures with many inconveniences because of the state, for the state serves largely to maintain the domination of a privileged minority that exploits the general population. But in societies of this intermediate type, public services are developed: the government builds highways, railroads, canals, seaports, and airports, and provides telephone service and electricity; it stimulates and regulates the use of credit; and it undertakes programs requiring large capital investments (irrigation projects, dams, and mining development). However, these services primarily benefit a minority of the population—the aristocracy and the bourgeoisie. The splendid highways of certain underdeveloped countries serve only those who own automobiles, modern knights who comprise a tiny minority compared with the mass of pedestrians. Above all, the services benefit only city dwellers; the bulk of the rural population is virtually excluded from the advantages of power.

Even so, in comparison with primitive societies, some progress is being made toward integration; more people now benefit from government power. The circle of social integration is growing. Originally, it was only a handful of aristocrats; but now there is also a bourgeoisie that is gradually expanding into a middle class, and even some elements of the peasantry and working class, who have profited from schools, welfare assistance, and social security. (But for these last groups, the benefits of the state remain well below the hardships the state imposes on them; nevertheless, they are becoming more sensitive to social problems—a fact that increases feelings of integration.) This intermediate type of situation corresponds to the first phase of capitalism. Nineteenth-century Europe, a part of Latin America, North Africa and the Middle East, and noncommunist Asia can be placed in this category.

In the industrially developed societies of the West, political integration is much more advanced. The generally high standard of living reduces antagonisms and increases social consensus. Public services provided by the state continue to multiply, and political power expands its role in the organization of society. Even if the state does not completely plan the economy, it plays an ever greater regulatory role, anticipating crises and alleviating their effects, and correcting imbalances caused by private initiative. Common services and collective organization no longer affect only a limited "inner circle" of the universal society, but are progressively extended to include all segments of the society. This is primarily the result of a higher living standard. Highways, which affect only a privileged minority in Latin America, are of interest to almost everyone in the United States and Western Europe. This situation is also a result of the development of social security, which is to say, public services designed to correct inequalities among men by helping, in particular, the poorest and weakest members of society.

In addition, the state tends to escape from the control of a particular class that uses it to maintain its domination and its privileges. This is so because, first of all, technological progress makes class division increasingly complex, with the result that power is never in the hands of a single homogeneous class, but always in the hands of several classes. Then too, the mass of the population exerts increasing pressure on political power because of the development of universal suffrage on the one hand, and the development of political parties, trade unions, and other mass organizations on the other. The state can no longer be entirely controlled by minority groups. Finally, the evolution of society and the state tends to develop a class of administrator-technicians who identify with the general interest, and who really emobdy it, at least in part, as Hegel had predicted. The Marxist idea that high government officials serve the interests of the ruling class, from which, moreover, they are generally recruited, was valid for a long time. In general, it is still true, but in certain countries, administrators increasingly constitute a special class, which consciously refuses to serve the interests of capitalism, and which tends to play the role of impartial arbiter.

We might apply to this group the famous dictum of Charles Maurras, a half-century ago, on the superiority of monarchy: a regime in which the personal interest of the ruler is inseparable from the interest of the country, since the nation is the king's patrimony. We must not exaggerate the extent of this phenomenon. Although still quite limited and containing some dangers of technocracy, it is significant. Let us cite as an example the arbitration in 1962 of the miners' strike by the "Sages." No one has questioned the impartiality of their conclusions. Some have suggested that high government officials should be permanently entrusted with "telling the facts," just as judges interpret the law in questions concerning the allocation of national income. You will note that the dominant classes, with their influence threatened, are quick to criticize such actions by government administrators. They generally camouflage their criticism behind the myth of "technocracy," exaggerating a danger that is real in other respects. When administrators or technical experts of the government intervene in the decision-making process, they again raise the issue of technocracy, but they are silent on that subject when the intervention comes from technical experts and administrative personnel employed by private firms. The difference is symptomatic (see the notes to Chapter 2).

LIMITS OF THE INFLUENCE OF TECHNOLOGICAL DEVELOPMENT ON INTEGRATION   The influence of technological development on political integration, though undeniable, should not be exaggerated. Two other factors that are often very important enter the picture.

We have already noted that the distinction between stable societies and societies in a state of accelerated change is probably as important as the distinctive between underdeveloped and highly developed societies. In this connection, we examined the influence of the speed of development upon social and political antagonisms. It also plays a role in integration. In stable societies—that is, societies with a slow rate of change, scarcely perceptible in the structure of human life—the sense of integration is much stronger. A social order that has been in existence for several generations seems natural, however unjust it may be, and, as such, tends to be accepted. Societies in the process of rapid change are, on the other hand, societies that are only partially integrated. The established order no longer seems to be an order, from the moment that it ceases to be established and its disintegration has become apparent. At the same time, injustice is no longer regarded as natural and becomes unacceptable. Latent antagonisms flare up and produce serious conflicts. The great class struggles of the nineteenth and twentieth centuries correspond to a change in the rate of evolution. Although they were not as well developed technologically, aristocratic societies of the seventeenth century were more closely integrated than the bourgeois societies of 1850.

Integration varies, moreover, depending on the types of societies involved. At a very early stage in human development, the fusion of the individual into the community appears to have reached a degree it will never again experience. The primitive individual is totally absorbed into the group of which he is an essential element. He cannot conceive of an existence apart from the group and sees himself as a member of the collectivity rather than as an individual. Sociologists of the Durkheim school have described the individualization of power: authority that first belonged to the entire group, to the collectivity as such, was progressively appropriated by certain members of the group who thus became its leaders. We could describe, in a parallel manner, the process of individualizing citizens. Marxists link this process to the appearance of private property. Whether or not this is so, no subsequent society seems to have been as integrated as primitive society, with the exception of certain monastic communities or the first Israeli kibbutzim, which practiced extreme communism.

The development of integration, under the influence of technological development, appears only in modern societies, constituted according to the individualization of the citizens. In an early phase of the history of mankind, technological progress seems to have had the reverse effect. It was probably the cause of an awareness of individuality, which partially separated men from the community and provoked conflicts among them and between the group and its members. Even if one rejects Marxist reasoning—explaining the dissolution of primitive communism by the appearance of private property, produced in turn by advances in the techniques of production—technological progress appears to have played a great role in the phenomenon of individualization.

The Myth of Total Integration

Men have always dreamed of a fully integrated society, where everyone would find complete fulfillment without conflicts or antagonisms, where each individual would merge with the entire community without alienating his own personality. Some believe they find this lost paradise in the past: certain descriptions of the Middle Ages or of the *ancien régime* endow them with colors of the Golden Age. Others envisage the eventual arrival of a future paradise, a widely prevalent tendency today. Optimistic theories of the indefinite progress of humanity, formulated in the eighteenth century, are transposed and given new life both by Marxists, with their concept of the "final phase of communism," and by certain Western theorists, with their notion of the society of abundance.

WESTERN THEORIES OF THE SOCIETY OF ABUNDANCE   Even before 1939, certain theoreticians were predicting the imminent arrival of a society in which all human needs could be satisfied, thanks to the formidable increase in production made possible by technological advances (in France, it was Jacques Duboin with his "abundancy" theory that no one took seriously). During the past decade or so, these ideas have gained wide currency. We have the popular image of a "society of consumers," in which all members can satisfy almost all their needs, not only the basic ones (food, clothing, health, and housing), but also the secondary ones (security, comfort, leisure, and culture). Certain countries—such as those of North America and Western Europe, plus Australia and New Zealand—are already approaching this goal. It is believed that economic abundance will eliminate political antagonisms and will lead to fully integrated societies. The weakening of political conflicts—known as "depoliticization"—which is noticeable in the most advanced nations, is considered a step on the road to total integration. However, these theories appear far too optimistic.

In the first place, human needs are no sooner satisfied than additional needs are felt. The pursuit of abundance resembles somewhat the race of Achilles and the tortoise. New needs arise as the old ones disappear. To be sure, they are less urgent, less vital, objectively speaking. But subjectively speaking, are they any less deeply felt? It is hard to say. Among privileged classes who have known economic abundance for centuries, questions of prestige, luxury, clothing, and jewelry assume considerable importance. They produce violent conflicts: it is interesting to read social philosopher Henri de Saint-Simon (1753–1821) in this connection. In very highly developed societies, commercial advertising tends to encourage this unending expansion of human needs. Men nearly always have the impression of lacking one thing or another in the midst of abundance. Constantly changing patterns of fashion and style, which include an ever larger number of commodities, augment these feelings of frustration: right after you buy a new automobile, for instance, a new model appears, and you feel unhappy about owning an older model. And so it is with other things.

Moreover, certain scarcities cannot be eliminated. Not every Frenchman can own a villa on the Riviera, because space is limited. One day, every Parisian will have a comfortable apartment, but they cannot all live in equally convenient locations (near one's office, factory, recreational facilities, and so forth). All workers will be able to earn a satisfactory income, but all work will not be equally interesting or equally bearable. Supervisory positions will always be more sought after than subordinate positions, but there will always be fewer of the former. The more gifted will always win out over the less gifted, which will inevitably produce resentments and frustrations. These privileges will be materially less important than they are in underdeveloped societies, but they will perhaps involve a more painful adjustment. because they will be more incompatible with the established system of values. In an egalitarian society, a slight inequality is more deeply resented than a glaring inequality in a nonegalitarian society.

Even if the Golden Age could really be achieved in some highly developed societies, these would resemble oases lost in the sands of the desert, or islands surrounded on all sides by the sea. Only a few countries can hope to attain a state of abundance in the near future. For others, the notion remains a mirage, while the problem of accumulating capital and the population explosion aggravate social and political antagonisms. Thus conflicts will arise between rich nations and poor nations, and these conflicts will heighten tensions within the wealthy nations, that is, within the societies of abundance.

Moreover, and above all, the abundance in question involves only economic goods. But poverty in other aspects of society also generates social tensions, which naturally tend to increase when economic antagonisms disappear. A man with an empty stomach thinks only about food and struggles to survive. A man who has eaten his fill no longer thinks about food, but strives to satisfy other desires.

Arthur Koestler relates that, as a prisoner suffering from hunger, he dreamed at night about dinners and banquets with the same intensity that he dreamed about women as an adolescent. Societies of abundance put an end to the first privation, but not to the second. Now certain psychoanalysts consider the second type of privation more important than the first in the development of antagonisms. In their view, the conflict between social imperatives and human desires, between the reality principle and the pleasure principle, is more basic and more general than disagreements about the distribution of national wealth or questions about freedom of expression. It becomes so, in any case, when these freedoms exist and when economic abundance relegates material needs to a secondary plane. It would be interesting to study from this angle the contemporary development of eroticism and what American sociologists call—with much exaggeration—the "sexual revolution." Might it not be the demand for and gradual conquest of a form of freedom, a struggle against a privation, which develops as other freedoms are consolidated and other privations disappear?

Finally, many antagonisms are not tied to the question of abundance, economic or otherwise. The basic conflict between the individual and the group, the contradictions between individualistic tendencies and the need for communion with others, depends far more upon psychological factors than upon a scarcity of consumer goods. Ideological differences sometimes conceal the struggle for material things, but they generally go beyond it. We may indeed wonder whether, once the problems of food, shelter, and clothing are solved, those of ideology will not become more urgent. Conflicts, which today seem secondary, may thus occupy stage center and assume great importance—the conflict between men and women, for example, or the conflict between the generations.

Women are an oppressed class by comparison with men, but this oppression does not appear to be connected with economic poverty or with the system of private ownership of the means of production. Changes in the law rectifying women's legal inequities and ending discrimination in salaries and employment cannot prevent motherhood and child care from imposing additional responsibilities upon women. If a wife remains at home, she finds herself economically dependent upon her husband. If she works, she adds family and housekeeping duties to her professional responsibilities. Equality seems just as difficult to achieve in other domains because it always depends as much upon psycho-physiological conditions, which are hard to change, as upon economic conditions. American statutes regarding the relationships between the sexes place the man at the mercy of the woman, which is hardly more satisfactory than French law, which places the woman at the mercy of the man, or Italian law, which locks both the man and the woman in a state of permanent hypocrisy.

Conflicts between the generations seem just as difficult to eliminate. The entrance of young people into society will always set them, to some extent, against the older generation, who are naturally in no hurry to give up positions that young people are impatient to take away from them. The prolongation of life, thanks to medical and scientific advances, aggravates the conflict instead of alleviating it. It tends to give the advantage to the new generations and to reduce the older generations to the status of an oppressed class. By surrounding the elderly with prestige and respect, traditional civilizations relieved somewhat the sadness usually associated with old age. In highly developed societies, old age becomes a two-fold oppressor—through the effect of nature and through social causes. Anyone past the age of forty-five who has lost his job has great difficulty finding another, and he risks becoming a kind of social derelict in a capitalistic society. But everywhere, the lowering of the retirement age, plus the constant lengthening of human life, creates a class of elderly citizens whom society reduces to inferior status. Yet these people are able and willing to participate fully and to live an active life for a good many more years. They are thus "alienated" in the Marxist sense of the term.

But above all, the antagonisms between citizens and governmental power are not eliminated by technological progress and its resulting economic abundance. "Depoliticization" is more apparent than real.

We are witnessing a change in the forms of political life rather than its disappearance (see the notes to this chapter). Technological progress tends to strengthen the power of government and the state, making them more oppressive for the citizenry—which increase the alienation of the people by arousing their opposition to the government's power. We will shortly explore this subject further.

THE MARXIST THEORY OF THE "FINAL PHASE OF COMMUNISM"   Like Western theory, Marxism links social integration with the development of technology and economic abundance, but in a less direct manner. For Marxists, the principal result of technological progress is to change the conditions of production, namely, the property system and the class relationships it creates. Modern production methods make it possible to socialize the means of production and abolish social classes, and these steps, by themselves, lead toward a fully integrated society. Economic abundance is linked not only to technological progress but also to the elimination of capitalism.

According to Marx and Lenin, the future evolution of humanity will therefore occur in several successive phases. Capitalism will destroy itself as a result of its internal contradictions, and the working class will come to power. The bourgeois state, an instrument for the domination of one class, will be replaced by the revolutionary state, which will destroy private ownership of the means of production, put an end to the division of classes, and so eliminate all the causes of antagonisms and alienation. Then, the final phase of communism will be achieved, and will wither away and men will live in a fully integrated society.

For Marxists, antagonisms and alienation are linked to the private ownership of the means of production and to the resulting division into social classes. All antagonisms are more or less consequences and reflections of the struggle of the oppressed class against its oppressor, and of the efforts of the latter to maintain its oppression. Alienation results first from the fact that the capitalist appropriates the plus-value of an employee's labor—the essence of his creative activity—thereby robbing the employee of a part of himself. Alienation also arises from the fact that capitalism orients production and all social activity toward the pursuit of each person's selfish interest, which is turned against the collective interest. Salaried workers are obliged to pursue their own self-interest in their relationships with their employers; all of society is focused on the development of egocentric attitudes, which prevent the establishment of genuine community life. Once private ownership of the means of production is abolished, the class struggle no longer has any foundation and will therefore disappear with the gradual elimination of old reflexes acquired in the framework of the former capitalistic society. Likewise, egotistical habits will disappear little by little, while a sense of community spirit will develop in a society oriented toward the collective interest.

The notion of abundance, so fashionable in the West today, is not absent from this process of social integration. Lenin is said to have remarked: "Communism is the Soviets, plus electrification." By "Soviets," he meant the instruments of production in the hands of the workers, not in the hands of private ownership. "Electrification" was, at the time of the remark (about 1920), the symbol of technological progress and the increased production it made possible. Moreover, in the final phase of communism, the distribution of goods will be based on the principle "To each according to his needs." This obviously assumes that there will be enough goods available to cover all human needs— the very definition of abundance. It will be recalled that Marxists do not believe abundance is possible under a capitalistic regime because of its Malthusian tendencies, and that only a socialistic society can attain a large enough level of production to permit unrestricted consumption. Thus the development of socialism causes the disappearance of antagonisms and alienations produced by poverty and scarcity.

The previous criticisms of the Western theory of the abundant society can be applied here—except for the one concerning antagonisms between the individual and society. Marxists saw capitalism as an obstacle to integration because it directs all human activity toward the pursuit of selfish interests. By thus encouraging selfishness, by turning egotistical conflict into the motivating force of production and social life in general, capitalism prevents the development of a true human community. Even total abundance in a capitalistic society would not end the isolation of individuals enclosed in their private satisfactions and egos, an isolation that fosters antagonisms and alienations. Only when altruism replaces egoism, and the collective goal replaces private interest as the basic motive for human actions, can true integration result. Capitalism prevents this development, while socialism permits it. But nothing guarantees that this necessary objective will be sufficient. It is by no means certain that the elimination of capitalism will be enough to destroy human selfishness and the pursuit of personal interests. It is not certain that it will succeed in making human labor a free, creative activity again, one in which man will find joy and fulfillment, as Plato had hoped long ago. It is not certain that this unalienated labor will automatically work for the interest of the whole.

Other criticisms of the theory of the abundant society are valid for the theory of the "final phase of communism." The end of the class struggle will not eliminate most of the psychological factors in political conflicts. It will alleviate ideological antagonisms to the extent that they are a reflection of the class struggle, but they are only partly a reflection of this struggle. It will not mark the disappearance of the battle of the sexes or of conflicts between the generations. Like economic abundance, it will eliminate many conflicts linked with the satisfaction of material needs. But let us repeat that once the necessities of life are assured, the antagonisms associated with ideology are likely to arise. Finally, the conflict between citizens and governmental power will not disappear with the elimination of the class struggle. This point deserves closer examination because it is in direct contradiction with an important element in the Marxist theory of the final phase of communism: the doctrine of the withering away of the state.

For Marxists, the state is an instrument of coercion. In a society based on the class struggle, this instrument is in the hands of the dominant class (bourgeoisie, aristocracy, or slave owners), which uses the state to maintain its domination. In a socialist revolution, the workers take possession of the state apparatus and use it, thereafter, to destroy all domination of one class by another, and to create the conditions of communism: such is the role of the revolutionary state. Once private ownership of the means of production is entirely eliminated, all the consequences of capitalism have disappeared, and class divisions no longer exist, the state will then fade away. Purely and simply, it will tend to disappear. Since all conflicts emanate from the class struggle, and there are no more classes, there will be no more conflicts. Therefore, the apparatus of constraint and instruments will no longer be needed; all men will comply with the common rules; since they hurt no one and benefit everybody. The state will be no more than an administrative body, handling administrative matters somewhat like the police directing traffic. As Saint-Simon predicted: "The administration of things will replace the government of men." Power will disappear as power per se, and politics will come to an end.

Now this theory does not seem very tenable. We note, first of all, that socialism in the Soviet Union did not cause the state to wither away, but caused it to expand excessively, as the dictatorship of Stalin demonstrated. Marxists declare that that was partly the result of internal difficulties in building socialism, and partly due to outside pressure from the capitalist world. But other fundamental objections to their thesis of the fading away of the state remain. First, it assumes that all antagonisms and all forms of alienation will disappear. We have just seen that this situation seems quite impossible. As long as there are antagonisms or alienations of any kind, men will not comply freely with social rules and regulations, and political power will persist. Moreover, technological progress tends to strengthen political power, making an abnormal expansion of the power of the state a greater possibility, rather than a gradual withering away.

Let us review the main features of this process (previously described on pp. 55–67). In the first place, the modern state intervenes in many more domains than the traditional state. In a socialist regime, moreover, this extension of government authority reaches even further since it includes the entire economy (except for a decentralization that is always difficult to achieve because of the concurrent need for social planning). "I forgive the Republic for governing badly, because it governs little," novelist Anatole France has one of his characters remark. The modern state governs better, but it governs more. In ancient societies, men had little contact with governmental power. It remained remote, and they got along without it in most areas of life. In modern societies, on the contrary, every citizen depends upon the state for a large part of his existence. Relationships multiply between the government and the citizenry, along with opportunities for the former to take advantage of the latter.

In the second place, governmental power becomes more oppressive. Technological progress increases the possibilities of state control over the citizenry. Modern means of communication and propaganda give today's dictators a hold on the people that has no parallel among the ancient tyrants. Moreover, when the latter became intolerable, they were in danger of being overthrown. Today, technological advances give governmental power virtually irresistible means of coercion, making any resistance on the part of the people far more difficult. When the military and police were armed with sabres and lances, revolt by the masses was always a possibility. Against tanks, machine guns, aircraft, and armored cars, the population is practically powerless, as we saw in the Spanish Civil War.

In the third place, the psychological oppression of governmental power, which is a function of the ruler's desire for power, is reinforced in highly developed societies by sociological oppression, a consequence of the evolution of the power structure. The proliferation of officials —that is, people who force others to obey them—constitutes only one of its aspects. The extension of the state's apparatus involves an increase in the number of those who make decisions in the name of the state. The circle of government officials expands, thereby increasing the number of persons whom citizens must obey. Instead of a single tyrant and a few lieutenants, we are confronted with thousands of little tyrants, each with a limited sphere of authority. But the combined pressure from all of them results in virtually paralyzing the people's freedom of movement—reminding one of Jonathan Swift's Gulliver, bound to the earth by thousands of Lilliputian ties, each one insignificant by itself, but extremely effective when applied collectively.

And we have been speaking only of an expansion of the desire for power by multiplying the numbers of those who wield it. But the modern state is gradually changing from a collection of rulers, administrators, and department heads, who can individually abuse their power, into an enormous machine whose total activity exceeds that of each of its component parts. The mechanism itself is oppressive, quite apart from the desire for power of those who operate it. We have already noted this tendency toward bureaucracy in Chapters 1 and 2. It is not confined to the state, that is, to power within the nation; it reaches out to encompass all forms of power in large modern communities—giant industries, political parties, and organizations with mass memberships. Although it is mechanical, impersonal, abstract, clean, sterilized, organized, and free of physical violence, the oppression it creates is no less heavy-handed than the oppression of rulers driven by a desire for power. The enormous growth of state power and its bureaucratization directly contradict the notion of any "withering away of the state." The actual trend gives rise to the rebirth of liberal theories regarding resistance to oppression, by providing these theories with greater scope and relevance.

Notes

Introduction

A good overall résumé of the development of sociology is to be found in A. Cuvillier, *Manuel de sociologie*, 3d ed., Vol. I (1958), pp. 1–96, including numerous bibliographies; we have used it quite extensively. One should also consult J. Touchard et al., *Histoire des idées politiques*, 2 vols. (1959). For a fuller treatment, see G. Gusdorf, *Introduction aux sciences humaines* (1960); T.N. Bonner, D.W. Hill, G.L. Wilber, *The Contemporary World: The Social Sciences in Historical Perspective* (Englewood Cliffs, N.J., 1960); F. Znaniecki, *Cultural Sciences: Their Origin and Development* (Urbana, Ill., 1952); F.N. House, *The Development of Sociology* (New York, 1936); E. Bogardus, *The Development of Social Thought*, 3d ed. (Los Angeles, Calif., 1955); H.E. Barnes and H. Becker, *Social Thought from Lore to Science*, 2d ed., 2 vols. (New York, 1952); H.E. Barnes, *An Introduction to the History of Sociology* (Chicago, 1947), and *Historical Sociology* (New York, 1948); and A.W. Small, *Origins of Sociology* (Chicago, 1924). Also the brief résumé by G. Bouthoul, *Histoire de la sociologie* (1951).

On current scientific ideas, see J. Ullmo, *La pensée scientifique moderne* (1958); J. Cavaillès, *Sur la logique et la théorie de la science* (1960); and G.-G. Granger, *Pensée formelle et sciences de l'homme* (1960).

Concerning the notion of political sociology, see M. Duverger, *Méthodes de la science politique* (1959), pp. 1–58; G. Burdeau, *Méthode de la science politique* (1960); J. Meynaud, *Introduction à la science politique* (1959), and *La science politique: fondement et perspectives* (Lausanne, 1960); UNESCO, *La science politique contem-poraine* (1950); F. Barbano, *Sociologia della politica* (Milan, 1961); W.A. Robson, *The University Teaching of Social Sciences: Political Science* (UNESCO, 1955); R. Bendix and S.M. Lipset, *Political Sociol-ogy* (a special issue of *Current Sociology,* No. 6, 1957); D. Waldo, *Po-litical Science in the U.S.A.* (UNESCO, 1956); B. Crick, *The American Science of Politics* (1960); S. Hoffmann, "Tendances de la science poli-tique aux Etats-Unis," *Revue française de science politique,* 7195, p. 913; V. Van Dyke, *Political Science: A Philosophical Analysis* (Lon-don, 1961); and the interesting criticism by H.J. Storing et al., *Essays on the Scientific Study of Politics* (New York, 1962).

Concerning the concept of power as the basis for political science, see the articles by J. Lhomme, in *Revue économique* (1958), p. 859, (1959), p. 481; and by J. Gaudemet, "Esquisse d'une sociologie histo-rique du Pouvoir," *Politique* (July–December 1962); F. Bourricaud, *Esquisse d'une théorie de l'autorité* (1961); B. de Jouvenel, *Du pouvoir* (Geneva, 1945); the small volume by J.W. Lapierre, *Le pouvoir poli-tique* (1953); the books by Charles E. Merriam, *Political Power* (New York, 1934), and *Systematic Politics* (Chicago, 1945); the works of H.D. Lasswell, *Politics* (New York, 1936), and *Power and Personality* (New York, 1948); H.D. Lasswell and A. Kaplan, *Power and Society* (London, 1952); and the publications of the Institut international de Philosophie du Droit, *Le pouvoir,* 2 vols. (1956–57).

The thesis that "political science = science of the state" has been care-fully analyzed by M. Prelot in *La conception française de la science politique* (course in political science given at the Faculté de Droit de Paris, 1956–57, mimeographed) and in his short volume *La Science politique* (1961); see also A. Carro Martinez, *Introducción a la ciencia política* (Madrid, 1957). The view set forth by David Easton, *The Po-litical System* (New York, 1953)—that political science is the science of the authoritarian distribution of values in a society—returns, in effect, to the concept equating "political science" with "science of the state," as Hans Morgenthau has clearly shown in his article "Reflections on the State of Political Science," *Review of Politics,* No. 4 (1955). Con-cerning Easton's theories, see also D. Easton, *A Systems Analysis of Po-litical Life* (New York, 1965), and *A Framework for Political Analysis,* U.S.A. (1965). Intermediate views have been set forth by F. Bourri-caud, "Science politique et sociologie," *Revue française de science poli-tique* (1958), pp. 249ff.

On the concept of power, one should compare the notions of "social control" and "social constraint." See, on this point, E. Durkheim, *Les règles de la méthode sociologique,* 1st ed. (1895) (reprinted since); also the results of the comprehensive study conducted between 1926 and 1930 by G.L. Duprat on the various forms of social constraint, published by the *Revue internationale de sociologie* (1927–30); Duprat provided a careful summary of all forms of constraint in the January 1928 issue. See also American works dealing with social control, very close to the notion of social constraint, especially J.S. Roucek et al., *Social Control,* 2d ed. (Princeton, N.J., 1956); T.T. Segerstedt, *Social Control as Sociological Concept* (Upsala, 1948); L.L. Bernard, *Social Control and Its Sociological Aspects* (New York, 1901); and collected studies published by the American Sociological Society, *Social Control,* Papers and Proceedings, Vol. XII (Chicago, 1930), especially the bibliography on power on p. 61.

One should also compare the notion of power with that of "leadership": see F. Bourricaud, *Esquisse d'une théorie de l'autorité* (1961), and "La sociologie du 'leadership,'" *Revue française de science politique* (1953), p. 445; J. Maisonneuve, "L'étude psychologique des petits groupes," *Année sociologique* (1951); D. Cartwright and A. Zander, *Group Dynamics* (Evanston, Ill., 1953); P. Morre, E.F. Borgata, and R.F. Bales, *Small Groups* (New York, 1955); A.W. Gouldner, *Studies in Leadership* (New York, 1950); J. Klein, *The Study of Groups* (London, 1956); and G.J. Homans, *The Human Group* (London, 1951).

There is no work in any language that considers simultaneously the entire range of problems examined in this book. It is therefore not possible to provide the reader with a truly general bibliography. Accordingly, we will limit ourselves to a few representative titles on this subject. On the other hand, extensive bibliographies will be given in conjunction with each problem examined.

For a comparative study of the Western and Marxist approaches to political sociology, the reader is strongly advised to read S.M. Lipset, *Political Man* (1959), and the manual *Les principes du marxisme-léninisme* (translated from the Russian), 2d ed. (Moscow, n.d., probably 1962). For a comparative study of developed societies and so-called primitive societies, see the excellent work by G. Balandier, *Anthropologie politique* (1967).

See also M. Duverger, *Introduction à la politique* (1964); R. Aron, *Dix-huit leçons sur les sociétés industrielles* (1962), *La lutte des classes* (1964), *Démocratie et totalitarisme* (1965); and the brief study by G. Bouthoul, *Sociologie de la politique* (1965). The work by H.D. Lasswell, *The Future of Political Science* (New York, 1963), is interesting on the question of participation by political scientists in political decision-making, but his views of the future are open to question. One may also consult M.G. Lange, *Politische Soziologie* (Berlin, 1961); S.S. Ulmer, *Introductory Readings in Political Behaviour* (1961); S.M. Lipset, *The Social Bases of Politics* (1960); H. Eulau, *Political Behaviour* (1956); and F. Barbano, *Sociologia della politica* (1961).

It would be worthwhile to consult the general sociological studies mentioned in M. Duverger, *Méthodes des sciences sociales,* 3d ed. (1964), pp. 84ff., as well as the works on political science cited in the same book, p. 61. Among the many titles listed there, G. Gurvitch et al., *Traité de sociologie,* 2 vols. (1958–60), is especially worthwhile. Finally, there are fairly detailed bibliographies in UNESCO, "La sociologie contemporaine," *Sociologie politique* (1957).

Chapter One: Physical Structures

GEOGRAPHICAL STRUCTURES

Concerning the political importance of geographical structures, see J. Gottmann, *La politique des Etats et leur géographie,* 1952 (a study devoted exclusively to geographical influences on foreign policy); J. Brunhes, *Géographie humaine,* 3d ed., 3 vols. (1925), abridged edition in one volume, 1947; M. Sorre, *Rencontre de la géographis et de la sociologie* (1957), and *Les fondements de la géographie humaine,* 4 vols. (1943–52); A. Le Lannou, *La géographie humaine* (1949); A. Demangeon, *Problèmes de la géographie humaine* (1957); L. Febvre, *La terre et l'évolution humaine* (1922); M. Derbruau, *Précis de géographie humaine* (1961)—the most recent précis, which deals very little with political influences; H. and M. Sprout, *The Ecological Perspective on Human Affairs* (Princeton, 1965). Concerning the ties between geography and underdevelopment, see Y. Lacoste, *Géographie du sousdéveloppement* (1965); P. Gourou, *Les pays tropicaux* (1966); and especially the essay of P. Lavigne, *Climats et sociétés* (1966).

The Ways in Which Geographical Factors Act Upon Social Phenomena

It is interesting to recall, in this connection, several theories formulated during the first half of the twentieth century.

DETERMINISM OR "POSSIBILISM" The action of geographical factors was first conceived as a form of determinism. Such was the traditional position of Aristotle, Jean Bodin, and Montesquieu, and, more recently, of the followers of Le Play, who studied the relationship between geographical data and the structure of the family. This was also the position of F. Ratzel, who influenced the entire German school and part of the American school of political sociologists. Certain formulations by Ratzel are quite striking: "The earth regulates the destiny of peoples with a blind brutality," he wrote. And again: "Man's apparent freedom seems to be annihilated by the action of the earth." American writer Ellsworth Huntington makes statements in the same tone: "Man is but a piece of clay in the hands of nature."

Following Vidal de la Blache, the French school of human geography completely rejects this determinism. It does not regard the influence of geographical factors on political and social life as mechanical, automatic, and irresistible. A certain soil, a certain climate, or a certain kind of territory does not necessarily imply a certain political regime or a certain social relationship. A given soil, climate, or region is more conducive to one political regime than to another, but that is all. It would be better yet to say, "more conducive to such and such kinds of political regimes and less conducive to other kinds," for there is always a wide range of possibilities, a broad spectrum of choices. Whence the well-known, frequently quoted formulation of Vidal de la Blache: "At all levels and in all degrees, nature offers possibilities. Man chooses from among them. Geography furnishes the canvas on which man traces his designs."

DIRECT INFLUENCE AND INFLUENCE BY REACTION The French school of human geography seems to consider only the direct influence of the various possibilities offered by geographical factors: a certain type of political regime, institution, or society being more likely to develop under natural conditions most favorable to its development. But there is probably another kind of influence, which we may call "influence by reaction."

In this connection, we must examine the famous theory on "challenge," formulated by the great contemporary English historian Arnold J. Toynbee. According to Toynbee, "facility is harmful to civilization." All great civilizations, he argues, developed in difficult natural surroundings, and they did so precisely by reacting against natural difficulties. Man's energy, creativity, and capacity to invent social and political structures would be weak indeed if there were no obstacles to overcome, no natural difficulties to surmount. Men, on the contrary, become strong and powerful precisely when confronted with such obstacles. Consequently, Toynbee writes, "the stimulus to civilization grows in proportion to the hostility of one's environment."

This theory systematizes very old ideas about sybaritic societies and "the downward slope of ease." To be sure, it contains an element of truth. Great civilizations and highly organized political systems have developed under hostile geographical conditions through a reaction against or a challenge from the environment. The Amerindian empires of the Andes are striking examples of this phenomenon. Equally striking is the contrast between Boeotia, materially rich yet barely civilized, and the Greek empire, relatively barren but an admirable laboratory for different forms of civilization. However, Toynbee tends to exaggerate. There is nothing "proportionate" between "the stimulus to civilization" (a very vague notion) and the hostility of the environment. We must not imagine a kind of determinism in reverse. The truth is simply that natural conditions not only act directly upon a society; they also exert an indirect influence by provoking reactions.

Are Geographical Structures Physical or Social?

Nature has a direct influence on social and political life: the influence of climate on the human organism and on whatever is cultivated; the influence of the soil on vegetable, animal, and mineral resources; the role of rivers and seas as means of transportation and communication, and so on. But geographical factors are not only physical; they are sociological, as well.

THE ROLE OF POPULAR IMAGES   The great American geographer I. Bowman wrote at the end of his career: "All my life, I have tried to explain to people that natural environment has meant only what people wanted it to mean." The statement is an exaggeration. Natural environment has a reality of its own, whatever ideas people may have about it. But the ideas people have are extremely important. We have already indicated that there are few frontiers which can be described as physically natural borders. However, national rivalries, propaganda, and the course of history develop certain notions about natural boundaries; these may be geographically false, but they end up becoming sociologically true since everyone believes they conform to nature.

There is no more striking example of this tendency than the different systems of cartographic projection. The way the terrestrial globe is represented on a flat surface has had a notable influence on certain geo-political theories, and even upon certain current beliefs in this field. Mackinder's ideas about "the island of the world" and the heartland derive quite clearly from a world map that is centered simultaneously on the equator and on a longitudinal meridian located between 30° and 35° east of Greenwich. In this depiction of the earth, the American continent is set far over to the edges of the map with the Euro-Afro-Asian block occupying the center, and with European Russia at the very heart of the block. The position of Western Europe in the rivalry between the United States and the USSR is very different, depending on whether one looks at a map based on the traditional equatorial projection or one utilizing the polar projection, which has become so popular in the last twenty years. On the first map, Europe is situated between the two giants and even looks like a subject of contention. The idea of any European "disengagement" seems absurd. On the second, the United States and Russia are face to face and very close to each other on both sides of the North pole, with Europe pushed to one side. When viewed on this map, the notion of a European neutrality does not seem at all absurd, geographically speaking.

THE TRANSFORMATION OF NATURE BY MAN   Irrespective of the pictures or maps men make, the present-day geographical environment is, in most cases, a result of human action as much as of preexisting physical conditions. Of course, in the Sahara, in the deserts of central Asia, in the forests of the Amazon, and in equatorial Africa, man still finds himself confronted by a true, natural environment. But in most inhabited areas today, the environment has been fashioned as much by man as by nature. Large numbers of trees, vegetables, and animals have been imported from the outside. Clearing the land of trees and timber, deforestation, and crop cultivation have changed the climate as well as the landscape, setting in motion a chain of additional transformations. Even what we call "nature"—aside from cities, buildings, canals, highways, and so on—is as much the result of history as of geography.

Meanwhile, it is this contemporary environment that influences social life and political phenomena today. It is futile to try to separate primitive physical factors from those incorporated in the total picture by human action. All of it has now dissolved into an inextricable mixture. Moreover, there is little reason to attempt to dissociate them. The important thing is to observe that geographical factors are not only physical factors, but sociological factors as well. This is the profound truth in the term "human geography," adopted by the French school of sociologists.

LIBERATION FROM NATURE   Not only has man transformed nature so that its original features have become increasingly difficult to discern; man is also progressively freeing himself from nature. In the complex milieu of human geography, the influence of purely physical factors tends to diminish because of technological developments. We have mentioned how technology enables man to struggle with climate, how it abolishes or reduces distances. All this creates political repercussions, among others. For instance, the notion of "the great state" and "the small state" has changed considerably since the eighteenth century. In France, the *département* was considered a large territorial division when the Constituent Assembly created it in 1791, basing its size on the principle that one should be able to travel from its administrative seat to the departmental border in one day. Today one can cover the distance in less than an hour, and the *département* is too small.

The influence of technology has assumed great importance in connection with natural resources. In the past, a country's economy depended primarily on geography. Today it depends far more on technology. Developed nations are not those with the greatest quantity of natural resources, but those with the greatest technological equipment.

Finally, the distinction between "underdeveloped countries" (also referred to as countries "in process of development" or "in accelerated development") and "developed nations" (synonomous with "industrialized nations") is very important from the standpoint of geographical factors and their influence. This influence is more important in underdeveloped than in developed countries. Thus the influence of geography decreases to the extent that technological progress advances.

Concerning the views of the French school of human geography, see P. Vidal de la Blache, *Principes de géographie humaine* (1922), and especially L. Febvre, *La terre et l'homme* (1922); also the studies by American geographer I. Bowman, in particular, *Geography in Relation to the Social Sciences* (1914), and the article on Bowman by G.M. Wrigley in *Geographical Review* (1951), p. 7.

For a brief study of determinism, see E.C. Semple, *Influences of Geographic Environment* (London and New York, 1911). Arnold Toynbee's theories on "challenge" have been developed in his nine-volume *Study of History,* in process of publication since 1933. The first six volumes were abridged into one by D.C. Somervell (1947).

Some General Theories About Political Geography

It is worthwhile mentioning here, if only for historical interest, a few general theories concerning the influence of geography on politics. Except for those of Aristotle, Bodin, and Montesquieu already referred to, they are scarcely to be taken seriously any longer. Several, however, have served to camouflage the claims and ambitions of certain states.

Probably the most valid is Jean Brunhes' theory regarding the conflict between nomadic and sedentary peoples.

THEORIES ON THE CONFLICT BETWEEN NOMADIC AND SEDENTARY PEOPLES   A study of civilizations in the Asiatic steppes prompted the disciples of Le Play, at the end of the nineteenth century, to formulate a theory regarding the influence of nomadic life on politics. In their view, living conditions among nomads imposed a society with a patriarchal family structure, resulting in political authoritarianism. Later geographers, historians, and sociologists were more impressed by the warlike character of nomadic peoples, by their tendency to subjugate sedentary civilizations. Ethnographic studies in North Africa, Black Africa, and the steppes that border portions of the Sahara desert have revealed similar phenomena. A plausible theory (provided it is not carried too far) on the conflict between conquering nomadic peoples and vanquished sedentary peoples has been based on these studies. Here is how the great geographer Jean Brunhes expressed it: "The herbaceous steppes of central Asia, with their severe winters, do not allow for intensive cultivation. Only on the fringes of the mountains, where oases of irrigation have been established, can crops grow and flourish. Everywhere else, the natural terrain is best suited to the pastoral art, to tending flocks and herds. And such has been the particular domain of herdsmen on horseback, small groups of men scattered with their livestock over a vast area. But faced with the necessity of constantly moving about and having to know in advance about available grazing lands and water resources for great distances, they acquire a sense of tactical movement and strategy which predisposes them to sovereignty over space and domination of their neighbors. Some of the greatest and boldest conquerors of history have emerged from the steppes— Genghis Khan, Tamerlane, Kublai Khan. It is safe to conclude that the qualities and capabilities responsible for their power were acquired on the steppes, from the skills they conferred on a pastoral people, and from their geographical subordination to their environment. It was these wandering bands of herdsmen, not the masses of small farmers who swarmed all over southern and eastern Asia, who led the world. For several centuries, China, and India herself, were under the domination of the Mongols or the Manchus, that is, the nomads, the great Asiatic herdsmen."

HUNTINGTON'S THEORIES ON THE DRYING UP OF THE EARTH   With theories of this kind we enter the domain of imaginary fantasies, brilliant ones at that. The American geographer Ellsworth Huntington, struck by the contrast between the mighty civilizations of central and south-west Asia in antiquity and the wretched conditions of these regions at the dawn of the twentieth century, thought that this decline might have been due to changes in climate. The present-day aridity of these lands seemed to him incongruous with their former position as centers of great empires, and he began to think that their earlier climate must have been more humid, that this area must have undergone a progressive dehydration. But such a process could only have been part of a larger, more general phenomenon. Accordingly, Huntington was led to postulate a theory on the general drying-up of the earth, which occurred in rhythmic "pulsations," with alternating periods of dry and humid weather.

With this grandiose theory, Huntington claimed to explain a vast number of historical events. The story of the wanderings of the Hebrew people, related in the Bible, was linked to the midpoint between a period of dryness and one of humidity. The expansion of the Mogul empire, the barbarian invasions of Western Europe, resulted from the drying up of the original habitat of the invaders. Huntington also argued that the progressive dehydration of the earth followed a certain direction from east to north to west. This would account for the displacement of the great centers of civilization: from Egypt and Babylonia to Greece, from Greece to Rome, from Rome to France, from France to England, and from England to the United States (writing before 1940, Huntington was not very conscious of Russian power). You will note that this theory by an American geographer was quite favorable to America. But unfortunately for Huntington, archeological studies have proved that world climates have been stable for the past several thousand years.

MACKINDER'S THEORY OF THE "HEARTLAND" The English imagination has been no less fertile than the American. The theory of the "heartland," formulated in 1919 by the great British geographer Sir Halford John Mackinder, is more famous than Huntington's theory because of its strategic implications. It is no longer taken seriously.

Mackinder begins with a concept of the rivalry between continental powers and maritime powers, a rivalry that had already impressed many historians, sociologists, and geographers, notably Ratzel, who published a book entitled *The Sea as a Source of Political Power* in 1898. Its appearance was well timed to justify the maritime and expansionist aims of Kaiser Wilhelm II. Mackinder believed that the means of political power were different for maritime and continental states, but that they balanced one another. In order for one state to dominate the others, it must combine both land and sea power simultaneously.

This would explain why Russia has tried to acquire bases on the sea, and why maritime powers have tried to prevent Russia from doing so.

Mackinder's ideas, formulated in 1907, were reformulated in 1919 in his principal work, *Democratic Ideals and Reality,* and systematized into a general theory. Simplifying the reading of a world map, he considered Europe, Asia, and Africa as a single block, the center of the earth's political life, which he called "the island of the world." It consisted of highly developed, densely populated maritime nations on the periphery of the map, with the more sparsely populated, less civilized regions in the interior. In this enormous continental mass, one zone occupies a critical location from which it can dominate all other regions. Mackinder called it the "heartland" and situated it on Russian territory (it is well to remember that Mackinder was the British commissioner to the Ukraine in 1919). On the basis of these divisions and this terminology, Mackinder summed up his theory in a terse, frequently quoted statement: "Whoever holds Eastern Europe commands the heartland; whoever holds the heartland commands the island of the world; and whoever commands the island of the world commands the world." This theory, whose poetic value is not to be denied, remains wholly imaginary from any realistic point of view. It is belied by history and by the political changes that have occurred since its formulation. The United States, relegated to a marginal position by Mackinder because it was outside the island of the world, is at present in a strong position for world domination. But Mackinder's theories have often been used by European politicians, especially between 1919 and 1945, to justify their demands concerning central Europe, as well as by those opposing such demands.

GERMAN THEORIES ABOUT LEBENSRAUM ("LIVING SPACE") Long before National Socialism, a German school of geographers developed a theory of *Lebensraum,* and though it has no scientific value, its political influence has been remarkable. The beginnings of this theory go back to Ratzel himself. He believed that the political power of a nation depended on two geographical factors—location and the amount of space at a nation's disposal. But Ratzel added a third factor, not geographical, which he called "the sense of space" (*Raumsinn*). He regarded it as a natural sense, like sight, hearing, or touch, which is especially well developed among certain peoples, and far less so among others. The former are more capable than the latter of appreciating the amount of space they require, and, consequently, are more adept at territorial expansion.

Following the war of 1914, the Institut für Geopolitik at the University of Munich, under the direction of General Karl Haushofer (who later became one of Hitler's advisers), developed a rather obscure but politically effective theory of *Lebensraum* on the basis of Ratzel's ideas. It held that every nation should have the right to conquer the space it needed for its own self-fulfillment. People endowed with a "sense of space" have a right to expand at the expense of those who lack this ability and who are, therefore, less capable of developing the *Lebensraum*. Along with serious geographers, like Haushofer himself, the Institut für Geopolitik assembled pseudoscholars, who were motivated solely by their political passions. These men became increasingly numerous from 1933 on. The institute itself became a propaganda office, pure and simple, whose function was to conceal the German drive for expansion behind a smokescreen of pseudoscientific arguments. The following is typical of the kind of reasoning that came out of the institute: "A nation can no more manage to get along without the mouths of its rivers than the owner of a house can get along without the key to his door!"

Concerning Huntington's theories, see E. Huntington, *The Pulse of Asia* (1907), *Palestine and Its Transformation* (1911), *Civilization and Climate* (1915); and the critique by J. Gottmann in "L'homme, la route et l'eau en Asie sud-occidentale," *Annales de géographie* (1938), pp. 575ff. Concerning Mackinder's theories, see H. Mackinder, *Democratic Ideals and Reality* (London, 1919), and his article "The Geographical Pivot of History," *Geographical Journal* (1907). Ratzel's theories on the sense of space are developed in F. Ratzel, *Politische Geographie* (1897).

DEMOGRAPHIC STRUCTURES

Concerning population problems in general, consult the works of A. Sauvy, especially, *La population*, 6th ed. (1961), and *Théorie générale de la population*, 2 vols. (1952–54); L. Chevalier, *Démographie générale* (1951); A. Landry, *Traité de démographie*, 2d ed. (1949), and *La révolution démographique* (1934); P. Fromont, *Démographie économique* (1947); M. Halbwachs, *Morphologie sociale* (1938); M. Reinhard, *Historie de la population mondiale de 1700 à 1848* (1949); and P. Ariès, *Histoire des populations françaises* (1948). Concerning population influence on the power of nations, see K. Organsky and A.F. Organsky, *Population and World Power* (New York, 1961). For the theory of demographic pressure, see G. Bouthoul, *La surpopulation* (1964).

Concerning the distinction between "micropolitics" and "macropolitics," see J. Meynaud, *Bibliographie sur les problèmes de changement d'échelle dans les sciences sociales* (UNESCO, 1958); this should be compared with the writings of George Gurvitch on the subject of microsociology and macrosociology, and particularly the basic distinction in economic science between microeconomy and macroeconomy. Concerning bureaucracy, see M. Crozier, *Le phénomène bureaucratique* (1963)—a very interesting work, not only for its analysis of bureaucracy, but of authority in general, and especially the Frenchman's attitude toward authority; P.M. Blan, *Bureaucracy in Modern Society* (New York, 1956); R.K. Merton, *Reader in Bureaucracy* (Glencoe, Ill., 1952); G. Tullock, *The Politics of Bureaucracy* (Washington, 1965); the bibliography on "Bureaucracy and Bureaucratization," in *Current Sociology*, 2 (1958), 98–164; and the bibliography on technocracy, as well as a general discussion of the subject, in the notes to Chapter Two.

Concerning political decentralization, the bibliography is vast and difficult to establish because the problem is linked to the question of federalism. As an introduction to the problem in France (where it is especially acute), see J. Rovan, *Une idée neuve: la démocratie* (1961); P. Mendès-France, *La République moderne* (1962); and J. Rivero, "La décentralisation: problèmes et perspectives," *Etudes* (January 1950).

Concerning inequities in representation, see the work by J.-M. Cotteret, C. Emeri, and P. Lalumière, *Lois électorales et inégalités de représentation en France (1936–1960)* (1960), and the preface by M. Duverger, which constitutes the first draft of a general theory. Concerning political attitudes according to age groups, we are reduced to analyzing opinion polls, which do not always probe very deeply. See, for example, the results of the 1958 investigation in Fondation Nationale des Sciences Politiques, *Le réferendum de septembre et les élections de novembre 1958* (1961), pp. 119ff. On the political behavior of women, see M. Duverger, *La participation des femmes à la vie politique* (UNESCO, 1955); J. Narbonne and M. Dogan, *Les Françaises face à la politique* (1955); G. Bremme, *Die politische Rolle der Frau in Deutschland* (Göttingen, 1956). Concerning the problems of multicommunity states, compare the reports on "polyethnic societies" presented at the World Congress of Political Science, Paris, September 1961 (mimeographed); see also the collected studies published by the Faculty of Law, University of Aix, *Le fédéralisme* (1956), and C. Durand, *Confédération d'Etats et Etat fédéral* (1955).

Concerning neo-Malthusian theories, see especially M.G. Schimm et al., *Population Control: The Imminent World Crisis* (New York, 1961), and the summary treatment by G. Bouthoul, *Les guerres* (1951), based on the demographic theory of wars. Theories about birth rates were defended in France, prior to 1939, by the Alliance Nationale Contre la Dépopulation, which published several brochures under the signature of its president, F. Boverat. Depopulation, at that time, had generated in peoples' minds a genuine "population anxiety" (Louis Chevalier), well expressed by Jean Giraudoux: "All the fears and anxieties besetting the French imagination at this moment derive, unconsciously, from the same feeling: Frenchmen are becoming rare. This solitude that we find terrifying and which we persist in thinking of as an international solitude, is actually an internal one. The solitude of our deserted rural areas, of our smaller families, of our colonies from which we eliminated sleeping sickness, only to introduce sleep itself, and this almost morbid reaction occasioned by the announcement of any outbreak of war, whether in Europe or in Africa, is not so much an anxiety for the surviving generations of Frenchmen as an unconscious appeal to the generations that remain unborn" (*Pleins pouvoirs,* 1939). These sentiments explain the publication of the 1939 *Code de la famille* and the passing of legislation encouraging an increase in the birth rate since that year. After 1944, birth-rate theories were given a more scientific formulation by Alfred Sauvy, who linked general social dynamism to population growth. This thesis was originally expressed by Sauvy in *Richesse et population* (1944), and was later developed in other works by the same author.

Concerning the special problems of underdeveloped countries, one book in particular has been very influential: J. de Castro, *Géopolitique de la faim* (1955); see also P. Moussa, *Les nations prolétaires,* 2d ed. (1961).

On the theories of differential fecundity and eugenics, see J. Sutter, *L'eugénique* (1950), and the study conducted in France, in 1944, of 95,237 elementary school children, *Le niveau intellectuel des enfants d'âge scolaire,* 2 vols. (1950–54). The following is a summary, drawn from this study, of the scores obtained on the tests, according to the child's age and the father's profession:

AGE	FARMERS	WORKERS	CLERICAL WORKERS & CIVIL SERVANTS	BUSINESSMEN & INDUSTRIALISTS	INTELLECTUAL & LIBERAL PROFESSIONS
6 to 6½ yrs.	42.1	47.7	54.1	62.3	72.1
7 yrs.	55.3	61.3	70.6	75.9	89.1
8 yrs.	74.8	81.2	87.6	97.4	111.3
9 yrs.	91.3	98.7	106.4	115.0	128.6
10 yrs.	107.3	112.2	121.2	128.6	141.4
11 yrs.	120.6	125.3	132.9	139.6	146.2
12 yrs.	128.6	131.1	140.6	144.0	152.7

Chapter Two: Social Structures

TECHNOLOGICAL SKILLS

Theories opposed to technological progress are presented with great power and insight in the work of J. Ellul, *La technique ou l'enjeu du siècle* (1954)—highly recommended reading; also included is a detailed bibliography. See also Ellul's *L'illusion politique* (1965). Concerning the enslavement of man to the organization, see W.H. Whyte, *The Organization Man* (1959), which contains a supplement showing an excellent method "for cheating on personality tests." The champions of technological progress have yet to find defenders with views that are as profound; one of the most interesting and modern treatments in this connection is that of L. Armand and M. Drancourt, *Plaidoyer pour l'avenir* (1961); see also the books by J. Fourastié, especially *La civilisation de 1975* (1960), and J. Fourastié and A. Laleuf, *Révolution à l'ouest* (1957). Other works dealing with this debate include Lewis Mumford, *Technics and Civilization* (1950); R. Duchet, *Bilan de la civilisation technique: anéantissement ou promotion de l'homme* (1955); and J. Lebret, *Suicide ou survie de l'Occident* (1959). Concerning the transformation of the state as a result of technological evolution, the basic work is the collective study of the Club Jean-Moulin, *L'Etat et le citoyen* (1961). On the essential nature of technological influence upon economic and social development, see J. Fourastié, *Le grand espoir du XXe siècle,* definitive ed. (1963).

Concerning the political influence of the level of economic development, see in particular W.W. Rostow, *The Stages of Economic Growth* (1962); R. Aron, *La société industrielle et la guerre* (1959), and works by the same author listed in the notes to the Introduction; the doctoral course given by A. Hauriou, *Régimes politiques et structures économico-sociales* (Foreign Constitutional Law, 1960–61); and M. Duverger, *De la dictature* (1961). One should also consult the general bibliography on underdeveloped countries, which is immense. As an introduction, see Y. Lacoste, *Les pays sous-développés,* 2d ed. (Collection "Que sais-je?" 1962), and *Géographie du sous-développement,* (1965); P. Moussa, *Les nations prolétaires,* 2d ed. (1961); R. Barre, *Le développement économique* (1958); F. Perroux, *La coexistence pacifique,* 3 vols. (1959); G. Myrdal, *Une économie internationale* (1958); and R. Nurske, *Problems of Capital Formation in Underdeveloped Countries* (1953).

The Difficulties of the Transition Period

Technological progress is not accomplished without difficulties, without jolts, shocks, and contradictions that heighten, temporarily at least, political antagonisms. We must emphasize, in this connection, the difficulties that arise during the initial stage of a country's development—the stage a majority of the nations of the Third World are now going through, as they emerge from prolonged torpor and an age-old social order to undertake rapid social evolution. The task of transforming the country imposes new sacrifices on the people during the transition period when they are building the framework of a modern society. During this period, when capital funds are being accumulated, poverty increases instead of decreasing. At the same time, the drop in the death rate, but not in the birth rate, produces great population pressure, increasing the number of mouths to feed. Thus the general population is a bit worse off than it was just as it is beginning to become aware of its plight and of the possibilities of a change for the better. Political antagonisms are greatly intensified. The situation is not unlike conditions in Europe in the nineteenth century, when Karl Marx observed the development of the class struggle.

At the same time, contact with modern technology produces a violent disruption of traditional civilizations. Societies based on a balanced system of human relationships, slowly established over the centuries, with a deeply rooted culture and civilization, are brutally destroyed by the sudden impact of technological civilization. Traditional ways of life vanish; ancient values are rejected, without being replaced by new values or by an acceptable way of life. Germaine Tillion has invented a very vivid word to describe this situation: "clochardisation" ("beggarization"). The members of these societies literally become beggars, uprooted, wretched, rejected simultaneously by an ancient society they no longer acknowledge, and by a new community that is too far above their living standard and their cultural level.

A new social balance will eventually be established. A new kind of community life will be born within the framework of a technological civilization. But a long delay is necessary before its achievement, for the introduction of this technological civilization encounters obstacles to the modernizing process, which we have already indicated. Consequently, the "transition period" may be very long. Throughout this period, tensions between the "beggarized" masses and the few privileged groups, whose living standard is very high, will naturally be acute. Hence the tendency to establish authoritarian, even dictatorial, regimes. Hence the jealousy and resentment of developed nations. Similar phenomena of "beggarization," with the same tensions and the same political implications, occurred in Europe in the nineteenth century in societies in process of rapid industralization. The dissolution of traditional rural societies, under the onrush of technology, presented an analogous situation.

Concerning the transition period and "beggarization," see G. Tillion, *L'Algérie en 1957* (1957).

"Technocracy"

According to some sociologists, advances in science and technology put supreme power into the hands of scientists and technicians. Next to military might, wealth, and numbers, knowledge has become the primary political weapon, destined to culminate in the enthronement of technocracy.

It was thus that Ernest Renan, in *L'avenir de la science* (*The Future of Science*), imagined a world dominated by scientists. At the beginning of human history, magicians and priests also exercised considerable political influence because they possessed secrets—so it was believed—enabling them to command mysterious forces. Today, scientists, technical experts, and intellectuals tend to exercise a similar power. These new magicians possess the true secrets enabling man to control nature, secrets that remain, however, as mysterious and as incomprehensible to the ordinary man as those of their predecessors.

This analysis is only partly true. It is true that scientists, technical experts, and intellectuals possess the sources of fundamental power in the modern world. A society that persecutes them, or denies them the means to pursue their studies, weakens itself at the same time. But it is very doubtful that scientists use this power in political struggles. Scientific research is, by its nature, neutral, disinterested, and objective. Scientists do not seek to conquer political power, but sometimes to influence it only in matters pertaining to human welfare. What we call "technocracy" is something quite different. It refers to the fact that only the top officials in the specialized services of government are capable of making certain analyses, of gathering certain information, and of making certain decisions, because of the highly technical nature of the problems involved. Accordingly, they do wield a certain amount of political influence. In a system of economic planning, for instance, the decisions are much more the responsibility of technical experts than of political parties, parliaments, or government officials. But the influence of technocrats remains confined to certain areas. Some sociologists, moreover, believe their influence is beneficial. For technocracy to exercise an autonomous power, it would have to consist of a closed membership, a group intent on acting by itself, and this is not the case. Defined thus, "technocracy" remains a limited phenomenon. Scientists and technical experts do not constitute a major element in the struggle for political power.

But "technocracy" may also be defined in another way; it can be used to describe the transformation of political power, under the impact of technological progress, which tends to depersonalize real authority in the interest of a huge organization, an enormous machine. However, this phenomenon is usually called "bureaucracy," the term we have chosen to use in this text.

Concerning technocracy, see J. Meynaud, *Technocratie et politique* (Lausanne, 1960); R. Boisdé, *Technocratie et démocratie* (1964); OCDE, *La science et la politique des gouvernements* (1963); J.L. Cottier, *La technocratie, nouveau pouvoir* (1959); the collective study *Politique et technique* (1958); M. Rivière, *Economie bourgeoise et pensée technocratique* (1965); also J. Billy, *Les techniciens et le pouvoir* (1960); the article by B. Gournay, in the *Revue française de science politique* (1960), p. 880; the notes of J. Meynaud, *ibid.* (1961), p. 673, and of R. Cornevin, *ibid.* (1961), p. 684; the information contained in the collected works of B. Chapman, *The Profession of Government* (London, 1959)—a collective study of public office-holding in Europe; and the book of the Club Jean-Moulin, *L'Etat et le citoyen* (1961). See also our bibliography on bureaucracy in the notes to Chapter One.

Technological Progress and the Social Economy

Does technological progress move in the direction of free enterprise and the capitalist system, or in the direction of socialism? In the West, it is often pointed out that the most technologically advanced societies are capitalistic (the United States), and a conclusion is drawn correlating the two factors. The conclusion is debatable. At the time socialism was established in the countries of Eastern Europe, they were very backward in comparison with North America and Western Europe. Since then, they have considerably narrowed the gap, which is quite a remarkable achievement, considering that the distance separating industrialized nations from underdeveloped nations generally tends to grow wider.

SOCIALISM AND THE SOCIETY OF ABUNDANCE Technological progress can be considered as moving in the direction of socialism from two

points of view: first, it permits man to visualize a society of abundance in which his primary needs (food, housing, and clothing) and
his secondary needs (comfort, leisure, and culture) can be satisfied.
Without this abundance, the equal distribution of goods, a basic principle of socialism ("To each according to his needs"), is impossible.
But Marxists believe that this society of abundance cannot be attained
without first abolishing capitalism, for the latter is considered an obstacle to the total development of technological progress. For Marxists,
genuine abundance is not possible in a capitalistic society, since it is
still Malthusian by nature. Alienation of the worker reduces the productivity of labor. The industrialist delays the application of new technology because it is more profitable to wait until old machinery, already paid for, is completely worn out, rather than make new, costly
investments that will take a long time to liquidate. A great many new
inventions and new techniques are kept off the market by mutual
agreement between the firms controlling the market. Finally, and
above all, at a certain point in technological progress, the necessary research, organization, and planning cannot be done by private enterprise, but only within the framework of a production plan formulated
and directed by the state. The greatest discoveries of the last decades
—atomic fission, rocketry, and so on—have been the result of socialized research, and not of capitalistic research (nuclear studies in the
United States were conducted by the government because of the war;
they could not have been done by the private sectors of the economy).

Now this thesis appears to be contradicted by the facts. The most
highly developed nations, those closest to the society of abundance in
the present world, are capitalistic societies and not socialist. This argument, however, is not conclusive. Until now, socialism has been applied to underdeveloped or semideveloped countries which, when they
abandoned capitalism, were very far behind North America or Western Europe in economic development. That the gap has not yet been
bridged proves very little. Under a capitalistic system, it would probably be even wider.

LONG-RANGE PLANNING AND TECHNOLOGICAL PROGRESS Technological
progress seems to imply a socialist organization of the economy, as was
noted by the great Western economist, J. Schumpeter. The reasoning
behind a system of private enterprise is to permit the individual owner
of a business to be his own boss, to organize production as he sees fit,
as a function of the profits he derives from it. By nature, capitalism is
"microeconomic," which is to say, it considers the economy in terms of
each unit of production. But there is no doubt that "macroeconomy,"

which takes an overall, national or international view of production, is considerably more effective. A coordinated, planned, organized economy is certainly innately superior to a disorganized, anarchical economy, which corresponds to the very nature of capitalism (setting aside possible errors in planning and organization that can be corrected). But coordination, organization, and planning are possible only after reaching a certain level of technological progress. Accurate means of collecting data and estimating long-range economic prospects are needed, and large-scale production, not possible with small firms and average-sized industry, must be set up.

Overall economic planning cannot really be developed in a capitalistic framework. The system of corporate agreements, cartels, and trusts can achieve a partial organization, effective in a given sector of the economy, but only with respect to the interests of this sector, not with respect to the interests of the population as a whole. The worldwide petroleum cartel, for example, organizes the petroleum market with great effectiveness, but does so in the interest of the oil industry, which is not necessarily the public interest. An overall organization of the economy presupposes that the individual entrepreneur will be obliged to follow the decisions stipulated in the plan. A plan that is simply "suggested" or "recommended" is not genuine planning. Now, private ownership of the means of production implies a freedom of decision on the part of the owner. Hence, obligatory compliance with the overall plan would mark the end of a truly capitalistic society.

However, socialist planning is currently undergoing a crisis in the most technologically developed countries. It has proved very effective in enabling backward or partially retarded countries to reach the level of modern industrial societies in a short period of time. But once they have reached that level, socialist planning functions a good deal less efficiently. In a consumer society, centralized planning cannot adequately satisfy the great variety of public needs and demands. This accounts for the economic difficulties of the USSR and the Eastern European people's democracies during the past few years. Technological progress thus implies an evolution in socialist methods which will combine overall planning with the mechanics of the market place. This does not mean a return to capitalism, but rather an adaptation of socialism; in this connection, see H. Denis, *Histoire de la pensée économique* (1966), pp. 737–39.

INSTITUTIONS

Originally, the word "institutions" meant (according to the Littré dictionary) "anything that is invented or established by men, as opposed to what is created by nature"; the sexual act, for instance, is a natural phenomenon, while marriage is an institution. But for Durkheim and his followers, institutions are the ideas, beliefs, customs, and social practices that the individual finds already established in society. It is "the sum total of acts or ideas, *completely instituted,* which confront the individual and more or less force upon him their acceptance" (Fauconnet and Mauss); far from being opposed to "nature," institutions are thus the natural facts of the social universe. However, the Durkheim definition is too broad.

Around 1900, sociology was preoccupied with the question of institutions: see P. Lacombe, *De l'histoire considérée comme science* (Hachette, 1894), and J.W. Powell, "Sociology, or the Science of Institutions," *American Anthropology* (1899), pp. 475ff. During the years 1925–30, an original theory of institutions was developed by M. Hauriou, *Théorie de l'institution et de la fondation (essai de vitalisme social),* IVe Cahier de la Nouvelle Journée (1925). For Hauriou, "an institution is an idea of work or enterprise which acquires physical reality and a legal existence in a social environment; to realize this idea, power is organized to procure agencies for it; in addition, among those interested in the realization of the idea there is evidence of concerted action, directed by these agencies of power and regulated by procedures." This theory, which is rather obscure, is based on insufficient observation of the facts; it attaches too much importance to the rational and conscious element and to the legal aspects of the question. The theory was adopted and developed by a disciple of Hauriou, Georges Renard, who again stressed its idealistic and ethical nature; G. Renard, *La théorie de l'institution; essai d'ontologie juridique* (1930); *Philosophie de l'institution* (1939); and "Le droit constitutionnel et la théorie de l'institution," in *Mélanges Carré de Malberg* (1933).

A number of contemporary sociologists have returned to the question of institutions: see, for example, R.T. Lapierre, *Sociology* (New York and London, 1946), and especially B. Malinowski, *Freedom and Civilisation* (London, 1949), whose concepts are interesting to compare with those of Hauriou (for a brief summary, see A. Cuvillier, *Manuel de sociologie,* [1958], p. 217). However, the word "structure" is currently more fashionable than the word "institution." Their meanings are closely related, as we have noted. Concerning present debates over the notion of "structures," see J. Viet, *Les méthodes structuralistes dans les sciences sociales* (1965); *Notion de structure et structure de la connaissance* (Recueil de la XXe Semaine de Synthèse, 1957); T. Parsons and E. Shils, *Toward a General Theory of Action* (1951); the summary of the 1958 UNESCO Symposium, in the *Bulletin international des sciences sociales* (1958), pp. 481ff.; the analyses of C. Lévi-

Strauss, *Anthropologie structurale* (1958); G. Granger, "Evénement et structure dans les sciences de l'homme," *Cahiers de l'Institut de Science économique appliquée*, No. 55 (1957), p. 25; T. Parsons, *Structure and Process in Modern Societies* (Princeton, N.J., 1952); A.R. Radcliffe-Brown, *Structure and Function in Primitive Society* (London, 1952); and M. Fortes, *Social Structure* (New York, 1949).

Concerning role and status, see A.M. Rocheblave-Spenlé, *La notion de rôle en psychologie sociale* (1962); R. Linton, *The Study of Man* (New York, 1936), and *The Cultural Background of Personality* (1945); and N. Gross, W.S. Mason, and A.W. McEachern, *Explorations in Role Analysis* (New York, 1958).

Concerning the notion of legal institutions and its connections with sociology, see first the works in juridical sociology: H. Lévy-Bruhl, *Aspects sociologiques du droit* (1955); Colloque de Strasbourg, *Méthode sociologique et droit* (1958); G. Gurvitch, *Eléments de sociologie juridique* (1940); N.S. Timasheff, *Introduction à la sociologie juridique* (1939); Colloque de Toulouse on *"Droit, économie et sociologie"* in the *Archives de la Faculté de Droit de Toulouse*, Vol. VII (1959); the Eighth International Congress on Sociology, *Sociología del derecho* (Mexico City, 1957); G. Nirchio, *Introduzione alla sociologie giuridica et diritto* (Milan, 1946); F.W. Jerusalem, *Soziologie des Rechts*, Vol. I, (1925); and E. Ehrlich, *Grundlegung der Soziologie des Rechts*, 2d ed. (Munich, 1929). One should also consult works that are more properly juridical, especially F. Gény, *Science et technique en droit privé positif*, 4 vols. (1914–24); L. Duguit, *Traité de droit constitutionnel*, 3d ed., Vol. I (1927); M. Hauriou, "Théorie de l'institution" in the *Archives de philosophie du droit* (1930), Nos. 1 and 2; G. Ripert, *La règle morale dans les obligations civiles*, 3d ed. (1936); see also M. Réglade, *La coutume en droit public interne* (1919), and the more general works by L. Julliot de la Morandière, P. Esmein, H. Lévy-Bruhl, and C. Scelle, *Introduction à l'étude du droit* (1947); C. du Pasquier, *Introduction à la théorie générale et à la philosophie du droit*, 2d ed. (Paris and Neuchâtel, 1942).

Concerning the typology of political regimes, see R. Aron, *Démocraties et totalitarismes* (1965); G. Burdeau, *Traité de science politique*, 7 vols. (1949–57); and M. Duverger, "Introduction à une sociologie des régimes politiques," in the *Traité de sociologie*, under the direction of G. Gurvitch, Vol. II, pp. 3ff.; *La VI⁶ République et le régime présidentiel* (1961), and *Institutions politiques et droit constitutionnel*, 8th ed. (1965). You will find in this last work a detailed bibliography on the problem, and a fairly thorough analysis of each type of political regime, also with bibliographies. Actually, the courses in

"Sociologie politique" and "Institutions politiques" complement one another: political regimes are discussed in the second course, but they also figure to some extent in the first one.

Concerning the Marxist theory of political regimes, see the Soviet text *Les principes du marxisme-léninisme,* 2d ed. (1962); and G. Vedel, *Les démocraties marxistes et populaires,* a course given by the Institut d'Etudes politiques de Paris, mimeographed (every two years); Lenin, *L'Etat et la Révolution* (1917); H. Kelsen, *The Political Theory of Bolshevism* (Berkeley, 1949); B. Mirkine-Guetzévitch, *La théorie générale de l'etat soviétique* (1928); see also the general bibliography on Marxism in the notes to Chapter Four. It is interesting to compare *Les principes du marxisme-léninisme* with *Le Petit Dictionnaire philosophique* (Moscow, 1955), and works more directly concerned with economics, especially R. Fossaert, *L'avenir du capitalisme* (1961), and F. Sternberg, *Le conflit du siècle* (1958) (translated from the German). Concerning the relationship between democracy and the level of economic development, see M. Duverger, *De la dictature* (1961).

The "Modes" of Political Regimes

The different political regimes that exist today are all derived from one another, or more precisely, they all derive from a few basic models.

WESTERN REGIMES AND THE BRITISH MODEL   All so-called Western governments are built on the model of British institutions, but the copying occurred at two different moments in history. First, there was an imitation of the English regime in the middle of the eighteenth century, then again at the end of the nineteenth century. The first emulation of the British gave birth to presidential regimes; the second produced parliamentary regimes. When the men who drafted the American constitution at the convention in Philadelphia wanted to establish institutions for the new state, born of a rift with the mother country, they naturally drew their inspiration from the latter, the country with which they were familiar. They transposed the English system of 1750, or thereabouts, namely, the limited monarchy, to America. Some of the colonists wanted to reproduce the English system exactly, in other words, to establish a constitutional monarchy. In the end, the majority chose an adaptation of the English system within a republican framework. This produced the presidential system, giving the president powers and a governmental role comparable to those of a king in a limited monarchy. In Western Europe, the battle between conservatives and liberals, which raged throughout the nineteenth century, gradually ended with a weakening of royal powers and a development of the powers of assemblies chosen by electorates. In Great Britain, this political revolution took place without too many jolts or interruptions, and, by the end of the nineteenth and the beginning of the twentieth century, the parliamentary system we know today had appeared. In this system, the king is largely a symbol or figurehead and effective government is in the hands of a ministerial cabinet responsible to Parliament. The nations of northern Europe (Belgium, the Netherlands, Luxembourg, and the Scandinavian countries) then modeled themselves directly upon the British system in the framework of a monarchy. In 1875 France transposed the parliamentary system into a republican framework; this system was subsequently adopted by various countries, such as Italy, Austria, and the German Federal Republic.

COMMUNIST REGIMES AND THE SOVIET MODEL   The regimes of communist countries, on the other hand, are derived from the Soviet model, which was established gradually under revolutionary circumstances, almost from scratch (however, it was influenced by the French Jacobin Constitution of 1793). Marxist jurists recognize two current types of communist regimes—the Soviet regime and the "people's democracy" —but they acknowledge that the two are only variations of the same basic system, not much further apart than the English and French varieties of the parliamentary system.

In short, the English models of 1750 and 1900 and the Russian model of the mid-twentieth century are the three systems of political institutions from which almost all present-day regimes derive (except for certain archaic systems, like the type in Yemen, or very unusual regimes, like that of Switzerland). But differences are great within each of these "systems"—less because of institutional laws and regulations than because of political forces, their structure, and the competition between them.

CULTURES

Concerning the notion of cultures and the different kinds of cultures, see J. Leif, *Esprit et évolution des civilisations* (1950); R. Linton, *The Cultural Background of Personality* (1945); A.L. Kroeber, *Culture: A Critical Review of Concepts and Definitions* (Cambridge, Mass., 1951), and *The Nature of Culture* (1952); and T.S. Eliot, *Notes Toward the*

Definition of Culture (London, 1948). It is interesting to compare the concept of culture with that of "basic personality." The culture of a group defines the basic elements of the personality of its members; see A. Kardiner and R. Linton, *The Individual and His Society* (New York, 1939), and *The Psychological Frontiers of Society* (New York, 1945); and especially M. Dufrenne, *La personnalité de base* (1953).

Concerning the nation, see the famous discourse by Ernest Renan, "Qu'est-ce qu'une nation?" (1882), reprinted in his *Discourse et conférences* (1928). Concerning national "cultural ensembles," see G. Almond and S. Verba, *The Civil Cultures: Political Attitudes and Democracy in Five Nations* (Princeton, N.J., 1963), an attempt at a comparative analysis of the cultures of the United States, Great Britain, Germany, Italy, and Mexico, based on interviews with 5,000 individuals; regarding France, one may compare the foregoing study with the controversial book by R. Métraux and M. Mead, *Thèmes de culture de la France* (1957), published by the Institut havrais de Sociologie des Peuples. A number of interesting studies and bibliographies can be found in *Bulletin international des Sciences sociales,* No. 3 (1951), on "Stéréotypes nationaux et compréhension internationale"; and in H.C.S. Diujker and N.H. Frijda, *National Character and National Stereotypes* (Amsterdam, 1960), a "trend report" with bibliography; and in O. Klineberg, *Etats de tension et compréhension internationale* (1951). See also the section on "ethnotypes" in the notes to Chapter Four. Concerning the role of history in the formation of nations, see R. Rémond, "Les tempéraments nationaux, produits de l'histoire," *Revue économique* (1956), p. 439; C. Jullian, *De la Gaule à la France* (1922); and G. Dupont-Ferrier, *La formation de l'etat français et de l'unité française* (1929).

Concerning ideologies in general and their role, see the general bibliography on Marxism in the notes to Chapter Four; J. Fougeyrollas, *La conscience politique dans la France contemporaine* (1963); and J. Meynaud, *Destin des idéologies* (Lausanne, 1961). Concerning the study of ideologies, see the outline and bibliography by N. Birnbaum in *Current Sociology* (1960), pp. 91–172; concerning the various political ideologies, the basic work is that of J. Touchard et al., *Histoire des idées politiques,* 2 vols. (1959); one should also consult P. Janet, *Histoire de la science politique dans ses rapports avec la morale,* 2 vols. (1858), 5th ed. (1924); J.-J. Chevallier, *Les grandes œuvres politiques, de Machiavel à nos jours* (1959). The basic work in English is that of G.H. Sabine, *A History of Political Theory,* 3d ed. (New York, 1961).

Concerning values, see G. Myrdal, *Value in Social Theory* (London,

1958); L.R. Ward, *Ethics and the Social Sciences* (Notre Dame, Ind., 1959); E. Durkheim, "Jugements de réalité et jugements de valeur," *Revue de Métaphysique* (1911), p. 437 (reprinted in the collection *Sociologie et philosophie,* 1924); F. Adler, "The Value Concept in Sociology," *American Journal of Sociology* (1956), p. 272; A.M. Rose, "Sociology and the Study of Values," *The British Journal of Sociology,* No. 1 (1956); and B.M. Anderson, *Social Values* (Boston, 1911). Concerning the concept of value in general, see J. Piaget, *Le jugement moral chez l'enfant* (1932); S.C. Pepper, *The Sources of Value* (California, 1958); A. Stern, *La Philosophie des valeurs,* 2 vols. (1936); R. le Senne, *Obstacle et valeur* (1934), and "Qu'est-ce que la valeur?" *Bulletin de la Societé française de Philosophie,* conference of April–May 1945); E. Dupréel, *Esquisse d'une philosophie des valeurs* (1939); D. Parodi, *La conduite humaine et les valeurs idéales* (1939); R. Ruyer, *Le monde des valeurs* (1948); and the reports of the *IXe Congrès International de Philosophie* (1937) and of the *IIIe Congrès des Sociétés philosophiques de Langue française* (1947).

Concerning the notion of legitimacy, see M. Duverger, *Institutions politiques,* 8th ed. (1965), pp. 32ff.; and especially the book by G. Ferrero, *Pouvoir: les génies invisibles de la Cité* (1943); also B. Constant, *De l'esprit de conquête et de l'usurpation,* 3d ed. (1814). Concerning a belief in the "sacred" nature of power as a factor in its legitimacy, see the collected writings *Le pouvoir et le sacré, Annales du Centre d'études des Religions de l'Institut de Sociologie Solvay,* Vol. I (Brussels, 1962), and G. Dumézil, *Mitra-Varuna: essai sur deux représentations indo-européennes de la souveraineté* (1948). Concerning myths, see G. Sorel, *Réflexions sur la violence* (1907); R. Caillois, *Le mythe et l'homme* (1938); A.H. Krappe, *La genèse des mythes, rêves et mystères* (1957); and J. Pepin, *Mythe et allégorie* (1959).

The Origins of Nationalist Ideologies

Nationalist ideologies developed considerably after the period of the French Revolution of 1789. The word "nation" is borrowed from the revolutionary vocabulary: the cry "Vive la nation!" was first uttered in opposition to the cry "Vive le roi!" The idea that the nation is the depository of sovereignty served to define certain democratic doctrines, notably that of sovereignty designated as "national," as opposed to "popular" sovereignty (on this question, see M. Duverger, *Institutions politiques,* 8th ed. [1965], pp. 37ff.). Later, the principle of nationalities grew out of revolutionary ideas, affirming the right of peoples to choose their own destiny; it was in short, the transposition to a collective plane of the ideas of liberty and equality. Liberty and equality were applied to national communities, not merely to individuals.

However, nationalist ideologies are also based on ideas that date back to ancient times. Patriotism is a natural feeling, known long before the time of the French Revolution. It reflects simultaneously an attachment to one's community and the cultural system to which one belongs, and a distrust of others, "foreigners." Since time immemorial, the foreigner has been more or less treated as an inferior person, deprived of rights granted to the members of the community; unless the person happens to be a guest passing through, and then he is entitled to the courtesies of hospitality. For the ancient Greeks, as for many other peoples, foreigners were "barbarians"—a word having a less derogatory connotation in antiquity than it does today, but derogatory nevertheless.

In the development of nationalist ideologies, hatred of the foreigner, of the outsider, sometimes played an important role; less, however, in the nationalisms directly inspired by the French Revolution than in the conservative neonationalisms of the twentieth century. "The hereditary enemy"—whether true or imagined—often played an important part in the development of nationalistic feelings; this is particularly true after a war, and especially after a war that has been lost. In France after 1871, anti-German feelings were very intense and became a fundamental theme of the right-wing, nationalist political parties. Moreover, it represented a change in "the hereditary enemy"; Great Britain had played that role in the previous century.

In some countries, the foreigner, the enemy, is not a rival nation, but a race. Racist attitudes played an important role in Germany even before Adolf Hitler, and today they constitute an essential element in the patriotism of the whites of South Africa. Racism also figures rather prominently in certain new African and Asiatic states. Sometimes religion replaces or reinforces racist feelings, or the idea of an enemy nation. Catholicism played a role in the formation of the French nation, Protestantism in the development of the Dutch nation. Moslem nationalism is based in part on the feeling of *umma,* the Islamic community.

Concerning nationalist ideologies, see R. Girardet, "Introduction à l'étude du nationalisme français," *Revue française de science politique* (1958), pp. 505ff. The principal works in the field appear in the English language: Royal Institute of International Affairs, *Nationalism* (London, 1939); H. Kohn, *Nationalism: Its Meaning and History* (New York, 1955), selected readings with a good introduction, and *The Idea of Nationalism* (New York, 1946); C.J.H. Hayes, *The Histor-*

ical Evolution of Modern Nationalism (1948); J.W. Deutsch, *Nationalism and Social Communication* (New York, 1953); and E.L. Snyder, *The Meaning of Nationalism* (New Brunswick, N.J., 1954).

Chapter Three: Individual Causes

Concerning Darwinism and politics, see R. Hofstadter, *Social Darwinism in American Thought* (Boston, 1955), and Michael Banton, ed., *Darwinism and the Study of Society* (Chicago, 1961). Theories linking economic competition with political antagonisms based on competition to satisfy the maximal needs in a society of scarcity are inherent in liberal thinking. One may refer in this matter to neoliberal theories: L. von Mises, *Le socialisme* (1938), translated from the German; F.A. Hayeck, *La route de la servitude* (1945), translated from the German; and Walter Lippmann, *The Good Society* (1937).

Concerning theories of the elite, see first J.-C. Lartigan, "L'élite du pouvoir: Le pouvoir et sa localisation dans l'oeuvre de C.W. Mills" (doctoral dissertation, Paris, 1965); see also C. Maurras, *Mes idées politiques* (1937), and especially *Dictionnaire politique et critique*, 5 vols. (1932–34); also L. Baudin, *Le problème des élites* (1943). Concerning the theories of Mosca and Pareto, see, in addition to the works of these two authors (G. Mosca, *Elementi di scienza politica*, 1st ed., 1896, rev. ed., 1923; V. Pareto, *Traité de sociologie générale*, 2 vols., 1917–19), the critical analysis of J.H. Meisel, *The Myth of the Ruling Class* (Ann Arbor, Mich., 1958); and the more controversial works of G.H. Bousquet, *Vilfredo Pareto: sa vie et son oeuvre* (1928), and *Précis de sociologie d'après Vilfredo Pareto* (1925). The positions of Mosca and Pareto have been adopted in the work of J. Burnham, *The Machiavellians* (1949). In the United States, theories on the elite and studies on the "movement of the elites" have been considerably developed. See especially H.D. Lasswell, D. Lerner, and C. Easton Rothwell, *The Comparative Study of Elites: An Introduction and Bibliography* (Stanford, Calif., 1952); D.R. Mathews, *The Social Background of Political Decision-makers* (New York, 1954); D. Marvick, *Political Decision-makers* (Glencoe, Ill., 1961), a comparative study; and especially the basic work of C. Wright Mills, *The Power Elite* (1956); see also the most recent work of S. Keller, *Beyond the Ruling Class* (New York, 1963). Concerning social mobility in general, see the report on research and bibliography by S.M. Miller in *Current Sociology* (1960), pp. 1–8.

Concerning animal societies and the political phenomena they reveal, see René Chauvin, *Les sociétés animales* (1963), and M. Sire, *La vie sociale des animaux* (1960). Consult also P. Guillaume, *Psychologie animale,* 2d ed. (1947); H. Piéron, *Psychologie zoologique* (1941); and the articles of D.O. Hebb and W.R. Thompson, "The Social Significance of Animal Studies," in G. Lindzey et al., *Handbook of Social Psychology,* 2d ed. (Cambridge, Mass., 1956), I, 552, with bibliography, and P. Crawford, "Social Psychology of the Vertebrates," *Psychological Bulletin* (1939), p. 407.

PSYCHOLOGICAL CAUSES

For an overall view of the subject of psychological factors in political phenomena, see the compact work by J. Meynaud and A. Lancelot, *Les attitudes politiques* (1962); for attitudes in general, see Association Scientifique de Langue Française, *Les attitudes* (1961), and R. Girod, *Attitudes collectives et relations humaines* (1953); see also J. Delay and P. Pichot, *Abrégé de psychologie* (1962), and P. Koubilsky, A. Soulirac, and P. Grapin, *Adaptation et aggressivité* (Paris, 1965). It is also worthwhile to consult several introductory works to psychoanalysis, especially D. Lagache, *La psychanalyse* (1955); N.O. Brown, *Eros and Thanatos* (1961); S. Nacht, *La psychanalyse d'aujourd'hui,* 2 vols. (1956); and E. Glover, *Technique de la psychanalyse* (1958).

On the applications of psychoanalysis to general sociology, see R. Bastide, *Sociologie et psychanalyse* (1952), p. 22; the article by M. Bonaparte in *Revue Française de Psychanalyse* (1952), p. 313; W. Munsterberger and S. Axelrad, *Psychoanalysis and the Social Sciences* (New York, 1955); J. Flugel, *Man, Morality, and Society: A Psychoanalytical Study* (New York, 1955); and M. Birnbach, *Neo-Freudian Philosophy* (Stanford, Calif., 1961).

Concerning the applications of psychoanalysis to political sociology, see the article by F. W. Matson in *Journal of Politics* (1954), p. 704; R. Loewenstein, *Psychanalyse de l'antisémitisme* (1952); and L. Berkowitz, *Aggression: A Social Psychological Analysis* (New York, 1962), a study of violence in the mass information media. One should obviously consult, in addition, the work of T. Adorno et al., *The Authoritarian Personality* (New York, 1950). For a critical evaluation, see the collective work *Studies in the Scope and Method of "The Authoritarian Personality"* (Glencoe, Ill., 1954).

Concerning character and temperaments, see R. le Senne, *Traité de*

Caractérologie (1945); G. Berger, *Traité pratique d'analyse du caractère* (1950), based on the Heymans and Wierzma classification; E. Mounier, *Traité du caractère* (1946); R. Linton, *The Cultural Background of Personality* (1945); E. Schreider, *Les types humains,* 3 vols. (1937); and the bibliography on basic personality in the notes to Chapter Two of this book. Certain writers have tried to classify temperaments on a biological basis, according to blood type: see L. Bourdel, *Groupes sanguins et tempéraments* (1960); and P. Grieger, *La caractérologie ethnique* (1961). This thesis has in no sense been verified. Concerning the theories of Eysenck, see H.J. Eysenck, *The Psychology of Politics* (London, 1954).

Chapter Four: Collective Causes

THE CLASS STRUGGLE

Concerning social classes in general, see the summary bibliography appearing as a supplement in M. Duverger et al., *Partis politiques et classes sociales* (1955), and particularly, G. Gurvitch, "Le concept de classes sociales de Marx à nos jours," mimeographed (1954); M. Halbwachs, *Esquisse d'une psychologie des classes sociales* (1955), and "Les classes sociales," mimeographed (1948); J. Lhomme, *Les problèmes des classes: doctrines et faits* (1938); E. Goblot, *La barrière et le niveau* (1925); and G. Bolacchi, *Teoria delle classi sociali* (Rome, 1963), which is interesting, but makes almost no mention of Marx! A good résumé, though unfortunately too brief, on Marxist doctrines can be found in the short work by P. Laroque, *Les classes sociales* (1959).

On Marxist doctrines in general, the bibliography is immense. One should consult first the short résumé by H. Lefebvre, *Le marxisme* (1948), and other works by the same author, especially *Pour connaître la pensée de Karl Marx,* 2d ed. (1956), *Pour connaître la pensée de Lénine* (1957), *Problèmes actuels du marxisme* (1958), and the work that marked the author's break with the Communist party, *La somme et le reste* (1959).

In-depth analyses, rather difficult but very interesting, by non-Marxists include those of Y. Calvez (a Jesuit priest), *La pensée de Karl Marx* (1957), and H. Bartoli, *La doctrine économique et sociale de Karl Marx* (1950)—the author is a Christian, politically on the left.

For selected readings from Karl Marx, see M. Guterman and H. Lefebvre, *Morceaux choisis de Karl Marx* (1934), and M. Rubel, *Karl Marx: pages choisies pour une éthique socialiste* (1948). Also recommended, among the works of Marx, in addition to K. Marx and F. Engels, *The Communist Manifesto* (1848), are his writings on France: *Les luttes de classes en France (1848–50)* (1895), *Le 18 brumaire de Louis-Bonaparte* (1852), and *La guerre civile en France* (1871).

Concerning caste systems, see L. Dumont, *Homo hierarchicus: essai sur le système des castes* (1966), and M.N. Srinivas, Y.B. Damle, S. Shahabi, and A. Beteille, "Caste: A Trend Report and Bibliography," *Current Sociology* (1959), pp. 135–183.

RACIAL CONFLICTS

A good summary is given in the work of UNESCO, *Le racisme devant la science* (1960); a collection of articles by eminent sociologists, anthropologists, and biologists. A fuller treatment is to be found in the UNESCO study *La question raciale devant la science moderne*, 5 vols. (1951); also *La question raciale et la pensée moderne*, 4 vols. (1955). Basic works in French include P. Maucorps, A. Memmi, and J.F. Held, *Les Français et le racisme* (1965); J. Finot, *Le préjugé de race et de couleur* (1949); F.H. Hankins, *La race dans la civilisation* (1935); and J. Juxley, *Nous, Européens* (1947). In English, see B. Berry, *Race and Ethnic Relations*, 2d ed. (Boston, 1958); R. Benedict, *Race, Science, and Politics*, 2d ed. (New York, 1945); F. Boas, *Race and Democratic Society* (New York, 1945); M.F. Montagu, *Man's Most Dangerous Myth: The Fallacy of Race* (New York, 1942); C. Kluckhohn, *Mirror for Man* (New York, 1949); and F. Helimann et al., *Handbook on Racial Relations* (Oxford, 1949). Regarding purely biological aspects of the racial problem, see L.C. Dunn and T. Dobztansky, *Heredity, Race, and Society* (New York, 1946), and W.C. Boyd, *Genetics and the Races of Men* (Boston, 1950).

The "Ethnotypes"

Racist theories appear in the contemporary French school of "the psychology of peoples." On the one hand, the adherents seek to explain the psychological traits they believe to be characteristic of each nation by sociocultural factors. Thus they use notions of "basic personality" and "national stereotypes," often in a very general way.

But on the other hand, these people tend to ascribe psychological characteristics to biological factors. On the basis of "ethnic characterology," a very debatable theory, they argue that the predominance in a nation of a certain blood type results in the domination of certain psychological characteristics. Thus they would explain democracy in Western Europe by the predominance of blood type *A*, and Eastern European dictatorships by the predominance of blood type *B!* See G. Heraud, *L'Europe des ethnies* (1963); A. Miroglio, *La psychologie des peuples* (1958); and P. Lavigne's criticism in *Climats et Sociétés* (1965).

CONFLICTS BETWEEN "HORIZONTAL" GROUPS

Concerning nations, see the notes to Chapter Two. Concerning local communities, see P. Rivet, *Cités Mayas* (1954); M. Fortes and E. Evans-Pritchard, *African Political Systems,* 2d ed. (London, 1943); and C. Petit-Dutaillis, *Les communes françaises, des origines au 18ᵉ siècle* (1947). Concerning the international community in general, see C. de Visscher, *Théories et réalités en droit international public* (1953), especially pp. 114ff., and the many publications regarding the United Nations; concerning particular communities, see P. Reuter, *Institutions internationales,* 4th ed. (1963), and especially *Organisations européennes* (1965).

The principal works on corporate doctrines are M. Elbow, *French Corporative Theory (1789–1948)* (New York, 1953); R. Bonnard, *Syndicalisme, corporatisme et etat corporatif* (1937); G. Pirou, *Essai sur le corporatisme* (1938); *Néo-libéralisme, néo-corporatismȩ, néo-socialisme* (1939); L. Salieron, *Naissance de l'etat corporatif* (1942); and G. Bourgin, *L'Etat corporatif en Italie* (1935).

Concerning ideological groups, see the bibliography in the notes to Chapter Two, under "Cultures."

The Political Influence of Churches and Religions

By and large, the influence of religions is directed primarily toward conservatism. But there are numerous exceptions to this general tendency, such as the case of an ethnic minority with a different religion from that of the majority. The minority's religion strengthens its sense of autonomy, and it is generally helpful in the struggle for national existence. The role of the clergy and of Catholicism is noteworthy in this connection, both in the nineteenth century and at the beginning of the twentieth century. Their efforts on behalf of Belgian independence in 1830 was of the same nature. But after the erstwhile minority has achieved its independence, the situation is usually reversed; then religion becomes a conservative force.

On the other hand, the lower clergy, which is in direct contact with the people, often plays an educational role, not only in religious but also in political matters. In Latin America in the nineteenth century, many priests assumed a function of this sort, sometimes taking a decisive part in the struggle for independence. In certain African countries, we see similar phenomena at the present time. But we also discover that in France in 1789 the parish priests and vicars were very influential in formulating the grievances and petitions of the Third Estate; they played a decisive role at the assembly of the States-General by joining the Third Estate, thus enabling this body to proclaim itself the "National Assembly."

The contemporary development of Christian-Democratic parties—to which the Roman Catholic church has contributed—is a more complex phenomenon. From 1940 to 1944, they fought courageously against Hitler's dictatorship; at the time of the Liberation, they figured as parties of the center-left, opposed to conservatism. But since then they have diluted their politics, and the church has often favored its most conservative factions. However, small Christian groups of the left have developed and enjoy a rather large intellectual following. In the Church of France, in particular, the forces of renewal tend to increase. From 1956 to 1962, the church's position on the Algerian war was much farther to the left than the socialists'.

Concerning the political influence of religious ideologies in France, see A. Latreille and A. Siegfried, *Les Forces religieuses et la vie politique* (1952); A. Dansette, *Histoire religieuse de la France contemporaine*, 2 vols. (1948–51), and *Destin du catholicisme français (1926–1956)* (1957); R. Remond, "Droite et gauche dans le catholicisme français contemporain," *Revue française de science politique* (1955), p. 267; C. Suffert, *Les catholiques et la gauche* (1960); E. Léonard, *Le protestant français* (1953); and L.-V. Mejean, *La séparation de l'eglise et de l'etat* (1959). Concerning religious influence in the United States, see G. Lenski, *The Religious Factor* (New York, 1961), and J.H. Fenton, *The Catholic Vote* (New Orleans, 1961).

Studies in electoral sociology have shown that the religious factor plays an important role in determining an individual's vote, usually—though not always—in a conservative direction. Political sociology is directly involved in studies of religious sociology, presently flourishing under the influence of Gabriel le Bras, *Etudes de sociologie religieuse*, 2 vols. (1955–56), *Introduction à l'histoire de la pratique religieuse en France*, 2 vols. (1942–45), and "Problèmes de sociologie des religions," (in *Traité de sociologie,* directed by G. Gurvitch, Vol. II, pp. 79 ff.); Canon Boulard, *Premiers itinéraires en sociologie religieuse* (1954); and the bibliography in the special issue of *Current Sociology: Contemporary Sociology* (UNESCO, 1956), devoted to the Sociology of Religions.

Chapter Five: The Forms of Political Conflict

THE WEAPONS OF COMBAT

Concerning the political power of armies in traditional societies, see M. Crouzot, *Histoire générale des civilisations,* 6 vols. (1953–58), especially the earlier volumes; on the problem in the contemporary world, see M. Howard et al., *Soldiers and Governments* (London, 1957); *Guerre, armée, société,* special issue of the *Revue française de sociologie* (April–June 1961); the bibliography of R. Girardet, in the *Revue française de science politique* (1960), p. 395; and M. Janovitz, *The Professional Soldier* (1960).

On the influence of wealth, see first the bibliography on Marxism in the notes to Chapter Four, and the study by J.B. Shannon, *Money in Politics* (New York, 1959), with bibliography. By way of illustration, concerning the influence of economic forces in France, see the interesting, if partial, study by E. Beau de Loménie, *Les responsabilités des dynasties bourgeoises,* 3 vols. (1943–54); the documents compiled before the war by A. Hamon, *Les maîtres de la France,* 3 vols. (1936–38)—a writer of the far left; and the more recent studies by H. Coston, *Les financiers qui mènent le monde* (1955), and *La haute banque et les trusts* (1958)—a writer of the far right. These works must be used with considerable caution because of numerous errors in detail and because of arbitrary interpretations of the facts.

Regarding the influence of collective groups and organizations, see M. Duverger, *Les partis politiques* (1951), and J. Ellul, *La technique ou l'enjeu du siècle* (1959).

Concerning propaganda, see J. Ellul, *Propagandes* (1962); J. Domenach, *La propagande politique* (1950); S. Tchakhotine, *Le viol des foules par la propagande politique,* 2d ed. (1952); J.A.C. Brown, *Techniques of Persuasion* (London, 1963); H. Eulau, *The Behavioral Persuasion in Politics,* 2d ed. (New York, 1962); and L. Fraser, *Propaganda* (London, 1957).

Concerning the information media in liberal regimes, the basic work is by J. Kayser, *Mort d'une liberté: technique et politique de l'information* (1955); R. Clausse, *Les Nouvelles* (Brussels, 1963); see also B. Voyenne, *La presse dans la société contemporaine* (1955), which should be compared with the excellent legal study by R. Pinto, *La liberté d'opinion et d'information* (1955). Concerning the influence of the press on public opinion, note the material given in courses at the Institut d'Etudes politiques de Paris, by J. Stoetzel, "L'opinion publique et la presse," mimeographed (1947), and by A. Girard, "L'opinion publique et la presse," mimeographed (1959). Concerning the excesses of advertising, see V. Packard, *The Hidden Persuaders* (1958).

On the French press, see B. Voyenne, *Guide bibliographique de la presse* (1958); R. Manévy, *Histoire de la presse, 1914–1939* (1958); J. Mottin, *Histoire politique de la presse, 1944–1949* (1950); C. Ledre, *Histoire de la presse* (1958); B. Féron,• *Feu de la presse libre* (1952); Mouvement de Liberation du Peuple, *Les maîtres de la presse* (1959); the excellent review *Etudes de presse,* and the short studies in the "Kiosque" collection, published since 1959.

The Capitalistic System and Centralization of Information

Contrary to widely held opinion, capitalism does not necessarily result in a pluralism of information. In fascist dictatorships, many news media remain in the hands of private enterprise. If radio and television are generally state-controlled, most newspapers continue to be operated either by their former owners or by new owners. We can thus measure the weakness of economic power under pressure from political power, when the latter is forceful and when it also favors business interests. In Nazi Germany, except for the disappearance of the *Vossiche Zeitung* (a liberal newspaper comparable to the London *Times, The New York Times,* or *Le Monde*) because its owners were Jewish, the other great national organs were maintained (although the *Berliner Tageblatt* disappeared in 1937). All of them obediently complied with the government's directives: every day the editors-in-chief of the Berlin daily newspapers and the correspondents of provincial newspapers gathered at the Propaganda Ministry to be told what news was to be printed, what news was to be suppressed, what campaigns were to be undertaken, what editorials were to be written, and what headlines were to be emphasized. Although it operated on a capitalistic basis, the German press was even more submissive to governmental power than the Soviet press. Likewise, private publishers printed only those works authorized by government censorship.

Political Strategies

Concerning political strategies, see M. Duverger, "Introduction à l'étude des stratégies politiques," mimeographed (doctoral course at the Faculté de Droit de Paris, 1958–59), and W.H. Riker, *The Theory of Political Coalitions* (New Haven, Conn., 1962), based on a mathematical analysis starting with the game theory. Concerning strategies in international conflicts, see the article by J.B. Duroselle in *Revue française de science politique* (1960), pp. 287ff.; R. Aron, *Paix et guerre entre les nations* (1962), a critique, appears in the *Revue française de science politique* (1962), p. 969. Concerning strategies in social struggles, see F. Sellier, *Stratégie de la lutte sociale* (1962); M. Crozier, *Usines et syndicats d'Amérique* (1951); and J. Meynaud and B. Schroder, *La médiation: tendances de la recherche et bibliographie, 1945–1959* (Amsterdam, 1961).

Regarding the mathematical analysis of strategies, see T. Schelling, *The Strategy of Conflicts* (Cambridge, 1965); A. Rapoport, *Fights, Games, and Debates* (Ann Arbor, Mich., 1960); M. Shubik, *Readings in Game Theory and Political Behavior* (New York, 1954); and R.D. Luce and H. Raffa, *Games and Decisions* (New York, 1957). Useful French sources include the short introductory work by J.D. Williams, *La stratégie dans les actions humaines* (1956); J. Meynaud, "Les mathématiques et le pouvoir," *Revue française de science politique* (1959), p. 340—a good summary; and the collective study *La décision* (1961).

Concerning reformism in socialist doctrine, see first the basic work of E. Bernstein, *Socialisme théorique et socialisme pratique* (French translation, 1900; first German edition, 1899), which followed the debate between reformists and revolutionaries; concerning the problem today, see the article by M. Duverger in *Cahiers de la République* (January–February, 1959). Concerning the description of legitimacy and the revolutionary situation, see M. Duverger, *De la dictature* (1961).

On concepts of the political right and left and centrist strategy, see M. Duverger, *La démocratie sans le peuple* (1967), and "L'éternel marais: essai sur le centrisme français," *Revue française de science politique* (January 1964).

Chapter Six: The Development of Integration

THE NOTION OF INTEGRATION

We have presented a summary of the general concepts relating to social integration. The problem is vast and the relevant bibliography immense. We will limit ourselves to a few suggestions. The work by E. Morin, *Introduction à une politique de l'homme* (1965), approaches the question from a new perspective. For a traditional approach, see first G. Gurvitch, *L'idée de droit social* (1932), and "Problèmes de sociologie générale," in his *Traité de sociologie,* Vol. I (1958); also E. Durkheim, *De la division du travail social* (1893); F. Tonnies, *Communauté et société* (French translation, 1944; the German work appeared in 1887); M. Scheier, *Formes et nature de la sympathie* (French translation, 1929); and M. Bergson, *Les deux sources de la morale et de la religion* (1933).

The ideas of Thomas Aquinas on the "common good," rediscovered about forty years ago, have influenced contemporary Western thought, especially many theories on natural law. Concerning these ideas, see S. Michel, "La notion thomiste du Bien commun" (doctoral thesis, Nancy, 1931); A. Sertilianges, *La philosophie morale de saint Thomas d'Aquin* (1922), and *Les grandes thèses de la philosophie thomiste* (1928); J. Leclercq, *Lecons de droit naturel,* 4 vols. (Namur, 1927–36).

Theories of the state as integrator are defended by idealistic jurists. On this question, see especially G. Burdeau, *Traité de science politique,* Vol. I, *Le pouvoir politique* (1949). See also J. Dabin, *La philosophie de l'ordre juridique positif* (1929), *Doctrine générale de l'etat* (Brussels, 1929), and *L'Etat ou le politique: essai de définition* (1957); L. le Fur, *Les fondements du droit* (1925); and G. Renard, *Le droit, l'ordre, et la raison* (1929).

Concerning the reaching of compromises and the notion of justice, see *Compromis et résolution des conflits,* special issue of *Revue internationale des sciences sociales,* No. 2 (1963); R. Aron, *Paix et guerre entre les nations* (1962); J. Meynaud and B. Schreder, *La médiation: tendances de la recherche et bibliographie, 1945–1959* (Amsterdam, 1961); V. Dessens, *Essai sur la notion d'équité* (thesis, Toulouse, 1934); G. Ripert, *La règle morale dans les obligations civiles* (1927); F.

Gény, *Science et technique en droit privé positif,* 4 vols. (1914–24); and D. del Veccio, *Justice, Droit, Etat* (1938). Concerning propaganda, see the notes to Chapter Five. Concerning civic education, see J. Jousselin, *Pédagogie du civisme* (1963), and *Civisme et insertion sociale* (1962).

The Marxist theory of integration-camouflage was developed most vigorously by Lenin in *L'Etat et la Révolution* (1917); see also the general bibliography on Marxism in the notes to Chapter Four. Non-Marxist theorists have also described the state and power as a phenomenon of force; see especially the analysis by the great French jurist L. Duguit, *Traité de droit constitutionnel,* Vol. I (1928).

Regarding the ties between technological development and political integration, consult first the bibliography in the notes to Chapter Two. The subject is popular nowadays, and a large number of books and articles in scholarly journals deal with it. As an example of specific problems, see A. Marchal, *L'intégration territoriale* (1965). Concerning bureaucracy, see the bibliography in the notes to Chapter Two.

A Rebirth of Political Liberalism?

Conflict between the citizen and the state will probably remain the main source of antagonism in highly developed societies. As a state of economic abundance approaches, class conflicts and competition among individuals diminish, except for those described above. On the other hand, conflicts between power and the citizenry increase. The question of freedom thus tends to return to the center of the political stage, as it did for liberals in the nineteenth century.

FREEDOM AND ABUNDANCE   Liberals had posed the problem of freedom within the microcosm of the relative abundance that characterized the nineteenth century bourgeoisie, while the masses surrounding them were reduced to abject poverty. For the bourgeoisie, since material problems were solved, resistance to power on the part of the citizenry was deemed essential. For the working classes, however, the struggle for material existence, for equality and human dignity, was much more important. Political freedoms—which were real for the bourgeoisie, who had the means of enjoying them—were mere formalities for the proletariat. The class struggle was the primary cause of social antagonism.

In a society of abundance, the bourgeois microcosm expands to include all elements of the society. Important conflicts persist between groups and individuals; classes always tend to reappear in one form or another. But these antagonisms become secondary in comparison with the conflict between the citizens and the state. This latter conflict increases because, first of all, all citizens now have the means of exercising their freedom, so it assumes a greater value and significance for them. The conflict also increases because technological progress, by producing economic abundance and reducing the antagonisms caused by poverty, increases the might of governmental power and its ability to oppress citizens who resist its power. Once again liberty takes on its original meaning, formulated by the liberals of the nineteenth century. "Liberties are acts of resistance," said the French writer Benjamin Constant, who contrasted this modern concept with what he called "the freedom of the ancients . . . which consisted in the active participation in collective power."

CONCERNING FREEDOM-RESISTANCE AND FREEDOM-PARTICIPATION Actually, this "freedom of the ancients" gradually became the freedom of modern man, especially in Anglo-Saxon countries, in which democracy consists primarily in the active participation of each citizen in making collective decisions. The latter is accomplished through a decentralization of power and the existence of innumerable associations and civic organizations, which involve individuals more closely in community affairs. At the same time, socialism has shown that the state can be a liberating influence, contrary to capitalistic doctrines: "Between the rich and the poor, between the weak and the strong, it is freedom that oppresses and the law that liberates," as Lacordaire, the nineteenth-century French Catholic liberal, had already observed. The elimination of alienations is one form of liberation. The elimination of poverty is another. Alongside "freedom-participation," we find today what one might call "freedom-self-realization." Theories of the abundant society and of the final phase of communism are predicated on the idea that each man should develop according to his own nature, with all the means at his disposal to achieve self-fulfillment.

THE REBIRTH OF FREEDOM-RESISTANCE While these concepts of freedom were developing (liberation by the state, freedom-participation, and freedom-self-fulfillment) the idea of freedom as resistance was being slowly downgraded, especially in the Anglo-Saxon countries. The evolution of modern societies is helping to revive it, probably even to give it top priority. No doubt technological progress and relative economic abundance allow for greater fulfillment of each individual. No doubt the role of the state in opposing domination and exploitation by private interests is a liberating influence. No doubt participation by the citizenry at all levels of government is an essential factor in a country's freedom. But the more highly developed a society, the more certainly political power becomes entrenched and bureaucratic, and the greater the need to resist it. Freedom has always been an act of resistance. The society of abundance is not moving toward a withering away of the state, but to its enlargement and bureaucratization. The citizen's struggle against its power is becoming the principal source of social antagonism. Nothing warrants the assumption that it will disappear or even diminish. There is no foreseeable end to the political struggle as a means of fighting for freedom.

Theories of "Depoliticization"

The Marxist theory of the fading away of the state has found its counterpart, in recent years, in the Western theory of depoliticization.

OUTLINE OF THE THEORY In the most highly developed nations, certain observers believe there has been substantial evidence, since 1950, of a lessening of conflicts, a reduction in antagonisms, and a decline in political struggles. The weakening of the role of political parties and especially their tendency to draw together have greatly impressed these observers. The gulf separating conservatives from liberals, which was enormous in the nineteenth century, has almost completely disappeared. Differences between socialist and bourgeois parties, which were significant before 1914, are today relatively unimportant. Even the gulf between communists and noncommunists, still immense in 1945, appears to be diminishing. The idea of revolution, which dominated left-wing political parties for more than a century in certain countries, France in particular, is little more today than a nostalgic memory: the revolutionary spirit is fading among the working classes of economically developed nations. Many believe that this depoliticization is a direct consequence of the rising standard of living and the advance toward economic abundance. The partial depoliticizing of present-day societies, based on a state of abundance that is also partial, is thought to be a stage in society's evolution. The end of the process will be total depoliticization, produced by total abundance, in other words, the complete withering away of the state. Thus we have a generalized version of the Marxist theory, which envisaged the disappearance of the state only within the framework of socialism: now it is seen as a general phenomenon tied to the question of technological progress.

THE END OF REVOLUTIONARY METHODS The success of the notion of depoliticization can be attributed to its ambiguity. If it means that political antagonisms tend to assume less violent forms of expression in highly developed societies, and especially that revolutionary tactics are giving away to reformist methods, then it embodies an incontrovertible truth. This stage of depoliticization certainly results from a high standard of living, but also from other factors, particularly the complexity of modern societies, which is incompatible with the use of cruel and brutal methods. The notion that revolution would do incalculable harm to the production machinery—that it would take a long time to get back into operation and would inevitably result in a sharp drop in living standards—is widely shared in the working community. And in a sense this is true. Let us repeat: whether we are dealing with biological organisms, with machines, or with societies, the farther one advances into complexity and specialization, the more fragile the structures become and the greater the precautions needed in handling them. A single annelid can be made into two by cutting the worm in half, but this treatment cannot be applied to the higher vertebrates. One can repair a wagon with a hammer and nails, but not a Boeing 747. Revolutions are possible in fairly primitive societies, but not in France or the United States.

THE TRANSFORMATION OF POLITICS However, the term "depoliticization" remains questionable, because the elimination of violence and its replacement by processes of discussion and compromise are specific characteristics of the art of politics, which tends by its very nature to replace physical combat, armed conflict, and civil war with organized, nonviolent kinds of conflict. Instead of depoliticization, we should be talking about politicization. Instead of the withering away of the state, we should be talking about its restoration following its partial dissolution in the violence of nineteenth-century revolutionary struggles. Besides, if depoliticization means that conflicts are disappearing, that antagonisms are coming to an end, and that politics is almost nonexistent, this concept does not correspond to contemporary conditions in technologically advanced societies. Indeed, it is entirely erroneous. The lack of interest in politics, which some believe they perceive in Western Europe and North America, is a lack of interest in certain types of political expression which have become outmoded through changes in the social structures. It corresponds to an increased interest in *other* types of political expression (consider the participation by French citizens in the election of a president by universal suffrage in December 1965).

The decline of political parties in France, as well as the indifference to certain traditional forms of representation, coincides with the rise of labor unions, farm organizations, political clubs, and the development of new forms of representation. Moreover, this decline in the number of parties is not general throughout the West. In many respects, an interest in politics has been increasing rather than decreasing. In this sense, too, we could speak of politicization instead of depoliticization. Political methods have tended to eliminate the heroic or spectacular; the politics of the specific has replaced that of the grandiose; the struggle *over* the regime is giving way to the struggle *within* the regime; concrete demands receive more attention than sweeping indictments of the system itself; reform movements replace revolutionary movements: but politics goes on! Liberty and equality are defended less frequently today on the barricades than in committee rooms, less in grandiloquent speeches than in organized strikes: but the struggle for liberty and equality continues.

Concerning depoliticization and the problem of participation in political life in general, see the special issue of the *Revue internationale des Sciences sociales* devoted to "La participation des citoyens à la vie politique," No. 1 (1960), containing an important bibliography. Concerning depoliticization in France, see G. Vedel et al., *La dépolitisation, mythe ou réalité?* (1962); the brief work by J. Meynaud and A. Lancelot, *La participation des Français à la politique* (1961), pp. 609ff., which shows the absence of depoliticization; and the book by A.H. Hirsch, *Small-town Politics* (London, 1959). Concerning the United States, see R.B. Lane, *Political Life: Why People Get Involved in Politics* (Glencoe, Ill., 1959), and S.M. Lipset, *Political Man* (New York, 1960).

Index